On Mission With Jesus

On Mission with Jesus is vital 'unlearning' for the Church, rebooting our ecclesial imagination with the missionary dynamism of the New Testament. When I first heard Graham explain his thesis, I was persuaded; I'm delighted to see it now published. This is a compelling case for a new Christian default more deeply rooted in our gospel past and more radically oriented to the world in love. Comprehensively biblical, robustly theological – this is a whole library of missiological wisdom in one book, beautifully and wisely digested. As a mature reflection on the mission-shaped church and a pointer to the future it will make an important contribution.

Revd Canon Dr Mark Powley, Archbishop's Mission Enabler for the North

I consider Graham Cray to be a foundational thinker and leader in helping communities engage more missionally and faithfully in our time. This book, loaded with insights gleaned from the last few decades of activism, bolsters his legacy in a meaningful way. An important contribution.

Alan Hirsch, founder of the Movement Leaders Collective and author of numerous books on missional spirituality, leadership and organization

This is the book we have been waiting for Graham Cray to write! I am delighted it is here. He compellingly argues that the Western church has got its default all wrong, frozen in time, stuck. The images we have when we think 'church' have a gravitational pull back towards a Christendom default. We need to move beyond the idea that mission is simply a task of the church and see it as the activity of God in which the church is called to participate and so be missionary by nature. An adventure of the imagination is required if we are to respond to the challenges of our era. Cray refounds the church around the disarmingly simple notion of church as a community of disciples on mission with Jesus. To get outside of gravity you need rocket speed. This book might just be the rocket fuel we need.

Jonny Baker, Britain Hub Mission Director, Church Mission Society

On Mission With Jesus

Changing the Default Setting of the Church

Graham Cray

CANTERBURY PRESS

Norwich

© Graham Cray 2024

First published in 2024 by the Canterbury Press Norwich
Editorial office
3rd Floor, Invicta House
110 Golden Lane
London EC1Y 0TG, UK
www.canterburypress.co.uk

Canterbury Press is an imprint of Hymns Ancient & Modern Ltd
(a registered charity)

Hymns Ancient & Modern® is a registered trademark of
Hymns Ancient & Modern Ltd
13A Hellesdon Park Road, Norwich,
Norfolk NR6 5DR, UK

All rights reserved. No part of this publication may be reproduced,
stored in a retrieval system, or transmitted,
in any form or by any means, electronic, mechanical,
photocopying or otherwise, without the prior permission of
the publisher, Canterbury Press.

The Author has asserted his right under the Copyright, Designs and
Patents Act 1988 to be identified as the Author of this Work

Unless otherwise indicated, the Scripture quotations contained herein are
from The New Revised Standard Version of the Bible, Anglicized Edition,
copyright © 1989, 1995 by the Division of Christian Education of the
National Council of the Churches of Christ in the United States of America,
and are used by permission. All rights reserved.
Scripture quotations marked (NIV) are taken from The Holy Bible, New
International Version (Anglicised edition) copyright © 1979, 1984, 2011 by
Biblica (formerly International Bible Society). Used by permission of Hodder &
Stoughton Publishers, an Hachette UK company. All rights reserved.

British Library Cataloguing in Publication data
A catalogue record for this book is available
from the British Library

ISBN: 978-1-78622-541-2

Typeset by Regent Typesetting

Contents

1 Introduction: Missional Diplomacy 1
2 On Mission With Jesus: Sharing in the Mission of God 22
3 On Mission With Jesus: Making Disciples 38
4 On Mission With Jesus: Following the Spirit 64
5 On Mission With Jesus: Shaping the Church 87
6 On Mission With Jesus: Anticipating the Future 122
7 On Mission With Jesus: Joining the Family Business 139
8 On Mission With Jesus: A Pilgrim People 151
9 On Mission With Jesus: Identifying Jesus in the Church 166
10 Becoming a 'Jesus on Mission'-Shaped Church 189

Bibliography 214
Index of Names and Subjects 227

The past 20 or more years has seen an extraordinary flourishing of creative imagination and praxis, as churches of many different traditions have engaged in mission with the rapidly changing world around them. In writing this reflection I wish to honour the many pioneers, practitioners, missional thinkers and permission givers who have taken part in this move of the Spirit. I write in the hope that this contribution also will help us to follow the missionary Spirit.

I dedicate this book to my wife, Jackie, who has been my key companion, encourager and support along the way.

I

Introduction: Missional Diplomacy

This book reflects upon understandings of the church that have developed through, or as a consequence of, the Fresh Expressions movement and similar initiatives: part of 'the extraordinary creativity that is being expressed in communities, in churches, and in denominations themselves ... [where] the church is being reimagined as a myriad of new ecclesial forms burst upon the scene' (Ward, *Liquid Ecclesiology*, p. 2). In particular it asks what core underlying image of the church, what I call the default setting, is most appropriate for the day and context in which I write.

My vocation in the latter years of my ordained ministry has largely been one of missional diplomat or door opener, interpreting practitioners to permission givers and vice versa. I was once told, in a different context, that I was personally trusted by two parties, neither of which trusted the other. Fortunately I was not called to that particular ministry of reconciliation, but I have seen my role as that of diplomacy, of aiding mutual interpretation and understanding. One characteristic of many of those who pioneer new forms of church is that their calling is so self-evident to them that they find it hard to imagine why others cannot see it. Equally, permission givers can find it hard to see beyond novelty to the missional and theological rationale for new forms of church. So this is a book of missional diplomacy, aiming to provide theological foundations to give permission givers the theological assurances they need, but also the theological foundations that equip practitioners for the long-term work that pioneering requires.

My concern about the missional form of the church in

today's cultures began with the love of contemporary popular music, which began in my teenage years and continues today. That love developed into thinking and analysis when I attended a conference of the Theological Students Fellowship and heard Dr Francis Schaeffer give the lectures that were published as *The God Who Is There* and later, *Escape from Reason*. Schaeffer was the first person to introduce me to the history of western thought from the Enlightenment, and its shaping of our increasingly secular culture. I then read his colleague Hans Rookmaaker's book *Modern Art and the Death of a Culture*. Rookmaaker was Professor of the History of Art at the Free University of Amsterdam, but he was also the editor of a series of reissues of old recordings of jazz, blues and spirituals, and his reflections extended to what he called 'jazz, blues and beat' (*Modern Art*, pp. 184ff.).

It occurred to me for the first time that I could reflect on the music that moved me in the way that Schaeffer and Rookmaaker mainly reflected on philosophy and high art. From that came a series of talks (chiefly at the Greenbelt Festival, and later at Soul Survivor) and occasional articles, which have continued to the present day. The aim was always to listen to the music on its own terms and take seriously what it was communicating; to attempt to understand it from a biblical Christian world view, and to identify ways in which the Christian gospel could engage it with integrity. But music does not exist in cultural isolation. Popular music and all its accompanying culture is part of the wider culture that makes up the world we live in today and reveals its world view. I had studied the sociology of religion as part of my theology degree, and increasingly found myself thinking about the wider culture, particularly through the lens of the sociology of culture. The publication of Lesslie Newbigin's *The Other Side of '84* and the resulting The Gospel and Our Culture movement gave me new insights and impetus. Like most of those who have engaged in the missiology of western culture, I am standing on Bishop Lesslie's shoulders and return to his writings regularly. Hans Küng's application of paradigm theory to church history in *Theology* and *Christianity* and, in particular, its application to mission by David Bosch in *Trans-*

INTRODUCTION: MISSIONAL DIPLOMACY

forming Mission, provided an essential tool that helped me get to grips with the significance of context and culture change.

But both Newbigin's and Bosch's writing ended just as the transition in western culture labelled 'postmodern' began to take the foreground. Any era or period of culture labelled 'post' (modern, secular, colonial etc.) must, by definition, be a time of transition, when it is clearer what is being left behind, or receding in influence, than what is emerging. The term 'postmodern' was always contested, and used differently in different disciplines, but in the end the terminology was secondary. Whether arguing for postmodernity (David Lyon), late modernity (Anthony Giddens), the second modernity (Ulrich Beck), another modernity (Scott Lasch) or whatever, the various scholars were united in identifying a number of significant areas of cultural and social change, just disagreeing on the labels and the degree of continuity or discontinuity.

Three of the key elements of the emerging culture were:

1 The transition from identity being established by what we produce to what we consume. This was described by Giddens as 'a *novel* phenomenon, which participates directly in the processes of the continuing reshaping of the conditions of day-to-day life' (Giddens, *Modernity and Self-Identity*, pp. 4ff. and 199).
2 The emergence of new communication and information technologies, which according to Lyon 'contribute to *novel* contexts of social interaction' (Lyon, *Jesus in Disneyland*, p. 13). As this has developed through the internet, social media, gaming, ubiquitous mobile phones etc., it has created 'A media environment that is *unique* in its present form' (Couldry and Hepp, *The Mediated Construction of Reality*, p. 53).
3 The increasing significance of networks and the growth of a 'Network Society', and 'The emergence of a *new* social structure' (Castells, *The Rise of the Network Society*, p. 14).

Note the use of 'novel', 'new' and 'unique' by scholars who name this era differently from one another. Giddens wrote, 'The "world" in which we now live is in some profound respects quite distinct from that inhabited by human beings in previous periods of history' (Giddens, *Modernity and Self-Identity*, pp. 4ff.).

The way culture is understood has changed as these transitions have been observed and studied. According to Nick Couldry, 'The old model thinks of a culture as a "place" where certain things are collected together and ordered. But there is no such place. Our primary data are ... patterns of flows and the structural forces which shape them' (Couldry, *Inside Culture*, p. 103).

In practice, western culture is now 'glocal'. The ugly word 'glocalization' was coined by sociologists in the 1990s to describe the impact of the global on the local. It has become more important as scholars have increasingly recognized that globalization does not simply standardize or homogenize everything and everywhere, because 'We live in a world partially interconnected and interdependent, but where a multitude of different cultural arrangements coexist with one another' (Roudometof, *Glocalisation*, p. 138). So 'glocal' is 'The point of intersection between the global and the local' (Vanhoozer, *One Rule to Rule Them All*, p. 99). It is made even more complex by the massive spread of digital media, as a core element of everyday life and community. Couldry and Hepp write: 'As embodied human beings we have no choice but to act *from* a certain locality ... But these localities change their meaning in a world made up of ever more complex translocal connections' (Couldry and Hepp, *The Mediated Construction of Reality*, p. 87). It has to be local or it does not exist, but the local is impacted by the global.

Although each locality is distinct and cannot simply be standardized, a coherent contemporary world view, with great capacity for internal variety, has emerged through these changes. It is structured for individuals. Its core value is the right to individual choice: 'Individualization is becoming the social structure of the second modernity itself' (Beck and Beck-Gernsheim, *Individualization*, p. xxii). It has a satnav, consumer choice. The globalized consumer world provides multiple options, so consumer choice is the tool for individual navigation. Its controlling story is constructivist – create your identity through your individual choices. 'You can be whatever you want to be.'

INTRODUCTION: MISSIONAL DIPLOMACY

Furthermore its assumptions are 'secular'. There is plenty of room within it for religion or spirituality as a personal consumer choice for those who like that sort of thing but 'many people are happy living for goals which are purely immanent; they live in a way that takes no account of the transcendent' (Taylor, *A Secular Age*, p. 143). Charles Taylor has described in detail 'a move from a society where belief in God is unchallenged and, indeed, unproblematic, to one in which it is understood to be one option among others, and frequently not the easiest to embrace' (Taylor, *A Secular Age*, p. 143). He describes current western assumptions as an 'immanent frame' – 'A race of humans has arisen which has managed to experience its world entirely as immanent' (Taylor, *A Secular Age*, p. 376).

In other words, happiness is found through the multiple-choice options within the immanent frame, so there is no need to look beyond, even should there be anything there. Taylor's image of the frame demonstrates the promise and the limits of 'secular' life. Happiness, or whatever is realistically possible, is available within the frame. But the frame blinds those within it to the possibility that there might be more.

Summing up the implications of Taylor's work, James K. A. Smith wrote:

> Your 'secular' neighbours aren't looking for 'answers' – for some bits of information missing from their mental maps. To the contrary, they have completely different maps ... they have constructed webs of meaning that provide almost all the significance they need for their lives ... A way of being in the world that offers significance without transcendence. (Smith, *How (Not) to Be Secular*, pp. vii–viii)

My preferred metaphor for this era is Zygmunt Bauman's 'Liquid Modernity'.[1] According to Bauman, '"Postmodernity" and "postmodernism" have been hopelessly confused ... Hence my own proposition "liquid modernity" which points to what is continuous (melting, disembedding) and discontinuous (no solidification of the melted, no re-embedding) alike' (Bauman and Tester, *Conversations with Zygmunt Bauman*, pp. 97ff.).

'Liquid', as Bauman used it, is a useful term. It provides an accessible metaphor for the speed and complexity of the changes we have been living through. It makes us aware that structures, commitments, trust in institutions and patterns of life and work which were once taken for granted, are dissolving, and being replaced by an ongoing and acceleration process of change. This change is discontinuous. The assumptions of the past are no longer assured guides for decisions in the future. Giddens described this era as 'Modernity's surprising outcome'. 'Living in the modern world is more like being aboard a careering juggernaut rather than being in a carefully controlled and well driven motor car' (Giddens, *Consequences*, p. 53). This complex globalized world is unpredictable, almost by definition. Bauman says: 'the world we inhabit is as complex a system as can be imagined, its future is a great unknown, and it is bound to remain unknown whatever we do' (Bauman, *44 Letters from the Liquid Modern World*, p. 107).

Pete Ward has helpfully applied Bauman's metaphor to the church and ecclesiology, but admits that his use of the term is 'against the grain' (Ward, *Liquid Ecclesiology*, p. 9). For Bauman this liquidity is a matter of concern. This change is a reality, but not all of it is good. Some of this liquid is corrosive.[2] Patterns and institutions of mutual human commitment are being undermined. 'The solids which are in the process of being melted at the present time are the bonds which interlock individual choices in collective projects and actions' (Bauman, *44 Letters*, p. 6).

This sociology of the 'new' culture needs to complement not replace the understandings which preceded it. Whatever the realities of the consumer networked world may be, they have not replaced the earlier realities of disparities of wealth, poverty, power, opportunity, gender and racial inequality. The consumer choice world may have captured the hearts and imaginations of many people in the West, but there is little opportunity for equal access. Christian witness will need to affirm and engage much of the 'new' culture, but also counter aspects of it. This is acknowledged in the *Mission-Shaped Church* report. In the Introduction I wrote:

INTRODUCTION: MISSIONAL DIPLOMACY

The gospel has to be heard within the culture of the day, but it always has to be heard as a call to appropriate repentance. It is the incarnation of the gospel, within a dominantly consumer society, that provides the Church of England with its major missionary challenge. (pp. xi ff.)

But if the culture we live in today is 'in some profound respects quite distinct from that inhabited by human beings in previous periods of history' (Giddens, *Consequences*, p. 5), how do we engage it with the gospel? This 'gospel and culture' question leads inevitably to questions about the missionary shape of the church for this context: hence *Mission-Shaped Church*.

From my perspective the Fresh Expressions movement, originating in the UK, developed from the meeting of gospel and culture concerns with Anglican church-planting theory. Each enriched the other, the most significant further development being the emphasis on discernment in each local context, rather than just identifying wider cultural trends. How is the church to be here? We have moved from a model where, with a few allowances for churchmanship, the local Church of England looks more or less the same everywhere, to an approach where, with a shared Anglican DNA, it needs to take shape appropriate to its local context, and will therefore be diverse in form. The Church of England's House of Bishops speak of 'creating and normalizing a pattern of diversity, of parish and other traditional forms alongside newer forms. This pattern of diversity is the "new normal"' (*Church Planting*, para. 4).

This does not mean a complete disregard of scripture, or of the history and tradition of the church, or that of a particular tradition within it. Guided by the scriptures, pioneer leaders know that there are core characteristics of any church – worship, community, prayer, scripture, baptism, holy communion, mission and so on. They are asking what form these should take in the context to which God has called them. To use Douglas Gay's metaphor, practitioners 'remix' their historic resources for the new context they face (Gay, *Remixing the Church*).

Some 20 years have passed since the writing of *Mission-Shaped Church* and there is now sufficient distance, and sufficient quantitative and qualitative evidence gathered, for perspective, but sufficient proximity for relevance. What have we learned about the church for our culture and contexts? And as we engage with this cultural shift, what have we learned for the future cultural shifts, which inevitably will come, so that succeeding generations have some tools passed down from us for appropriate discernment and mission?

How are churches formed?

According to Duerksen and Dyrness, 'the entities we call "churches" emerge from the interaction of their cultural assumptions, their special historical inheritances and their understanding of God's revelation through scripture' (*Seeking Church*, p. ix). Similarly, according to Healey 'The distinctiveness of the church lies in its Spirit-guided participation in God's self-communication as this is mediated by scripture, the church's history, and its traditions of practice and enquiry' (Healey, 'Ecclesiology, Ethnography and God', p. 194). Cultural context, ecclesial tradition and scripture bear some resemblance to Anglicanism's scripture, tradition and reason, for reason is not detached objectivity. It is always contextual – how do people think and see from here?

Cultural context

Context is vital for two reasons.

First, as we will see later, the local church is intended to be incarnational – the body of Christ taking shape for this particular place in the light of Christ. Second, we are all culturally embedded people. 'Our culture is within us as well as around us. We cannot escape it, though it is possible to innovate, replace, add to, transform and in other ways alter our use of the culture that we have received' (Kraft, *Christianity in Culture*, p. 106). Our cultural assumptions, both good and bad, provide the place from which we see, assess and reason. There is nowhere else to stand but here, and 'here' is where we are called to live and minister as the church. Or if we are called to establish a fresh expression of church cross-culturally the assumptions we bring with us may not be the same as those of the context to which we have been called. If culture is 'the way we do things around here', as Archbishop Warlock of Liverpool put it, time needs to be taken to get our minds around those ways. To oversimplify, the gospel affirms some aspects of a culture, challenges others and is neutral to others, except to the extent that they are part of the character of the community where we are called to embody Christ.

Ecclesial tradition

But we also come as traditioned people, in my case as an Anglican. We bring the traditions we all share, and those of our particular tribes within them, with us. Very properly they will influence our plans and expectations. We will be shaped even by our reactions against part of our tradition. But tradition is always double edged. It bears the best of our DNA, and the essential practices which we share with most other Christian communities. But it can be in danger of preserving habits of church life which have lost touch with the people we are seeking to reach. Tradition is not a frozen asset.

According to Duerksen and Dyrness:

> Quite often the particular expression of an ecclesial marker becomes frozen in time, disassociated from the cultural, social and political influences that generated its emergence. Over time, the context in which those markers gained their particular salience fades from view, and the practices themselves come to be seen as pure markers of the church. (*Seeking Church*, p. 149)

'Pure' in the sense of having meaning within the church but no longer in the context. Tradition is not a fixed point used to ensure that there is no innovation. It is a dynamic, developing gift from the past with the capacity to ensure that missional innovation is properly rooted in the gospel.

Scripture

So from our context, shaped in different ways by our tradition, we turn to scripture.

Levison, for example, claims that 'The inspired interpretation of scripture, more than mission in a general sense or miracles ... is the principal effect of the Holy Spirit in the book of Acts' (*Inspired: The Holy Spirit and the Mind of Faith*, p. 152). As it was with the church in Acts, so we also can expect the Holy Spirit to open the scriptures to us in our missionary context and to show us how to open them for that context. We come to scripture, from our context (we have nowhere else to be), informed by our tradition, in order to bring scripture to bear on our context, in a way that both engages it with the gospel, and renews our tradition.

The Holy Spirit is in the whole process. 'Our theological understanding of church involves the real presence of God and the potential for a relationship between God and people ... thus God is actively at work as an agent in the emergent process of church' (Duerksen and Dyrness, *Seeking Church*, p. 71). Context, tradition, scripture – these are the component parts which shape the church, but only too easily they can become set, or even frozen, in what I call a default setting.

Default settings

Whenever Christians gather to talk about ecclesiology, about the nature of the church, you will find that different groups will assume the conversation will be about different things. So when the Church of England and the Methodist Church formed a joint Faith and Order working party to review fresh expressions of church, the initial emphasis was on faith, yes, but particularly 'Order': authority and authorized ministry, the authenticity of the church identified through its authorized leadership. A conference of Christians in a sacramental tradition will emphasize the proper administration of the sacraments of the gospel. A meeting of charismatic evangelicals will think of a gathering for

INTRODUCTION: MISSIONAL DIPLOMACY

worship, with an active encounter with the Holy Spirit. I worship with a group of village churches, where the imagination rarely goes beyond attending a traditional service in an ancient building.

Like mission, ministry and worship, ecclesiology is a 'greedy' theological concept. In one way or another it engages with the whole range of Christian belief and practice. Whatever the intention of their authors, all ecclesiologies are partial – they cannot cover the whole field in any more than the most general sense. Rowan Williams says: 'Every particular way we crystallize [the church] is going to lack something'; the church 'is not captured by any one institutional expression' (quoted in Taylor, *First Expressions*, p. 103). To be of more than a detached academic value, ecclesiologies have to have a focus for their time. It is not sufficient to simply cover the primary biblical metaphors – the people of God, the body of Christ, the temple of the Spirit and so on – and the historic marks – one, holy, catholic and apostolic – without contemporary application. How did these engage together for the times in which they were written? How do they function now? What new insights does a changing culture or fresh circumstance bring to view? Ecclesiologies must be contextual, if they are to be of service to the ecclesia. But they must also be recognizable as an authentic expression of the Church of Jesus Christ as revealed in the scriptures and creeds, and as seen in diverse cultures and contexts through the history of the church. This is not to be an attempt to create church from scratch, which is an impossibility; rather it is 'Re-Contextual Church'.[3] This combination of newness (fresh expression) and the family likeness is the key to any ecclesiology that has the capacity to envision and equip the church of its day.

Forms of church that are long established and regarded as 'normal' by many worshippers can leave the impression that 'normal' means universal: 'If it was good enough for St Paul ...!' All forms of church are contextual, 'no churches transcend culture' (Morris, *Flexible Church*, p. 7), and we easily forget that they have evolved over time within their historic context. This misperception becomes particularly critical during major times of cultural change, when a growing gap can emerge between the gospel community and the culture in which it bears witness. Any attempt to defend a particular form of church life at all costs is likely to widen that gap.

One consequence of this disconnect is that familiar biblical metaphors take on diminished meanings. Terms like 'the people of God', 'the body of Christ' or 'the temple of the Spirit' remain familiar but lose their power to envision or transform. They are assumed to fit the church as it is being practised, rather like Nietzsche's description of 'truths' as 'metaphors which are worn out and without sensuous power, coins which have lost their pictures and now matter only as metal, no longer as coins' (*On Truth and Lies in a Nonmoral Sense*, p. 13). To change the analogy, centuries of church life have created a sort of ecclesial arthritis, a lack of flexibility. A properly contextual ecclesiology needs to regain the transformative power of these biblical descriptions of the church for here and now.

It is now commonplace to recognize that the church and its mission have always been shaped in response to the primary cultural paradigms of different historical eras. As mentioned earlier, drawing on the paradigm theory of Thomas Kuhn (*The Structure of Scientific Revolutions*), in both *Theology for the Third Millenium* and *Christianity*, Hans Küng identified five eras and paradigms of the church. This was then applied to the mission of the church, first by David Bosch, who addressed a sixth emerging paradigm in *Transforming Mission*, and then by Bevans and Schroeder in *Constants in Context*, who identified the eras slightly differently, 13 years later. As their title indicated, Bevans and Schroeder emphasized the relationship between the 'constants' identifiable in each era, with the diversity of practice and emphasis required by or developed in the varied 'contexts'. But hindsight concerning past paradigms is easier than discernment in the present. Understandings of the church inevitably lag behind major periods of cultural change, but they dare not be left behind.

As I have described here, we have been living in such a period of cultural change. The missionary context of the church in the West has changed out of all recognition during my lifetime, and the pace of change is still increasing. Professor Eddie Gibbs,

INTRODUCTION: MISSIONAL DIPLOMACY

whose ordained ministry began in the Church of England, famously wrote, 'The ministry training I received over 40 years ago was for a world that now no longer exists' (Gibbs, *Leadership Next*, p. 9). The main features and direction of change are clear: modern to late or postmodern ('liquid modernity'), Christendom to post Christendom, solid to liquid, producer to consumer, local to glocal, the emergence of a global network society, from identity understood as a given to identity as a construct – and, as this book is being written, the impact of Covid-19, which brought much of everyday life as we know it to an abrupt halt.

The significance of this, and the study of cultural eras and paradigms, is because 'mission is the mother of theology ... an accompanying manifestation of the Christian mission' (Martin Kähler, quoted in Bosch, *Transforming Mission*, p. 16). The church's theology and theological imagination is renewed as the 'Great Tradition' engages with new contexts and eras with their assumptions, thought forms and ways of life. Missionary engagement refreshes the church's self-understanding and saves its theology from seeming frozen in time with apparent irrelevance.

Naturally enough, most Christians have a default setting which is taken for granted when they hear the word 'church', or which is at the back of our minds when we use the term ourselves. It is part of our world view, as Christians with a particular history, in a particular tradition, in a particular place. For many Christians their default setting finds its focus in a gathering for worship in a particular tradition and, for most, in an ecclesiastical building. Pete Ward calls this 'solid church', saying 'Solid church arises from the understanding that Church is a meeting. In other words, Church is a gathering in one place, at one time, with the purpose of performing a shared ritual.' This, he says, 'has a deep hold on the imagination of the Christian community such that it is almost impossible to think of Church as being anything other than a meeting' (Ward, pp. 9–10). As Anthony Thiselton says, 'From a *biblical* perspective today's commonly used phrase "go to church" would seem to verge on the ridiculous ... resulting from the regrettable custom of using the word "church" to denote a church building ... Not wrong but entirely secondary and unbiblical' (Thiselton, *Systematic Theology*, p. 311). But over the years, through customary practice, and our habits of speech, certain images of church life have imprisoned our imagination. As Elaine Heath reports:

> Whenever I talk about a church becoming missional and leaving behind its self-centeredness, when I talk about the poor, invariably I am told that what people like the Missionaries of Charity are doing is fine for them, but not practical for most people. They are a special interest ministry, not 'the church'. I am told that a normal church in the suburbs is a building with lots of programming to meet the needs of its members. (*The Mystic Way of Evangelism*, p. 114)

Often we know better theologically, but years of practice have frozen our imagination and make it hard to see whether we have default settings which may not best serve the vocation of the church today. What I call a default setting is the set of assumptions and unreflected habits of thought and church life which make up our world view,[4] as it is applied to our participation in the church. But a world view is something we think *with* and rarely think *about*. It's like a lens or pair of spectacles '*through* which, not *at* which a society or individual normally looks' (N. T. Wright, *The New Testament and the People of God*, p. 125). When my spectacles are working as they should, I hardly notice them. They facilitate my seeing, they are not the focus of it. A world view 'is not argued *to* but argued from' (Bosch, *Believing in the Future*, p. 49). This is not strange: to see anything you have to stand somewhere. But not all locations give the fullest view. As vicar of St Michael-le-Belfrey in York, I could stand outside my church building and see down the street. If I crossed the road and climbed the tower of York Minster, on a clear day, I could see halfway to the city of Hull. So the other consequence of a world view is that it controls what we do not or cannot see, acting more as blinkers than spectacles. We remain ignorant of what we cannot see. There is a much-quoted statement of the philosopher Ludwig Wittgenstein that 'A picture held us captive. And we could not

INTRODUCTION: MISSIONAL DIPLOMACY

get outside it, for it lay in our language and language seemed to repeat it to us inexorably' (Wittgenstein, *Philosophical Investigations*, p. 115). What he had to say about habits of language which prevented us from seeing differently is, I believe, true about our habit-formed imagination about the church. We have default settings which prevent us from seeing it differently. The years of Christendom provide the primary example, but so also are renewal movements from previous cultural eras; and even many models of fresh expressions can be restricted or held captive by a dominant default setting. According to Paul Hiebert, 'The problem with worldviews is that they are largely unnamed, unexamined and unassailable' (*Transforming Worldviews*, p. 320). But in times of significant cultural change our default settings about the church have to be re-examined.

The philosopher Charles Taylor coined the term 'social imaginary' as a way to capture a combination of assumptions, habits, stories and explanations. He applies it to western modernity as a whole pattern of life: 'Not a mere mental construct, but a way of being in the world. It is the water one swims in. It is the context in which one's reality, one's actions and one's identity are formed and have meaning' (*Modern Social Imaginaries*, p. 2). The importance of Taylor's term is its focus on the imagination: what we can or cannot imagine because of our current assumptions and way of life. He warns that our current social imaginary 'has now become so self-evident to us that we have trouble seeing it as one possible conception among others' (*Modern Social Imaginaries*, p. 2). It becomes 'obvious' rather than an option. This concept can be properly applied to our imagining of the church. Drawing on Taylor's concept, Scott MacDougall says: 'we cannot be church properly, we do not do Christian community well, if our ecclesial imagination is stunted' (*More than Communion*, p. 3).

Our current assumed imagining of the church is largely seen as the only possible one because we cannot imagine it differently. It is the way we have learned to think and feel about the church and behave in it. 'This imagination often remains invisible', MacDougall says (p. 1). It is taken for granted as normal and obvious. As Hiebert puts it, 'It's hard to think about what you are thinking with' (*Transforming Worldviews*, p. 320). Furthermore, when church attendance is in decline and its future seems threatened, the instinctive reaction is to defend our assumptions more strongly, to circle the wagons, either because its failure is unimaginable, or fatalistically because there is no realistic imaginative perception of an alternative. Centuries of church life have created a sort of ecclesial arthritis. Our default settings for the church are often too static. So it is harder to innovate when the mission of the church requires that we change. Few churches are capable of new initiatives from a standing start, let alone from ecclesial arthritis!

A further problem with a default setting centred primarily on a gathering for worship is that ministry can be seen primarily as the activities which take place within, or to facilitate, that gathering or which are the function of those who have special roles in that gathering. This can combine with an overemphasis on the laity/clergy distinction at the cost of the callings of all Christians. Discipleship can be marginalized or become the focus of 'special' Christians only. Which is unfortunate, as the term Christian was first given as a nickname for disciples of Jesus (Acts 11.26).

Which brings me to my primary concern, that current default settings about the church equip us very poorly for the primary challenge we face: the shape and praxis of a missional church in a changed and changing culture, recently reshaped by Covid-19. How can we most effectively embody Jesus in communities of his followers and share in his mission locally and nationally today? When the default setting for our perception of church no longer engages appropriately to the context in which the church is called, it is time to revise that default setting, without losing the essence of an authentic church. Just as in 'culture eats strategy for breakfast'[5] so default settings eat theoretical alternatives, however theologically sound. What is required is not just a renewed default setting in theory, but an accompanying set of appropriate practices. We will have to act our way to a renewed ecclesiology by developing appropriate practices until they become habit and reshape our imagination.

INTRODUCTION: MISSIONAL DIPLOMACY

Mission-Shaped Church

The cultural disconnect that I have described (apart, of course, from Covid-19) was central to the brief for the *Mission-Shaped Church* report. We wrote that 'We have allowed our culture and the Church to drift apart, without our noticing' (*Mission-Shaped Church*, p. 13) and spoke of a moment of repentance.

The brief for our working party was to revisit the 1994 'Breaking New Ground' report on church planting, in the light of the evident cultural and social change, and the emergence of new forms of church in response to it.

- Our report was to address 'changing cultural and ecclesial contexts – what is the environment in which we are called to be and do church? If we are in a "new" context for mission, how does that lead into new models/ways of church in mission?'
- It was to include 'an exploration of an Anglican missiological ecclesiology and practice, the relationship between Anglican theology/tradition and emerging church themes'. How do these various patterns 'fit' with Anglican ecclesiology and practice?
- There was to be an assessment of progress with 'church planting' as a mission model and dynamic, and of the variety of phenomena under the 'planting' label, of which we soon had a long list – youth congregations, cell church; multiple congregations; not-Sunday congregations; network, non-geographical church; 'alternative worship'; urban situations; community development-based plants; 'traditional' church plants; new monastic orders; café church; network (non-geographical) church; new 'traditional' churches; 'tribal' church planting/groupings; chaplaincy in prisons, workplace etc.; deaneries; ethnically and culturally homogenous church plants.
- The report would include an overview of church-planting methods, policy and practice within dioceses and seek to evaluate and reaffirm the validity and importance of 'planting' methodologies.

The notes of our meeting in May 2002 remind me that I said, 'We will need to sketch an Anglican missiological ecclesiology.' One of the later criticisms of the report was that we had not drawn sufficiently on Church of England sources. But there lay our difficulty. Our Church of England ecclesiological statements were of a particular social imaginary which had very little to say about the missionary nature of the church, which was assumed but rarely clearly stated. For example, in the 500-page volume *The Study of Anglicanism*, 'Anglicans and Mission' appears as the final chapter. It begins:

> Anglicans have made a considerable contribution to the mission of the Church Universal. Unlike the Roman Catholic Church, there is no body of theory to which the enquirer may turn for an understanding of the Church's mind ... By contrast the Anglican contribution has to be pursued by study of its practice and the writings of individuals, with occasional references in official documents. (Quoted in Yates, *Anglicans and Mission*, p. 430)

The joint Church of England and Methodist Faith and Order report *Fresh Expressions in the Mission of the Church* summarizes the Church of England's understanding of the church as 'both catholic and reformed', part of the one holy catholic and apostolic church (Declaration of Assent, Nicene Creed), 'a congregation ... in which the pure Word of God is preached and the Sacraments duly administered according to Christ's ordinance (The 39 Articles) with orders of bishops, priests and deacons' (Ch. 4). All correct, but where is mission in this foundational chapter of a book reflecting on the validity of fresh expressions of church?

But at the same time, in the Church of England, we have had:

- A Decade of Evangelism – at the initiative of the African bishops, the 1988 Lambeth Conference called the whole Communion to a 'Decade of Evangelism' from 1990. The primary fruit of the decade was not a great deal of effective evangelism, but the bringing of evangelism and mission to the top of the Church's agenda.

INTRODUCTION: MISSIONAL DIPLOMACY

- The 5 Marks of Mission, adopted by the Church of England's General Synod in 1996.
- Alpha, Emmaus and Pilgrim courses.
- Hundreds of food banks, debt counselling centres, toddler groups etc.

Since the publication of *Mission-Shaped Church*, the landscape has changed considerably. There has been:

- Research on 1,109 fresh expressions of church, covering some 20 different models in 21 dioceses.[6]
- The development of pioneer lay and ordained ministry.[7]
- The House of Bishops 2018 statement on church planting, which says: 'As bishops, we are committed to adopting an approach to mission and church growth within our dioceses that embraces both the contribution of traditional forms of ministry (e.g. through our parishes, chaplaincies and schools), and the contribution of newer forms (e.g. through our church plants, fresh expressions etc.). We see no binary divide between traditional and new, as forms of church evolve. In the Church of England today, bishops undertake to pursue and support the full range of contributions to mission and church growth creating and normalizing a pattern of diversity, of parish and other traditional forms alongside newer forms. This pattern of diversity is the "new normal".'[8]

Most recently, and significantly, the 'Vision for the Church of England in the 2020s' with its welcome, Christ-centred emphasis on 'a church of missionary disciples', 'a church that is younger and more diverse' and 'a church where mixed ecology (of traditional church and fresh expressions of church) is the norm'.[9]

In practice, much of the Church of England is and has been visibly committed to mission, both in traditional parochial ministry and fresh expressions of church. But that is not reflected in most ecclesiological statements. It is as though we see mission as a task to which we are committed, perhaps more from anxiety about numerical decline than any positive understanding, but not as of the essence of the church. What is missing is not some acknowledgement of the missionary task of the church, but a greater understanding of the missionary nature of the church. The danger otherwise is that missional praxis is purely opportunistic, rather than soundly founded on the Christian tradition.

There have been some notable exceptions (the 'occasional references in official documents' mentioned by Yates), which will be referred to as this book proceeds. Above all, the source of the term 'fresh expressions' (*Mission-Shaped Church*, p. 34) is the Declaration of Assent, made by all Church of England clergy at their ordination and at the start of every new role in ministry: 'The Church of England is part of the One, Holy, Catholic and Apostolic Church, worshipping the one true God, Father, Son and Holy Spirit. It professes the faith uniquely revealed in the Holy Scriptures and set forth in the catholic creeds, which faith the Church is called upon to proclaim afresh in each generation.'

This lack of attention to mission in ecclesiologies is not a uniquely Anglican problem. Most theologizing about the church in recent decades has been either in constructive ecumenical dialogue, or in defence of a particular denomination's ecclesiology. The focus has been unity rather than mission. In his book *Church*, Ephraim Radner from Wycliffe College Toronto says: 'Defending this or that version of the Church has in fact defined our thinking about the Church almost exhaustively until relatively recently' (ch. 1).

At the licensing of Phil Potter as my successor as Archbishops' Missioner and Leader of the Fresh Expressions Team, Archbishop Justin expressed his confidence: 'that Fresh Expressions will continue to lead the reimagination of the ministry of the church in this country'. That missional reimagining cannot be complete without a change of default setting. What comes first to our imaginations when we hear the word 'church'?

Sometimes, to go forward we have to go back to the beginning and reconnect the present to our founding events and above all to our Founder. In the chapters that follow I will propose what I regard as the original default setting as the one to reaffirm today. The church is 'a community of disciples on mission with Jesus'. This is not entirely an original suggestion. The church as

INTRODUCTION: MISSIONAL DIPLOMACY

'a community of disciples' was proposed by Avery Dulles when he released the second edition of *Models of the Church* in 1986 (ch. 13), but it seems even more potent today in our strange and unpredictable times. Each part of this proposal, which is more extensive than that of Dulles', is essential: mission, discipleship, community and above all the active presence and leadership of Jesus. We are the community who join Jesus in his continuing mission from the Father to the world.

Notes

1 Bauman followed this through with a series of 'Liquid' titles.
2 For example, see Richard Sennett, 1998, *The Corrosion of Character*, New York: Norton.
3 A term coined by Helen D. Morris in *Flexible Church*, pp. viii, 7.
4 By using the term 'world view' I do not mean purely intellectual understanding. For N. T. Wright, a world view has four levels: 1. The answers to life's key questions; 2. The symbols which represent our culture ('signs'); 3. The way we choose to live (praxis); 4. The underlying story. See 1992, *The New Testament and the People of God*, pp. 109–12, 122–6; 1996, *Jesus and the Victory of God*, pp. 136–43. According to Paul Hiebert, a world view has three dimensions: cognitive, affective and moral (beliefs, feelings, values) (Paul Hiebert, 2008, *Transforming Worldviews*, p. 27).
5 Attributed to Peter Drucker.
6 Canon Dr George Lings, 'The Day of Small Things', *Church Army*, https://churcharmy.org/wp-content/uploads/2021/04/the-day-of-small-things.pdf (accessed 11.8.23).
7 See 'Vocations to Pioneer Ministry', *The Church of England*, https://www.churchofengland.org/life-events/vocations/vocations-pioneer-ministry (accessed 11.8.23).
8 The paper 'Church Planting and the Mission of the Church', June 2018, is no longer available on the Church of England website.
9 The paper 'Leadership and Governance: Emerging Church' is no longer available on the Church of England website.

2

On Mission With Jesus: Sharing in the Mission of God

> One of the things I have particularly noticed about life in the Church ... is how little time people spend thinking about the nature of the Church. (Hardy, *God's Ways*, p. 217)

If we are to reset the default setting of the church, we need to spend some time thinking about its missionary nature, which is to be understood theologically but also needs to be embedded in our imaginations. For many Christians, mission is still seen as one of the tasks given to the church, mainly overseas, a task which some find uncomfortable and not very British. It can be seen as having bad history, whether through caricatures of manipulative evangelism or a compromised history of colonialism. But where there has been bad practice the only proper response is repentance and good practice, but the church is not excused mission for apparently un-British behaviour.

The gift of mission

But there is something much more fundamental to be grasped. Mission is more than a task, it is a gift from God, and it is of the very essence of the church itself. Christian faith begins with God's missionary initiative. We would not know God as we do if the Father had not sent the Son in the power of the Spirit. 'God's love was revealed among us in this way: God sent his only Son into the world so that we might live through him. In this is love, not that we loved God but that he loved us and sent his Son' (1 John 4.9–10). 'There is Church because there is mission, not vice versa' (Bosch, *Transforming Mission*, p. 390).

The church is first and foremost the people of God, brought into being by God, bound to God, for the glory of God. If we are going to rediscover the missional nature of the church, we have to begin with the most important finding of contemporary missiology. Mission is not simply an activity of the church, something that God commands the church to do (although he does), and for which we will have to give an account (although we will): mission is an activity of God, in which we participate. Mission is an essential consequence of being in Christ. The church is both the fruit of God's mission and a participant in it. The best theological starting point is the church's participation in the *missio Dei*, the mission of God (for a historical outline of the emergence of *missio Dei*, see Bevans and Schroeder, *Constants in Context*, ch. 9). The practice of what we call mission is as old as the church itself, but the term is a comparative newcomer. For much of the Church's history the word *missio* was a technical theological term in trinitarian theology for the sending of the Son and the Spirit. The contemporary usage, applying it to the church's activity only began in the sixteenth century, and as David Bosch indicates: 'Unfortunately the relationship between the original and the modern meaning of *missio* has for a long time not been recognized' (Bosch, *Witness*, pp. 239–40).

The idea of the *missio Dei* was a development inspired by the theology of Karl Barth and is one of the fruits of an ecumenical re-engagement with the doctrine of the Trinity in the twentieth century (see James Torrance, 'The Doctrine of the Trinity in our Contemporary Situation'; Thompson, *Modern Trinitarian Perspectives*; Greenwood, *Transforming Priesthood*, pp. 74–7). The idea, though not the term, was adopted by the Willingen conference of the International Missionary Council in 1952 (the International Missionary Council merged with the World Council of Churches in 1961). The statement of this conference affirmed:

> The missionary movement of which we are a part has its source in the Triune God himself. Out of the depths of his love for us, the Father has sent forth his own beloved Son to reconcile all things to himself ... We who have been chosen in Christ ...

are committed to full participation in his redeeming mission. There is no participation in Christ without participation in his mission to the world. That by which the Church receives its existence is that by which it is also given its world-mission. (*International Review of Mission* 92, no. 367 (2003), p. 464)

The final sentence from Willingen is worth careful consideration. The church is born through mission, and in the moment of birth receives its call to mission. Mission is of the essence of the church. This understanding of mission as *missio Dei*, the mission of God, rather than a mere activity of the church in obedience to God, is articulated in two of the most influential books on mission of our time, both mentioned in the previous chapter:

> Mission was understood as being derived from the very nature of God. It was thus put in the context of the doctrine of the Trinity, not of ecclesiology or soteriology. The classic doctrine of the *missio Dei* ... Was expanded to include yet another 'movement': Father, Son and Holy Spirit sending the Church into the world. As far as missionary thinking was concerned this linking with the doctrine of the Trinity constituted an important innovation ... In the new image mission is not primarily an activity of the church, but an attribute of God. God is a missionary God ... Mission is therefore seen as a movement of God towards the world; the church is viewed as an instrument for that mission. There is church because there is mission, not vice versa. To participate in mission is to participate in the movement of God's love toward people, since God is a fountain of sending love. (Bosch, *Transforming Mission*, p. 390)

Bevans and Schroeder concur:

> The result of this therefore is that mission is not a task that is one among several in which the church should be engaged; mission, rather, belongs to the very purpose, life and structure of the church – its 'royal charter'. (*Constants in Context*, pp. 290–1)

That mission is the church's 'royal charter' is now the common understanding among missiologists. Andrew Kirk, for example, wrote:

> Mission is so much at the heart of the Church's life, that rather than think of it as one aspect of its existence, it is better to think of it as defining its essence. The Church is by nature missionary to the extent that, if it ceases to be missionary, it has not just failed in one of its tasks, it has ceased being Church. (*What is Mission?*, p. 30)

But mission, understood as participation in the *missio Dei*, has been clarified by two important constructive critiques. First, it is essential that *missio Dei* be understood Christologically. That the mission of God is through, for and focused on the incarnate Lord. This has not always been the case. Bishop John V. Taylor, one of the great Church of England missionary statesmen, believed that the International Missionary Council settled on what he called 'the gloriously inclusive term' because 'there is an inherent, if not deliberate, vagueness in the term "Mission of God" which lays it open to abuse. It can be made to include anything under the sun that anyone considers a Good Thing' (Taylor, *The Uncancelled Mandate*, pp. 1-2). Taylor was reflecting on an interpretation of *missio Dei* which developed after Willingen, which saw it as providence, the general work of God in the world, irrespective of, or even excluding, the church. This, for Taylor, was to confuse or replace God's redeeming mission through Christ, with the overall providence of God. This, Taylor claimed, was:

> Confusing the particular scope of the Christian mission, however broad that might be, with the vast inclusiveness of the ultimate purpose of God for the creation. They were confusing the divine means with the divine end. For the mission which has been laid on the Christian community from its inception arose out of, and is forever focused upon, the historical event of Jesus Christ. (*The Uncancelled Mandate*, p. 2)

But Taylor was fully convinced that mission was God's mission, through Christ by the Spirit, in which we participate. In *The Go-Between God* he wrote, 'The chief actor in the historic mission of the Christian church is the Holy Spirit. He is the director of the whole enterprise. The mission consists of the things that he is doing in the world. In a special way it consists of the light that he is focussing upon Jesus Christ' (p. 3; see also Graham Cray, *Discerning Leadership: Co-operating with the Go-Between God*).

In some sense, God, as Bosch claimed, is a missionary God by nature. However, as John Flett has pointed out, the sending of the Son and Spirit into the world for its redemption can seem to be a second step, a remedial action necessitated by human sinfulness. In which case the mission of God in Christ is a 'second step' in response to the world, not a revelation of God's eternal nature (see Moynagh, *Church for Every Context*, pp. 124ff.). In *The Witness of God*, Flett warns that 'sending' (*missio*) is potentially too 'thin' a concept to demonstrate that mission is of the heart of God. For Flett divine giving, God's self-donation, more than sending, reveals the heart of mission, and the missionary nature of God. Mission is rooted in the trinitarian life itself:

> The Father's act in sending the Son and Spirit into fallen creation is not separate from who God is in himself. God is in himself the answer to the problem of the connection between the divine and the human. The missionary enterprise originates, not in historical contingences ... but in the being of God. (p. 211)

The sending of the Son and the Spirit for the sake of the world are evidence of the mutual self-giving which are the very character of the triune God: 'God has not withheld himself from true humanity as true being, but that He has given no less than Himself to humanity as the overcoming of their need, and light in their darkness – Himself as Father in His own Son by the Holy Spirit' (Flett, *The Witness of God*, p. 201). This coheres with Karl Rahner's much-quoted statement that 'the Economic Trinity is the Immanent Trinity and vice versa' (*The Trinity*, p. 309); that God's self-revelation for our salvation corresponds to and reveals God's essential triune nature. The triune God as revealed through the coming of the Son and the Spirit in human history fully reveals the nature of the triune God, at least to the extent that human beings need to grasp it.

In the New Testament, the Father's whole focus is on the Son, whom he has sent. He is 'my Son the beloved' (Mark 1.11, 9.7; Col. 1.13). It is only through the Son that we can know the Father (Matt. 11.27) or come to the Father (John 14.6-7). To see Jesus is to see the Father (John 14.9). 'The Father judges no one but has given all judgement to the Son' (John 5.22). The Father gave 'all things into his (Son's) hands' (John 13.3). God the Father's true nature is revealed in Christ. He is 'the image of the invisible God' (Col. 1.15). 'He is the reflection of God's glory and the exact imprint of God's very being' (Heb. 1.3). He is by very nature God and becomes by very nature human (Phil. 2.6-8). But equally, the Son depends upon the Father. It is the Father who reveals Jesus' true identity (Matt. 16.17). The Son's whole purpose on earth is to do the Father's will, whether that be in his daily ministry (John 5.19-20) or facing the costliness of the cross (Mark 14.36). St Paul tells us that the whole work of the Son is 'to the glory of God the Father' (Phil. 2.11). The same mutual self-giving is seen in the relationship between the Son and the Spirit and the Spirit and the Father. The birth (Luke 1.35), ministry (Acts 10.38), teaching (Luke 4.18-21), experience of the Father (Luke 10.21), atoning death (Heb. 9.14) and resurrection (Rom. 1.4) of Jesus are all dependent on the Holy Spirit.

But the Spirit is 'the Spirit of Christ' (Rom. 8.9), 'the Spirit of God's Son' (Gal. 4.6), whose whole focus in on Christ (John 15.26; 16.12-15). When the Son receives the Spirit from the Father, and pours the Spirit out at Pentecost (Acts 2.33), the Spirit's purpose is witness to Jesus (Acts 1.8; 5.32; John 15.26-7). The Spirit's purpose is to glorify Jesus (John 16.13-14). The Spirit is 'the Spirit of his (the Father's) Son', sent into our hearts that all who believe may share the Son's 'Abba' relationship with the Father (Gal. 4.6; Rom. 8.15-17).

The mutual, self-giving character of the triune God is revealed in the actions of Father, Son and Holy Spirit for our redemption

God is truly a missionary God. 'Through embracing God's mission in this world ... humans enter into the trinitarian life of self-giving love' (Heath, following Balthazar, *The Mystic Way*, p. 51).

Flett has made an important contribution, and strengthens our understanding of *missio Dei*. My one caution about his work is that 'sending' is too central a biblical word to marginalize unintentionally. In his commentary on St John, Lesslie Newbigin wrote:

> Forty times in this gospel Jesus is described as the one sent by the Father: now he sends them to continue and complete his mission. This mission wholly defines the nature of the church as a body of men and women sent into the public life of the world. (*The Light Has Come*, p. 268)

I agree that love, actualized in self-donation, reveals the heart of God's missionary nature. Bosch described God as 'a fountain of sending love' (*Transforming Mission*, p. 390). The sending of the Son and Spirit is the manner of that self-donation extended to the world.

So it has become commonplace, in missiological circles at least, to recognize that the Church's mission is a participation in the *missio Dei*, the mission of God. But that has not necessarily been translated into the self-understanding of the church as a whole, let alone shaped its praxis. One reason is that theological disciplines tend to live in silos, in isolation from one another. Missiologists, doctrine scholars and biblical scholars mainly operate in distinct academic communities when the Church needs to benefit from an integrated understanding of the fruits of scholarship.

Trinitarian ecclesiology

Missiology has not adequately shaped ecclesiology. The rich rediscovery of trinitarian theology since the middle of the last century has fed creatively into ecclesiology, with the emergence of 'communion' theologies which have also played a major role in ecumenical dialogue and reports. But John Flett warns that these ecclesiologies can result in a prioritization of the internal life of the church and the marginalizing of mission (Flett, *The Witness of God*, pp. 206–7). He refers to 'the absence of any reference to the missionary act within communion accounts of the church', claiming that 'it is not only possible, but normative, to develop full ecclesiologies based on a social account of the Trinity and to omit the missionary act as immaterial to the being of the church' (p. 207). As an example, he points to Miroslav Volf's influential book *After Our Likeness: The Church as the Image of the Trinity*, where Volf writes, 'the outside world and the church's mission are only in my peripheral vision' (p. 7). Rather, says Flett, 'the *koinonia* of Christian community has to be understood in terms of her own movement for the world. The church is a missionary community because the God she worships is missionary' (*The Witness of God*, p. 208).

A complementary challenge to some communion ecclesiologies comes from Scott MacDougall, an Anglican scholar from the USA, who also argues that the 'Communion' ecclesiologies are significantly lacking. Hence the title of his book *More than Communion*. For MacDougall these ecclesiologies focus to much on what the church is now, making it too self-interested, and focus too little on its calling to be a foretaste of God's coming kingdom. They need, in his view, an adequate eschatology. 'Unfortunately a robust, tensive and dynamic eschatology is often missing from communion ecclesiologies' (*More than Communion*, p. 40). Such an understanding is an essential part of the church's missionary vocation, as a witness and imperfect bearer in the present, of the future Christ has secured for the world.

Both Flett and MacDougall make the point that just to have a trinitarian ecclesiology does not mean that it will involve a missionary understanding of the church. But it can and should! And mercifully, sometimes it does. Jürgen Moltmann wrote that: 'It is not the church that has a mission of salvation to fulfil to the world; it is the mission of the Son and the Spirit through the Father that includes the church' (*The Church in the Power of the Spirit*, p. 64). Another notable exception is the Anglican theologian Daniel Hardy. For Hardy 'the nature of God is to be God by being in the world to confer true order – in Jesus Christ – and movement – in the Holy Spirit – within it' (*Finding the Church*, p. 249). He understood the mission of God as being manifest in both in creation and redemption. His former student Alistair McFadyen made a similar point: 'The quality of life within the triune being of God ... overflows ... in creation-redemption ... Through this trinitarian history of creation-redemption human being is invited and drawn into a form of life which is a creaturely reflection of the trinitarian being of God' (*The Call to Personhood*, pp. 29–30).

In 1987, I, along with all the other Church of England theological college principals, had to provide theological justification for our syllabus and programme of ordination training in response to a paper (ACCM 22) mainly drafted by Dan Hardy. The paper declared:

> The Church's task is to serve the mission of God in the world. So, regardless of the diversity of situations within which it does so, its task is fundamentally twofold: to proclaim the creative activity of God by which the world is constituted in its proper nature by God, affirming the world so far as it reflects its proper nature: and to proclaim the redemptive activity of God by which the world is once again given its proper being, thereby to be fulfilled according to God's purposes. In this task it follows, and by its nature seeks to conform to, the work of God – through Jesus Christ and by the Holy Spirit – in and for the world, in order to bring the world to its proper relation to God. (Advisory Council for the Church's Ministry Occasional Paper 22, 'Education for the Church's Ministry')

For Hardy this was not a purely academic matter. Theology's purpose was to serve the praxis of the church. 'The Church was not first an idea or a doctrine but a practice of commonality in faith and mission' (*Finding the Church*, p. 29).

The church is for the world because God is for the world. The church is missionary by nature because God is missionary by nature. Reflecting on Dan Hardy's work, Bishop Christopher Cocksworth wrote:

> The 'missionary energies' of the Church are inherent to the Church as the community of the Messiah, the one who is sent by the Lord God in the Spirit. They do not need to be created by the Church, still less by its leadership. They are given to the Church as Christ calls people to belong to his body, which is energized by the Spirit.[1]

So the church is not only missional by nature, but it has been gifted by God with 'the energies' it needs to carry out that mission. If its default setting blinds the church to this self-understanding then the default setting needs revisiting.

Participation in Christ

Although there are rich theological insights in applying the nuances of trinitarian theology to the missionary nature of the church, they are an obstruse intellectual debate as far as most Christians are concerned. Their value lies in the necessary work of the church's theologians as they debate and test out the theological claims which underly the church's ministry and mission, but they are little help in getting people from the pews into their communities as witnesses to Christ.

The most helpful and accessible statements I have found about this praxis come from the Scottish theologians Thomas and James Torrance. They were born in China as part of a missionary family. Thomas wrote, 'I was deeply conscious of the task to which my parents had been called by God to preach the Gospel ... This orientation to mission was built into the fabric of my mind, and has never faded' (Navarro, *Trinitarian Doxology*, p. 2). Their ecclesiology is Christ centred, meeting John V. Taylor's concern. Its great focus is the vicarious humanity of Christ, what he does for us, and our participation in him. 'Are we not in danger of forgetting', wrote James, 'that the real agent in the life of the Church is not ourselves but Jesus Christ?'

(Torrance, *Worship, Community and the Triune God of Grace*, p. 107). The brothers developed a Trinitarian theology of worship which, as we shall see, also informed their theology of mission. In it we benefit from Christ's work by the Spirit in two ways. We are recipients of his grace, restoring us to relationship with the Father through the cross and resurrection of the Son. But we are also participants in his risen and ascended life as, in his transformed humanity, he perfectly worships the Father. Thomas Torrance states:

> It is as our Brother, wearing our humanity, that He has ascended, presenting Himself eternally before the face of the Father, and presenting us in Himself. As such He is not only our word to God but God's Word to us. Toward God He is our Advocate and High Priest, but toward man He is the acceptance of us in Himself. (*Royal Priesthood*, pp. 14–15)

> Christian worship is properly a form of the life of Jesus Christ ascending to the Father in the life of those who are so intimately related to him through the Spirit, that when they pray to the Father through Christ, it is Christ the Incarnate Son who honours, worships, and glorifies the Father in them. (*Theology in Reconciliation*, p. 139)

James concurred with his brother:

> In Jesus Christ each and every one of us finds our worship, prayers, and intercessions lifted up, sanctified and presented by the one who is the sole Priest and Representative of each of us. The very nature of our ongoing life of worship and, indeed, ethics (worth-ship) is to be conceived, therefore, in terms of this very concrete participation, by the Spirit, in our sole priest, intercessor and leitourgos. (*Participatio*, pp. 9–10)

This latter emphasis on his current priestly ministry was an important feature of patristic theology, became less significant for the medieval church, and was reemphasized by the reformers, by Calvin in particular. James Torrance claimed that it was both a catholic and an evangelical doctrine. James' son, Alan

Torrance, shared his father's theology: 'Worship is a gift of grace which is realized vicariously in Christ, and which is realized and participated in by the Spirit.' He put it radically simply: 'The Father is the author of worship, the Son the worshipper and the Spirit the agent of worship' (*Persons in Communion*, p. 314). But one theological student put our participation in worship simpler still: 'Worship is joining with Jesus as he praises his Father' (Cocksworth, *Holy, Holy, Holy*, p. 159).

According to this understanding, there is only one true Priest through whom and with whom we draw near to God our Father. There is only one mediator between God and humanity. There is only one offering which is truly acceptable to God, and it is not ours. It is the offering by which he has sanctified for all time those who come to God by him (Heb. 2.11; 10.10, 14). Only Jesus – our great high priest – can worship the Father perfectly. 'The perfect human prayer and the perfect human praise are to be found on the lips of Jesus our brother. He is the perfect worshipper in the presence of the perfect God ... Our worship is participation in his worship' (Cocksworth, *Holy, Holy, Holy*, pp. 158–9). 'For this reason Jesus is not ashamed to call them brothers and sisters, saying, "I will proclaim your name to my brothers and sisters, in the midst of the congregation I will praise you"' (Heb. 2.11–12) and 'We have such a high priest, one who is seated at the right hand of the throne of the Majesty in the heavens, a minister in the sanctuary' (Heb. 8.1–2). 'Christ leads our songs and is the chief composer of our hymns' (John Calvin). Accordingly, James Torrance defined worship as 'the gift of participating through the Spirit in the incarnate Son's communion with the Father' (*The Forgotten Trinity*, p. 6 and *Worship, Community and the Triune God of Grace*, pp. 3 and 8).

But what has this to do with mission? A great deal, because James made a parallel statement: 'The mission of the Church is the gift of participating through the Holy Spirit in the Son's mission from the Father to the world.' The two are inseparable. James wrote: 'It means participating in what he (Christ) is *continuing to do for us* in the presence of the Father and in his mission from the Father to the world' (*Worship, Community and the Triune God of Grace*, p. 8). We participate not only in

Christ's communion with the Father but equally we participate in his mission from the Father to the world. James wrote: 'As Christ was anointed by the Spirit in our humanity to fulfil his ministry for us, so we are united by the same Spirit to share his ministry' (*The Vicarious Humanity of Christ*, p. 145). In a footnote he added, 'The Spirit lifts us out of any narcissistic preoccupation with ourselves to finds our true humanity and dignity in Jesus Christ, in a life centred in others, in communion with Jesus Christ and one another, in loving concern for the humanity of all.'

Thomas Torrance compared the sending of the Spirit at Jesus baptism to the day of Pentecost:

> What happened to Jesus at his baptism ... was given its counterpart in the church when the Holy Spirit sent by the Father in the Name of the Son came down upon the Apostolic church, sealing it as the people of God redeemed through the blood of Christ, consecrating it to share in the communion of the Father, the Son, and the Holy Spirit, and sending it out into the world united with Christ as his Body to engage in the service of the Gospel. (*Theology in Reconciliation*, p. 86)

We will give detailed attention to the New Testament in later chapters, but there is good New Testament support for this interpretation. In John's Gospel, Jesus says, 'Abide in me as I abide in you. Just as the branch cannot bear fruit by itself unless it abides in the vine, neither can you unless you abide in me. I am the vine, you are the branches. Those who abide in me and I in them bear much fruit, because apart from me you can do nothing' (John 15.4f.). There can be no fruit apart from abiding in him. And after his resurrection, '"As the Father has sent me, so I send you." When he had said this, he breathed on them and said to them, "Receive the Holy Spirit"' (John 20.21f.). By the Spirit we join in the risen and ascended Christ's continuing mission. Equally, the Great Commission of Matthew 28 is to be carried out *with* Jesus ('I am with you always'), not merely *for* Jesus. St Paul says he can only speak of 'what Christ has accomplished through me' (Rom. 15.18).

Worship and mission are the two primary movements of the church – towards God in worship and prayer, and towards the world in witness and service. The key word is 'participating'. The whole of Christian life is a participation, by the Spirit in the Son's relation to both the Father and to the world. The two are inseparable. Both worship and mission are gifts we receive before they are activities in which we participate. As a consequence all disputes about the priority of either worship or mission are fruitless as the two are inseparable and interdependent, two dimensions of one relationship as we participate in Christ. At is simplest the church is in its essence a worshipping and missional community simply because it is 'in Christ'. 'The mission of the Church is primarily a matter of our shared participation in the one ministry of Jesus and the Spirit' (Irving, *God, Freedom and the Body of Christ*, ch. 1).

A Church of England report acknowledged that 'Christians (even theologians) have not always sufficiently integrated their understandings of mission and of Church. It is however increasingly acknowledged that the mission of the Son and the Spirit creates the Church and that the Church only exists in relation to the *missio Dei*, whose instrument it is.' But that understanding, and its consequences, has not as yet become instinctive in the life of many churches. It does not shape their default setting. Where it has been engaged it has often been with a limited understanding, seeing it as providing a foundation, and a greater theological credibility, to the church's work of mission. So far so good; the missional nature of God the Holy Trinity is fundamental to the church's identity and vocation. We are missionary because God is missionary: 'the church belongs to the *missio Dei* rather than the *missio* to the church. Therefore mission precedes the church and is utterly fundamental. It is effectively the womb from which the church is called into being' (Badcock, *The House Where God Lives*, p. 328).

But the *missio Dei* is not merely the foundation of the Church's mission; it is its daily dynamic. The church's mission is not merely built upon the missional nature of God, its dynamic is to participate in the continuing mission of God to the world. In support of this I had frequently quoted Moltmann: 'It is not the church that has a mission of salvation to fulfil in the world; it is the mission of the Son and the Spirit through the Father that includes the church.' But I had not noticed how the quotation continued: 'creating a church as it goes on its way' (*The Church in the Power of the Spirit*, p. 64). Not creating 'the Church' once and for all foundationally, but 'a church as it goes on its way'. Earlier in the same book Moltmann wrote, 'It is not that the church "has" a mission, but the very reverse: the mission of Christ creates its own church' (*The Church in the Power of the Spirit*, p. 10).

As the mission of God 'goes on its way' it creates in, through and sometimes ahead of God's human partners in mission, a church appropriate to each era, culture and context. 'The church *is* "missionary by its very nature" [Vatican 2] and it *becomes* missionary by attending to each and every context in which it finds itself' (Bevans and Schroeder, *Constants in Context*, p. 2). Or, according to the missional church conversation which developed in the USA, 'The church is. The church does what it is. The church organizes what it does' (van Gelder, *The Essence of the Church*, p. 37). But if the church does not recognize what it is – missional by nature – if it has a different default setting, it will not act accordingly and what it organizes and does may not accord with its true nature.

Mission requires praxis not just a theological foundation, and that praxis requires a spirituality. Our participation in Christ has two implications. At one level it is simply the reality we need to recognize. According to Alan Torrance, 'It is neither a form of "praxis" nor a mode of *doing*, but a dynamic in which we find ourselves' (*Persons in Communion*, p. 320). Jesus called his disciples to 'remain' in him if they were to bear fruit. But in another sense it requires a conscious companionship with Jesus. 'Mission is primarily a matter of spirituality: it is a way of participating in the life of Jesus Christ' (Sunquist, *Understanding Christian Mission*, p. 173). Participating in the life of Jesus Christ requires more than a change in our understandings of church or mission. It requires the capture of our hearts, spirits and imagination. It creates a longing.

Mission is a longing to see all things renewed – our relationship with God and with one another, with our environment and species, with our societies, our world and our cosmos. It is the healing and redemption of all things under the Lordship of Christ.' (Ross, in Baker and Ross, *Imagining*, p. 49)

According to the World Council of Churches:

> The mission of God (*missio Dei*) is the source of and basis for the mission of the church, the body of Christ ... Thus mission becomes for Christians an urgent inner compulsion, even a powerful test and criterion for authentic life in Christ, rooted in the profound demands of Christ's love, to invite others to share in the fullness of life Jesus came to bring (John 10.10).

The document continues, 'Participating in God's mission, therefore, should be natural for all Christians and all churches, not only for particular individuals or specialized groups' (quoted in Kim, *Joining in with the Spirit*, p. 30). Which is all very well, but 'We are participating in the *missio Dei*' does not exactly run off the lips of the average churchgoer! But the content of the *missio Dei* is focused on the person and work of Christ. If worship is 'joining with Jesus as he praises his Father' (Cocksworth, *Holy, Holy, Holy*, p. 159), then mission is 'joining with Jesus in his mission from the Father to the world' (which makes the Gospels primary sources for a missional ecclesiology). Perhaps 'we are on mission with Jesus' could catch the imagination of ordinary Christians and the local church. To that we will now turn.

Notes

1 Cocksworth, 'Considering the Church with help from Dan Hardy: talking, walking and loving in the light of Christ', https://d3hgrlq6yacptf.cloudfront.net/5f3ffda5728e0/content/pages/documents/1595598040.pdf (accessed 25.11.23).

3

On Mission With Jesus: Making Disciples

Jesus of Nazareth gives God's loving mission a face, a voice and a pair of sandals. (Flemming, *Recovering*, p. 61)

If we are seeking a new default setting to capture the imagination of the church today, 'We are participating in the mission of God', despite its profundity, does not easily roll off the average Christian's lips. But 'we are a community of disciples on mission with Jesus' just might. Each part is important, discipleship, community and mission are inseparable. They form an organic whole. Discipleship has to be personal but is only really sustainable in a community of fellow disciples. Its primary context for growth is out of one's comfort zone on mission. Christian community becomes inverted if it is not participating in mission. The heart of mission is the making of disciples and needs a community of disciples to carry it out. It is all empty apart from the active presence and leadership of Jesus by the Spirit.

We have already been reminded that the mission of God has to be understood Christologically. Its centre and focus is Jesus Christ.

> This is the heart of *missio Dei*. '... to partake in God's life is also to share in his mission ... The Church goes with Christ in the power of the Spirit in the mission entrusted to Christ by the Father, to a world of broken relationships.' (General Synod, *Eucharistic Presidency* 2.13)

This puts discipleship and mission at the heart of what it means to be the church. To unpack it further we need to turn to the Gospels. They are an essential source of any missional ecclesiology. They are 'the foundational charter for the church's life' (Tom Wright, *How God Became King*, p. 119). But they have not always been treated that way.

> There would be no mission of the church without the mission of Jesus. The importance of Jesus own life and message for *our* mission in the world ought to go without saying. But historically the church has struggled with *how* its mission should relate to the ministry and mission of Jesus. (Flemming, *Recovering the Full Mission of God*, p. 61)

According to Dan Hardy, in this respect 'the Gospels are under-read' (*Wording a Radiance*, p. 87).

1 Called to discipleship by Jesus

We need to start at the beginning. The New Testament Church began, not on the day of Pentecost, although it took off like a rocket then, but when Jesus proclaimed the kingdom of God and called his first disciples on the shores of Lake Galilee. For Rowan Williams, 'What makes a Church is the call of Jesus Christ, and our freedom and ability, helped by grace, to recognize that call in each other' (Archbishop's Presidential Address, General Synod, York, 14 July 2003). According to Dan Hardy, 'The Church is born in the process that generates our gospel' (*Wording a Radiance*, p. 65). The Church of Scotland's 'Church Without Walls' report said bluntly, '"Follow me". These two words of Jesus Christ offer us the purpose, shape and process of continuous reform of the Church' (p. 9). Discipleship, not just forgiveness, has aways been at the heart of the church.

The core of Jesus' ministry was the inauguration of the kingdom, the reign of God. 'The time is fulfilled, and the kingdom of God has come near; repent, and believe in the good news' (Mark 1.15). His preaching, teaching and all his actions, whether healing the sick or rebuking religious hypocrisy, were for this purpose. And were intended to evoke a response. His preaching of the kingdom 'involves a call to discipleship ... The invitation to enter God's reign requires undivided devotion a new set of loyalties and relationships. Following Jesus takes priority over everything else' (Flemming, *Recovering the Full Mission of God*, p. 65). We cannot divorce Jesus' ethical teaching from his proclamation of God's reign: 'The announcement of the kingdom and the explanation of what it means to live as a citizen of the kingdom are part of one magnificent whole' (*Recovering*, p. 64). To be a disciple of Jesus was to participate in God's action to restore his reign over his broken creation, beginning, before the resurrection, with Israel. So today the church does not exist for itself but for the Jesus the King (to whom all authority in heaven and earth has been given) and his kingdom, his purposes for his creation.

The word 'disciple' appears 75 times in Matthew's Gospel. It is his standard word for a follower of Jesus; the word 'apostle' appears just once (10.2). Likewise in John's Gospel 'the twelve' only appear on two occasions (6.67–71 and 20.24) and 'apostle' never appears (Burridge, *Imitating Jesus*, p. 339). In the Gospels, the twelve are not just apprentice future leaders, but are primary examples of learning discipleship. The number 12 obviously refers to the tribes of ancient Israel. Jesus is reconstituting it around himself. But it is to be a nation of disciples. 'Disciple' basically means student or apprentice. Christian disciples are apprenticed to Jesus. Unlike in our day, first-century students did not enrol in a college or to study a discrete subject. They enrolled with a rabbi, a teacher (see Morris, *Matthew*, p. 746). In first-century Palestine potential disciples sought out their hoped-for rabbis. No self-respecting rabbi went in search of disciples. Jesus, by contrast, called his disciples by name as with Andrew and Peter, James and John in Matthew 4 and Matthew in chapter 8, and as he does with us today. He gives an open invitation: 'Come to me, all you that are weary and are carrying heavy burdens, and I will give you rest. Take my yoke upon you, and learn from me' (Matt. 11.28–29). There is a further contrast with Jesus' contemporaries. First-century disciples

MAKING DISCIPLES

stayed with their rabbi until they had advanced sufficiently to be able to attract disciples themselves. Jesus, by contrast, calls to lifelong discipleship (which, as we shall see, involves helping others to become not our disciples, but Jesus' disciples). 'In the gospel, we see people following Jesus as he wanders around Palestine; they re-find their identities as, following him, they come to participate in the process that generates gospel' (Hardy, *Wording a Radiance*, p. 64).

The heart of this discipleship was and is obedience to Jesus our teacher and Lord. He said, 'Take my yoke upon you and learn from me' (Matt. 11.29) because a disciple is a life-long learner from Jesus. He said, 'Why do you call me "Lord, Lord", and do not do what I tell you?' (Luke 6.46), that, 'Everyone then who hears these words of mine and acts on them will be like a wise man who built his house on rock' (Matt. 7.24) and contrasted with those who hear but never do. He said, 'You call me Teacher and Lord – and you are right, for that is what I am' (John 13.13). The motivation for such wholehearted discipleship is not obedience. Obedience is the fruit of something else. Its motivation is a vision of Jesus and his kingdom, and grasp of who he is and what he came to achieve. So we read that 'They [the disciples] were amazed, saying, "What sort of man is this, that even the winds and the sea obey him?"' (Matt. 8.27), and Simon Peter says, 'Lord, to whom can we go? You have the words of eternal life. We have come to believe and know that you are the Holy One of God' (John 6.18). Jesus is not just a rabbi. He is 'Emmanuel – God with us'. Jesus himself described the kingdom he was inaugurating as being worth far more than all his disciples had:

> The kingdom of heaven is like treasure hidden in a field, which someone found and hid; then in his joy he goes and sells all that he has and buys that field. Again, the kingdom of heaven is like a merchant in search of fine pearls; on finding one pearl of great value, he went and sold all that he had and bought it. (Matt. 13.44–46)

There is no sense of loss in these parables, although there is a great cost involved. Rather, there is a sense of immeasurable gain.

The heart of discipleship is to be with Jesus, in order to become like him. 'With Jesus we are not just learning how to "do" what he does, we are learning how to be like him' (Peppiatt, *The Disciple*, p. 1). To learn from him is to grow to be like him. He said, 'It is enough for the disciple to be like the teacher' (Matt. 10.25). According to Dallas Willard, 'If I am to be Jesus' disciple that means I am with him to learn from him how to be like him' (*The Divine Conspiracy*, p. 303) or 'how he would live my life if he were me' (p. 308). The underlying assumption is that Jesus knows how to live our lives better than we do! This furthers the contrast with contemporary student–teacher relationships:

> Discipleship may be being a student in the strict Greek sense of the word, but it doesn't mean turning up once a week for a course, or even a sermon. Discipleship is not an intermittent state; it's a relationship that continues. In the ancient world being a student was rather more like that than it is these days. If you said to a modern student or prospective student that the essence of being a student was to hang on your teacher's every word, to follow his or her steps, to sleep outside their door in case you missed any pearls of wisdom falling from their lips, to watch how they conducted themselves at the table, how they conducted themselves in the street, you might not get a very warm response. But in the ancient world, it was a rather more like that. To be the student of a teacher was to commit yourself to living in the same atmosphere and breathing the same air; there was nothing intermittent about it. (Williams, *Being Disciples*, p. 2)

Archbishop Rowan's words throw light on Jesus' saying, 'Abide in me' (John 15). Make my presence your home, your environment. In this matter Jesus had the same view as his rabbi contemporaries:

> The Jews believed that a teacher's example was as important as his words. Thus, in the absence of a ruling authority, it was permissible to report his actions and to deduce from them what his legal position would be on the matter. This was known as *ma'aseh* (precedent) ... From the master's action, something of Torah could be learned. (Burridge, *Imitating Jesus*, p. 73)

> The Jewish tradition that the imitation of the rabbi was an imitation of Torah, and this ultimately an imitation of God reflects the central command in the Torah, 'You shall be holy, for I the Lord your God am holy' (Lev. 19.2). (Burridge, *Imitating Jesus*, p. 75)

Contrary to some current usage, 'disciple' was not a term for 'special' Christians, or Christians who take their faith more seriously. Luke tells us that 'it was in Antioch that the disciples were first called "Christians"' (Acts 11.26). The idea of being Jesus' disciple predates the word 'Christian' and is a synonym for it. It is likely that 'Christian' was a term coined to mock the followers of Jesus in Antioch (rather like 'Quakers' in George Fox's day) but which stuck, because it contained more truth than its originators knew. Christians are disciples of Jesus the Christ.

2 Called into community by Jesus

The call to be a disciple of Jesus is a call to community. According to David Bosch, 'The disciple follows the Master but he/she never follows him alone.' And 'Disciples belong together in an indestructible fellowship' (Bosch, *The Scope of Mission*, p. 5). But disciples do not choose their fellow disciples, that is Jesus' prerogative alone:

> Jesus does not call people to follow him individually, but within the community of other learners and followers, which can be a very mixed group of people ... it was characterized

by not only relationship to Jesus and God, but also by the disciples' relationship to other disciples in the community. (Burridge, *Imitating Jesus*, p. 220)

Disciples accompanied Jesus in community. Their commitment to him implied their commitment to one another. To be called to follow Jesus was to be called to be with all the others who have been called by Jesus. Growth as a disciple requires the company of other disciples whom Jesus has chosen, not those whom we choose. With a Zealot and a tax collector in the company, this was not a self-select group. According to Flemming, 'At the very heart of the needed response to Jesus' kingdom proclamation is a wholehearted love for God and others ... It is inevitably social and relational' (*Recovering*, p. 66).

This community of disciples took two forms:

> As soon as he (Jesus) begins his public ministry he gathers a community of followers. Some, like Mary, Martha and Lazarus, follow him while remaining within their own towns and villages. They participate in God's mission by living out the alternative life of the kingdom in their local communities ... Jesus asks others to leave everything behind and follow him in a more literal sense. (Flemming, *Recovering*, pp. 78ff.)

So according to N. T. Wright:

> The evidence points towards Jesus intending to establish, and indeed succeeding in establishing, what we might call cells of followers, mostly continuing to live in their towns and villages, which, by their adoption of his praxis, his way of being Israel, would be distinctive in their local communities. (*Jesus and the Victory of God*, p. 276)

And according to Richard Bauckham:

> We should not imagine that this specially selected group of twelve were the only disciples of Jesus or the only ones that shared his itinerant ministry. Luke's Gospel, especially, pro-

vides a broader picture of many other disciples, most of whom remain anonymous, but some of whom are named and appear as quite prominent figures. The twelve had a special symbolic role, but many others also accompanied Jesus on his journeys around the country. No doubt the size and composition of the large group of disciples that travelled around with Jesus varied from time to time ... Luke's Gospel in particular stresses that several women also accompanied Jesus from an early stage of his ministry right up until his death ... Had they been only patrons of Jesus' movement, as some wealthy and influential women were of the Pharisees, they could have stayed at home and spared themselves the scandal of sharing the life of these vagrant men. They were with Jesus to learn, just as the male disciples were. (Bauckham, *Jesus: A Very Short Introduction*, pp. 51–2)

It is the combination of this dual pattern, a distinctive local community embodying and applying the way of Jesus, and a movement, a community on the move as Jesus directs which is, I believe, required of the church today.

The Church of Scotland report 'Church Without Walls' defines church as 'people with Jesus at the centre, travelling wherever Jesus takes us'. The full quotation goes:

> 'Follow me' ... That core calling takes us back behind the secondary identities of denomination or tradition and calls us to turn again to be people with Jesus at the centre, travelling wherever Jesus takes us. It is so simple we cannot miss it. It is so profound we can never exhaust it. This calling invites us to risk the way of Jesus. (p. 9)

This very public accompanying of Jesus was, indeed, intended to form a distinctive public way of life. It was to the disciples, not the crowds, that Jesus said, 'You are the salt of the earth ... You are the light of the world' (Matt. 5.13–14). This involved personal disciplines of prayer, giving and fasting, but also life in community, and missional practices. These were not just standard devotional practices. They result directly from Jesus' proclamation of the kingdom. The implication was that, 'Those who follow Jesus can begin to practice, in the present, the habits of heart and life which correspond to the way things are in God's kingdom – the way they will be eventually, yes, but also the way they *already* are because Jesus is here' (Tom Wright, *How God Became King*, p. 91, re the Beatitudes). Discipleship was to be public and corporate, as well as personal – because it was for the sake of the world. Willard wrote, 'The church is for discipleship and discipleship is for the world, as God's place.' This is a positive view of discipleship being for the glory of God and the blessing of others. 'My Father is glorified by this, that you bear much fruit and become my disciples' (John 15.8).

Discipleship is for the sake of the world because it is for the sake of God's purposes in the world. It is world transforming rather than withdrawing. It is salt and light. It is about being a Christian community which serves its community and is the best news its community has! Because it brings the presence of the king and a foretaste of the kingdom of God.

3 Disciples on mission with Jesus

Dean Flemming wrote, 'Jesus of Nazareth gives God's loving mission a face, a voice and a pair of sandals' (p. 61). It is time today for the church to put its sandals on. The overall context of the disciples' learning and growth, as presented in the Gospels, is with Jesus on mission. 'By accompanying Jesus at all times, they were to learn from him how to continue his own mission' (Bauckham, *Jesus: A Very Short Introduction*, p. 51). Immediately after his call to the pair of brothers by the Sea of Galilee (4.18–22), Matthew tells how:

> Jesus went throughout Galilee, teaching in their synagogues and proclaiming the good news of the kingdom and curing every disease and every sickness among the people. So his fame spread throughout all Syria, and they brought to him all the sick, those who were afflicted with various diseases and pains, demoniacs, epileptics, and paralytics, and he cured them. And

great crowds followed him from Galilee, the Decapolis, Jerusalem, Judea, and from beyond the Jordan.
When Jesus saw the crowds, he went up the mountain; and after he sat down, his disciples came to him. Then he began to speak, and taught them. (4.23—5.2)

They observe his mission and then receive his teaching in the light of it. 'The goal of Jesus teaching and preaching is to transform those who respond into people who look like the reign of God and who are caught up in the mission of God' (Flemming, *Recovering*, p. 66).

Mission is the essential context for learning discipleship. To remove growth in discipleship from the context of mission is to stunt it. Discipleship courses and programmes have little effect unless the participants are drawn out of their comfort zones into Jesus' engagement with local communities and networks. According to 'Church Without Walls', 'Being part of the Church in action leads to a deeper desire to be a disciple of Christ' (p. 15). Disciples, says Alison Morgan, 'learn on the hoof' (Morgan, *Following Jesus*, p. 90). Missionary disciples were on the move, because Jesus was on the move. Jesus said, 'Foxes have holes, and birds of the air have nests; but the Son of Man has nowhere to lay his head' (Matt. 8.20). Hauerwas comments, 'Jesus never tarries, like foxes and birds, he is always on the move, the kingdom is a movement that requires him to go to those to whom he has been sent' (*Matthew*, p. 103). In his final theological reflections, following a pilgrimage to the Holy Land, Dan Hardy reflected that 'Ecclesiology is embodied: in Jesus walking' (*Wording a Radiance*, p. 83). He spoke of the need for 'a moving ecclesiology' and 'the wandering church' (*Wording a Radiance*, p. 87).

Mark tells us that Jesus 'appointed twelve, whom he also named apostles, to be with him, and to be sent out' (3.14). In all four Gospels the balance of being disciples 'with him' and being 'sent out' is not between retreat and active ministry. The majority of the time the disciples spent 'with' Jesus was with him on mission, sometimes at the cost of planned times of retreat. To 'be with' Jesus was not static but active. It involved following and going – being sent. Jesus called them to be with him, they shared in his mission, and then were sent out in his name, in preparation for the time when they would share in his mission in a different way, with his promise to be with them always, 'to the end of the age'.

> Jesus' own call to discipleship also included the idea of doing what he was doing, namely, imitating him by joining in his ministry ... After being with Jesus for a while, the disciples are sent out to imitate him in preaching the kingdom of God, teaching and healing (Matt. 9.35—10.6). (Burridge, *Imitating Jesus*, p. 74)

They were his representatives. Just as Jesus was the person through whom people could encounter the Father, so they became the ones through whom Jesus could be encountered, even when he was not physically present. 'Whoever welcomes you welcomes me, and whoever welcomes me welcomes the one who sent me' (Matt. 10.40). Participation in mission, bearing Jesus to others, is an essential context for learning discipleship. There will be little discipleship apart from the following and the going.

Baptism is a public acknowledgement of the call of Jesus, and simultaneously a call to share in his mission. According to Pope Francis:

> In virtue of their baptism, all the members of the People of God have become missionary disciples (cf. Matt. 28.19). All the baptized, whatever their position in the Church or their level of instruction in the faith, are agents of evangelization ... Every Christian is a missionary to the extent that he or she has encountered the love of God in Christ Jesus: we no longer say that we are 'disciples' and 'missionaries', but rather that we are always 'missionary disciples'. (*Evangelii Gaudium*, p. 120)

Their calling then is 'characterized by *being* with Jesus, *telling* his message of God's reign, and *doing* his works. In short *their* mission mirrors *his* mission' (Flemming, *Recovering*, p. 79).

Such discipleship is costly. All four Gospels move towards the cross. 'Disciples of Jesus did not simply follow his teaching: rather, they were to "take up the cross" and follow him' (Burridge, *Imitating Jesus*, p. 183). 'He called the crowd with his disciples, and said to them, "If any want to become my followers, let them deny themselves and take up their cross and follow me"' (Mark 8.34). 'The incarnation of that divine love in a world of sin leads to the cross' (Volf, *Exclusion and Embrace*, p. 25). On the night he was betrayed he said to them: 'Remember the word that I said to you, "Servants are not greater than their master." If they persecuted me, they will persecute you; if they kept my word, they will keep yours also' (John 15.20). He said this in the full knowledge that they would fail him and went to the cross believing that through his death and resurrection they would be restored. Their and our failures do not withdraw the costly call, nor the expectation of grace and power to fulfil it. In all four Gospels 'he (Jesus) continued, up until his death, to train his disciples to extend his mission' (Bauckham, *Jesus: A Very Short Introduction*, p. 53).

4 As with them, so with us

But why should this pre-Passion account inform the post-Pentecost church today? Because it remains current. *Jesus is still on mission with his disciples.* In John 20, Jesus' Easter evening commission is 'As the Father has sent me, so I send you' (v. 21). He is not saying 'I have done my part, now it's over to you, and, by the way, you will need help from the Holy Spirit.' The Greek tense implies that the Father continues to send the Son who includes his disciples in his continuing commission (Beasley-Murray, *John*, p. 379). He has not stopped, because the work is not yet complete. Because of the cross and resurrection it can extend to the nations. It is by the Holy Spirit, in through and ahead of the disciples, that his mission will continue.

Matthew 28.16–20 is often called 'the Great Commission':

All authority in heaven and on earth has been given to me. Go therefore and make disciples of all nations, baptizing them in the name of the Father and of the Son and of the Holy Spirit, and teaching them to obey everything that I have commanded you.

This is not to be carried out *for* him, but *with* him; as he promises, 'I am with you always to the end of the age.' It is the continuing mission of Jesus with and through his disciples. As disciples we are called and empowered to join him.

The book of Acts, Luke's second volume, begins, 'In the first book, Theophilus, I wrote about all that Jesus did and taught from the beginning' or 'began to do and teach'. Jesus continues his mission, often by the Holy Spirit, often through the power of his name, which implies his presence. Occasionally directly.

The Ascension was not the completion of Jesus' mission, but the development of it. It is not completed it is expanded, extending now to 'the ends of the earth'. It is a real departure from the earth, but his ministry to the earth continues from heaven.

> The apostles do not so much substitute for an absent Jesus as they exemplify his present, on-going activity … Jesus' departure and absence do not prevent his involvement in the ongoing life of the churches or the mission of the gospel. However, at the same time we will see that his activity always remains activity from heaven or through agents (the Holy Spirit or the apostles). (Orr, *Exalted Above the Heavens*, p. 156, quoting Gaventa)

We will see in the next chapter the primary role of the Holy Spirit as the leader of the mission of the Church, but the Spirit was poured out by the ascended Jesus to equip the church for witness, as he had promised. But throughout Acts Jesus himself remains active from heaven. Think of Saul on the road to Damascus asking, 'Who are you, Lord?' And the reply is, 'I am Jesus.' Then a disciple called Ananias goes to him saying, 'Brother Saul, the Lord Jesus has sent me.' So Jesus still sends disciples. He appeared to Ananias 'in a vision' (Acts 9.10), charging him to commission Saul as 'a chosen instrument of mine to carry my name before the Gentiles and kings and the children of Israel' (9.15). Paul later reflects on this commission by telling the crowd in Pisidian Antioch that Christ commanded him, 'I have made you a light for the Gentiles, that you may bring salvation to the ends of the earth' (13.47). The Damascus Road is not the only time the exalted Christ appears to Paul. In chapter 22, as he recounts his conversion to the crowd in Jerusalem, he describes how, following his encounter with Ananias, he returned to Jerusalem to pray in the temple and fell into a 'trance' (22.17). As he did so, Christ appeared to him and told him to leave Jerusalem since his testimony would not be accepted (22.18) and that he would send him 'far away to the Gentiles' (22.21).

Similarly, in Corinth, the Lord encourages Paul by telling him, 'Do not be afraid, but go on speaking and do not be silent, for I am with you, and no one will attack you to harm you, for I have many in this city who are my people' (18.9–10). Further, in chapter 23 as Paul is imprisoned in Jerusalem, Luke tells us that 'the Lord stood by him and said, "Take courage, for as you have testified to the facts about me in Jerusalem, so you must testify also in Rome"' (23.11). The beginning of chapter 14 describes Paul and Barnabas in Iconium, where 'they remained for a long time, speaking boldly for the Lord who bore witness to the word of his grace, granting signs and wonders to be done by their hands' (14.3). That is, it is the Lord himself who 'bore witness' and the Lord who granted 'signs and wonders to be done'. However, he does so through Paul and Barnabas: the signs and wonders that Christ grants are 'done by their hands'.

The one obvious difference is that the four Gospel narratives culminate in Jesus' death and resurrection, whereas the post-resurrection church proclaims it. They had walked with him physically, confined to one place at a time. We walk with him in us wherever his people are sent. Hauerwas writes, 'There can be no substitute for the sending of people. A church that is not a missionary church is not a church. The book of Acts witnesses to the necessity for disciples of Christ to, like Jesus himself, be on the move' (*Matthew*, p. 103).

Mobility with Jesus continues into the story of the early church. He had declared himself to be 'the Way' (John 14.6) and their movement is known as 'the way'. John the Baptist's task had been to prepare 'the way of the Lord'. Followers of Christ in Acts belong to 'the Way' (9.2), are instructed in 'the Way of the Lord' or 'the Way of God' (19.25–26). There were those who 'spoke evil' of the Way (19.9) and it could cause 'disturbance' (19.23). Speaking in response to accusations Paul claims: 'I worship the God of our ancestors, believing everything laid down according to the law or written in the prophets, according to the Way' (Acts 24.14).

Luke Timothy Johnson reflects on the relationship between Jesus' itinerant ministry in Luke's Gospel and that of the early church in Acts. 'This constant movement and mission', he says, 'depicts a church that responds to the promptings of the Spirit and is not defined in terms of place' (*Prophetic Jesus*, p. 117). Then, once the church became settled in a particular place 'the corollary of itinerancy is responsiveness to the Holy Spirit' (*Prophetic Jesus*, p. 127). The geographically located church, as a parallel to the first disciples who remained in their local communities, starts each day, not asking Jesus which town are we going to today, but asking the Holy Spirit of Jesus, what activity we are to join the Lord in today.

5 Making disciples on mission with Jesus

Making disciples is at the heart of being on mission with Jesus. It is the central command of the passage many call the Great Commission to which we have already referred.

This was a crucial passage for the Protestant missionary movement. It has been used to motivate missionary vocations since 1792 when William Carey published his *Enquiry into the Obligations of Christians to Use means for the Conversion of the Heathens*. But not all applications of the Commission have paid careful enough attention to the text.

First: the text is not so much a command to be obeyed as an announcement that the time for this mission has come. When the twelve were first sent out they were told to go 'nowhere among the Gentiles', the non-Jewish nations. Now they are told to make disciples of 'all nations'. The risen Son of God, having made atonement through the cross, says to his disciples, in effect, 'I have done everything necessary, is time for you to go now.'

Second: the central command is not 'go' but 'make disciples'. The imperative, the command, is 'make disciples' the participles, the ways in which the command is to be fulfilled, are by going, baptizing and teaching. The reduction of 'make disciples' to make converts is one of the tragedies of the church in many places. Dallas Willard wrote about 'the Great Omission from the Great Commission in which the Great Disparity is firmly rooted' (*The Great Omission*, p. xii). The great disparity being between: 'the hope for life expressed in Jesus and the actual day to day behaviour, inner life and social presence of most of those who now profess allegiance to him' (*The Great Omission*, p. x). Jim Wallis wrote that, 'The great challenge of modern evangelism is in calling many to belief but few to obedience' (*Agenda for Biblical People*, p. 23). The offer of salvation has too often been severed from the call to follow. This gives the impression that discipleship, as understood in the New Testament, has become optional or self-select. But Jesus said 'Take my yoke upon you, and learn from me' (Matt. 11.29). The commission needs to be understood in its context. The commission in Matthew is not an add-on or postscript to that Gospel. It is the climax of it. 'These verses are the key to the understanding of the entire book ... They sum up everything Matthew wrote in his gospel' (Bosch, *The Scope of Mission*, p. 3). Disciples are to be taught to obey everything Jesus has commanded his first disciples throughout the Gospel. The whole Gospel, all that Jesus does and teaches, and teaches them to do, becomes a manual for discipleship. We read it for the first time, for ourselves, as disciples, and then read it again, as a manual of disciple making: 'Teaching them to obey everything that I have commanded you.' To do everything I have taught you to do.

Third: the language of discipleship is sometimes thought of as primarily negative, as majoring on what we must not do if we are Christians. There are indeed some behaviours which are not consistent with Christian discipleship. But we have already seen that the kingdom is presented as an overwhelming gain, of superb worth, putting the sacrifices it entails into perspective. But even more than that, Christopher Wright has shown that the greater purpose of discipleship is the bringing of Christ's blessings to the world. The purpose of discipleship is to be and bring blessing. The commission in Matthew is a fulfilment in Christ of God's original commission to Abraham. Three times to Abraham and once each to Isaac and Jacob (Genesis 12.1–3; 18.18; 22.18; 26.4; 28.14) the promise is that through them 'all the families' or 'all the nations of the earth' will be blessed. God tells Abraham to 'go' and promises 'you will be a blessing'. Jesus is the great descendant of Abraham. The Gospel of Matthew had Abrahamic bookends. It opens as 'An account of the genealogy of Jesus the Messiah, the son of David, the son of Abraham' (Matt. 1.1). It concludes with the son of Abraham, risen with all authority repeating the call to the nations. 'Go therefore and make disciples of all nations' (Matt. 28.19).

In effect, 'Go ... and be a blessing.' For Christopher Wright, 'Blessing is the umbilical cord that links creation and redemption, for redemption is the restoration of the original blessing inherent in creation' (*Mission*, p. 219). On the basis of the same Genesis text, St Paul believed that God declared the gospel beforehand to Abraham. 'And the scripture, foreseeing that God would justify the Gentiles by faith, declared the gospel beforehand to Abraham, saying, "All the Gentiles shall be blessed in you." For this reason, those who believe are blessed with Abraham who believed' (Gal. 3.8–9).

This is a positive view of discipleship, as being for the glory of God and the blessing of others. 'By this is my Father glorified, that you bear much fruit, showing yourselves to be my disciples.'

'Christian goodness or spiritual fitness is developed not primarily for our own sake but for God's and other people's' (Tomlin, *Spiritual Fitness*, p. 103). Discipleship is for the sake of the world because it is for the sake of God's purposes in the world. It is world-transforming rather than withdrawing. It requires a Christian community which serves its community. Which earns the right for its good news to be heard because it is the best news its community has got. This is what it means to be the salt of the earth and the light of the world. But to be a blessing we have also to be appropriately distinctive. Salt that loses its savour, and lights under boxes, cannot fulfil the purposes of God. That is why discipleship and mission can never be separated. 'The Abrahamic promise is a self-replicating gene. Those who receive it are immediately transformed into those whose privilege and mission it is to pass it on to others' (Christopher Wright, *Mission*, p. 236).

We make disciples as he made disciples:

> Jesus is the expert disciple-maker. When he was on earth, his disciples learned by watching him, listening to him, and doing the practical assignments he gave them (Matt. 10; Luke 9.1–6; 10.1–17). Jesus' example shows us that discipling revolves around the relationship between disciples and discipler in which they spend a lot of time together. (Hibbert and Hibbert, *Walking Together*, p. 16)

If we are to teach others to do all that Jesus has taught us, we are to make disciples as Jesus has made disciples, and how he has discipled us. 'The founding of the whole Christian movement was initiated through the simple acts of Jesus investing his life and embedding his teachings in his followers and developing them into authentic disciples' (Hirsch, *The Forgotten Ways*, p. 102). Our practice of 'making disciples' has to be the same. The Gospels are our training manual. 'If the church is to carry out its commission faithfully, it must draw its models, inspiration, motivation and wisdom from the earthly ministry of Jesus, in relation to his Father and the Holy Spirit' (Gibbs, *Leadership Next*, p. 32).

The implication is that only disciples can make disciples. We have already seen that a distinctive feature of Jesus' disciple making was that his disciples never graduate. They remain with him, and on the Great Day they will become fully like him, because they will see him as he is. Until that day we are apprentices of Jesus, still 'on the Way'. The commission on the mountain was not their graduation from discipleship, but the next stage of it. 'We are to be disciples before we can make disciples. Those who are learning the Way will accompany contemporary searchers in the Way. We are to be communities of the Way' ('Church Without Walls', p. 9). Scarily, Christopher Wright claims, 'He commissions his own disciples to go out and replicate themselves by creating communities of obedience among the nations ... Mission is replicated discipleship, learned through ethical obedience and passed on through teaching' (*Mission of God*, p. 391). So questions of disciple making and mission begin inescapably with a challenge about the quality of life of those who would make disciples. 'We have nothing to share with the world than what we are sharing with each other. We can effect no change in the ways of the world, unless we ourselves are being converted from those ways' (Wallis, *The Call to Conversion*, p. 125). Lives of costly discipleship evoke a response of similar depth.

Being on mission with Jesus is the vocation of all Christians, not just the ones who seem to have it all together. Remembering that in Matthew the twelve are presented as representative disciples more than special leaders, it is notable that immediately before the Great Commission the remaining eleven meet Jesus on the mountain and 'when they saw him, they worshipped him; but some doubted' (verse 17). The call to missional discipleship is given to all Christians with their doubts and struggles. It is *not yet fully formed* disciples who are to make disciples. Otherwise no one would!

Worship and mission

This concluding scene in Matthew also addresses the relationship of worship to mission. 'When they saw him, they worshipped him.' Worship is the first and instinctive response to the risen Lord. If the heart and motivation of discipleship is a vision of

Jesus and his kingdom it has to be so. But worship alone is not enough. In the closing verses of Luke's Gospel, 'they worshipped him, and returned to Jerusalem with great joy; and they were continually in the temple blessing God' (Luke 24.52–53). But this was to be 'until you have been clothed with power from on high' (verse 49). Worship and mission are inseparable, they are parallel responses to Jesus, they form the rhythm of church life, the ecology of the life of the church. Authentic worship leads to mission. Authentic mission wins worshippers.

'A prioritization of worship results, not in the marginalizing of mission, but in the energizing of it' (Gibbs, *Leadership Next*, p. 76) and 'A praising community preaches to answer the questions raised by its praise' (Watson, *I Believe in Evangelism*, p. 166).

My proposal for the new default setting to be 'a community of disciples on mission with Jesus' seems to lack any reference to worship. But if authentic mission is in the company of Jesus, dependent on his presence and power, then prayer will be at the heart of it:

> Abide in me as I abide in you. Just as the branch cannot bear fruit by itself unless it abides in the vine, neither can you unless you abide in me. I am the vine, you are the branches. Those who abide in me and I in them bear much fruit, because apart from me you can do nothing ... If you abide in me, and my words abide in you, ask for whatever you wish, and it will be done for you. (John 15.4–7)

It is the presence of the risen Lord which evokes worship. 'When they saw him they worshipped him.' A community on mission with Jesus will vibrate with worship and wonder.

By 'going'

Disciples are made, says Jesus, by 'going'. 'In order for the good news about Jesus to be proclaimed beyond the groups of people where the church is already established, Jesus' followers have to cross cultural boundaries. The discipling they do is intercultural discipling' (Hibbert and Hibbert, *Walking Together on the Jesus Road*, p. 14). In the *Mission-Shaped Church* report we wrote, 'The change is to an outward focus: from a "come to us" approach to a "we will go to you" attitude, embodying the gospel where people are, rather than embodying it where we are, and in ways we prefer' (p. 41). Our preferred way, our default settings have been shaped by centuries of Christendom. But in our post-Christendom age we can no longer depend on people coming to us. Eddie Gibbs writes:

> Churches have operated on a come-to-us philosophy, but this is no longer adequate when the church finds itself marginalized and existing as just one piece in a complex social kaleidoscope in which the pieces are constantly realigning ... The church must be not only inviting but infiltrating the groups it seeks to introduce to the Saviour. (*Church Next*, p. 167)

'Infiltrating' sounds rather sinister, but otherwise the point is well made.

Disciple making requires incarnational mission:

> Irreplaceable as the foundational ministry of Jesus is, we are related not simply historically through time to a 'past Christ' but by means of the Spirit to the living Christ now, in whose continuing ministry we participate. The Spirit enables fidelity to and continuity with apostolic faith but constantly actualizes and particularizes this tradition afresh in the present so that the truth of Christ is brought alive for the ever new situations with which the Church engages in its missionary calling. (General Synod, *Eucharistic Presidency* 2.28)

Tex Sample warns, 'The issue is not relevance so far as the church is concerned. The issue is incarnation. When so called "traditional" churches are out of touch with the people who live around them, the problem is not that they are irrelevant, but that they are not incarnational' (*The Spectacle of Worship in a Wired World*, p. 105). A church on mission with Jesus is, by definition, committed to an incarnational life. It seeks to embody the life of Christ in the place, or complex of places, to which it is called.

There are values and practices of discipleship which are common to all Christians in all contexts, but this incarnational engagement means that the local balance, emphases and priorities of discipleship will only emerge as the local context is engaged. 'Discipleship emerges out of prayer, study, dialogue, and worship by a community learning to ask the questions of obedience, *as they are engaged directly in mission*' (Roxburgh, *The Missionary Congregation*, p. 66).

By 'baptizing them in the name of the Father, the Son and the Holy Spirit'

Disciples are made by baptism, literally 'into' the name of the Father, the Son and the Holy Spirit.

This has at least three dimensions.

First, it is personal. The focus is not on the words which accompany baptism, but on a parallel to Jesus' baptism. Matthew reports that:

> when Jesus had been baptized, just as he came up from the water, suddenly the heavens were opened to him and he saw the Spirit of God descending like a dove and alighting on him. And a voice from heaven said, 'This is my Son, the Beloved, with whom I am well pleased.' (3.16–17)

So with us: through the Son, and by the Spirit we share the Son's relationship with the Father – which is the key to his discipleship. That identification is made possible only by his death on the cross, with which he identified as he was baptized. Baptism marks both the joy and the cost of discipleship. It is as though Jesus says: 'You have watched my relationship with the Father, now you can share it.' In this sense God has no grandchildren, only sons and daughters.

Second, it is corporate, incorporating people into the community called the church. As St Paul says, 'For in the one Spirit we were all baptized into one body' (1 Cor. 12.13). Disciples belong to the community of disciples, even when they have to travel alone. It is striking that when Jesus instructed his disciples to have disciplined times of personal, even secret, prayer, he told them to pray *our* Father, not *my* Father (Matt. 6.5–9), although our faith is personal, and he is Father to each of us. According to Evelyn Hibbert:

> This is the primary task of discipleship – meeting Jesus through another's experience of him. It is not so much what I have to give, but what I have to learn through another person's discovery of Jesus. Discipleship is a mutual exploration of what it means to be an authentic follower of Jesus in the various contexts we find ourselves in. The Holy Spirit is the teacher. We walk together alongside him. (*Walking Together on the Jesus Road*, p. 11)

Third, it is missional. As we have already heard from Pope Francis, 'In virtue of their baptism, all the members of the People of God have become missionary disciples.' It is baptism into the mission of God as active participants. 'As members of Christ's body they are baptized into his mission, equipped by the Spirit to make their distinctive contribution to the totality of the ministry of the church' (Gibbs, *Leadership Next*, p. 33).

To be true to itself this community of the baptized can never be focused just on its own survival. It finds its direction and identity in what God – Father, Son and Holy Spirit – is doing in the world.

By 'teaching'

According to Richard Bauckham, this instruction is evidence of 'the impact Jesus made on his disciples, who shared his life and committed his teaching to memory' (*Jesus: A Very Short Introduction*, p. 38). This is not limited to initial instruction, important though that is. It is a commitment to lifelong learning from Jesus, as those who will continue to learn from Jesus, until they see him face to face, pass on their learning to others. The curriculum is 'All that I have commanded you', whether that be the Sermon on the Mount, the teaching on marriage and divorce and the value of children, or the teaching about wealth and the exercise of power, reconciliation, justice and righteousness. It is not restricted to ethical values alone, but includes the missional practices which Jesus had taught the twelve and the 70: healing and deliverance, care of the poor, compassion for the sheep without a shepherd, and so on. The whole Gospel of Matthew becomes a manual for discipleship and for making disciples. It would be a mistake to read this as a compiled list of discipleship requirements. That was the mistake the Pharisees made with their list of commandments (later, according to the rabbis, 613 in all). Torah was understood the gift of a wholesome and integrated life in relationship with God. Its characteristic was *shalom*, not simply 'peace' as we understand it, but harmony and well-being in all relationships – with God, your neighbour, yourself and the earth – and joy with it.

One theme in Matthew is the superiority of Jesus to Moses. The teaching of Jesus is set out in five blocks, parallel to the five books of the Torah. His teaching provides an integrated way of living under God's blessing, sustained by his presence. It is in every sense whole life discipleship. The Great Commission passage helps us overcome some of the dichotomies and disagreements in the Church's thinking about mission. Word and deed, evangelism and social action, healing and deliverance are integrated in the practices of missional discipleship.

Although baptism is mentioned before teaching, there is no hint of the ethical implications of following Christ only being introduced at a later stage. Growing as a disciple – learning to do everything that Jesus has taught – will continue for the whole of life, but authentic evangelism will include teaching about the Jesus way of living. The offer of forgiveness should not be separated from the call to follow. Otherwise repentance and commitment would be hollow.

Only through Christ

The purpose of this chapter is not merely to propose a new default setting for our understanding of the church. Because the setting proposed has deep implications. It requires a spirituality, a praxis of ecclesial life which is founded on a deep trust in and obedience to the presence of Christ by the Spirit. 'Jesus came and said to them, "All authority in heaven and on earth has been given to me ... And remember, I am with you always, to the end of the age"' (Matt. 28.19–20). Only through Christ can the church be missional. Our participation in his mission is based on his achievement. He gave the commission to his church having 'given his life as a ransom for many' (20.28) and conquered death. 'The "defeat" of Golgotha is transformed into the triumph of Galilee, and on that transformation the church's mission is based "to the close of the age"' (France, *Matthew*, p. 410). So now he stands before his disciples and speaks from the place of supreme authority. Our participation can only then be under his authority and at his direction. The extent of his achievement and of his authority is seen in the scope of the word 'all' – '*all*' authority, to *all* nations, keeping *all* the things that I have commanded you, with you (*all*)ways. Christ's authority is cosmic – there is no part of the universe over which he has not written 'mine'. That is the fundamental truth which undergirds the church's mission. 'Those who believe in Jesus, who are witnesses to his resurrection, are given the responsibility to go and make real in the world the authority which he already has' (Tom Wright, *Matthew*, p. 207). His universal Lordship leads to his universal mission. He taught his disciples to pray to the heavenly Father saying, 'Your will be done on earth as it is in heaven.' Now they are to be involved in bringing it about.

But this mission can only be effectively carried out in his presence. I am with you always, to the end of the age. Which is 'not so much a cosy reassurance as the essential equipment for mission' (France, *Matthew*, p. 416). It is, thank God, his mission in which we share. The risen and now ascended Lord is of the same self-sacrificial character as when he walked the roads of

Galilee. His universal authority does not permit his church any form of triumphalist mission. It has to be Christ's mission in Christ's way. This is only possible because of Christ's presence. It is that presence which tops and tails Matthew's Gospel. The promise is of 'Emmanuel – God with us' (1.23). The fulfilment is 'I am with you always to the end of the age' (28.20)

Conclusion

In the Foreword to *Mission-Shaped Church* Rowan Williams wrote, 'If "church" is what happens when people encounter the Risen Jesus and commit themselves to sustaining and deepening that encounter in their encounter with each other, there is plenty of theological room for diversity of rhythm and style' (p. vii). I have simply added, 'and the Risen Jesus is on mission'.

4

On Mission With Jesus: Following the Spirit

Missional ecclesiology is only as good as its theology of the Spirit. (Hill, *Salt, Light and a City*, p. 239)

Mission is a heartfelt but the spontaneous outworking of the inspiring, transforming, life-giving work of the Holy Spirit. (Kim, *Joining in with the Spirit*, p. 30)

Before we consider the role of the Holy Spirit as the one who leads and empowers the church's mission, it is important to establish that 'The Spirit is not the church's auxiliary' (Newbigin, *The Light Has Come*, p. 208). The Holy Spirit is not an aid to the church. Without the Spirit there is no church!

Apart from the Spirit there is no church. There is a just a human collective that can be entirely explained sociologically, and which can achieve nothing of eternal value. This is affirmed across the Christian traditions:

> The Spirit is not something that 'animates' a Church which already somehow exists. The Spirit makes the Church be ... the very essence of the Church. (Zizioulas, *Being as Communion*, p. 132, Orthodox)

> The church owes to the Spirit its origin, existence, and continued life, and in this sense the church is a creation of the Spirit. (Küng, *The Church*, p. 172, Roman Catholic)

> The church enjoys 'fellowship with Christ' as the Spirit reveals Christ, unites the church with Christ, glorifies Christ, and

forms the church for the sake of Christ's messianic mission. (Moltmann, *The Church in the Power of the Spirit*, p. 197f., Lutheran)

The church is and is visible because God the Holy Spirit is and acts. (Webster, 'The Visible Attests the Invisible', p. 104, Anglican)

If there is no Spirit, it does not mean that the community lacks its missionary commission, but that there is no community at all. (Radner, *Church*, p. 165)

These reflections have strong scriptural support – for example, Romans 8.9. Anyone who does not have the Spirit of Christ does not belong to him (1 Cor. 12.3). No one can say, 'Jesus is Lord' except by the Holy Spirit (1 Cor. 12.13). For in the one Spirit we were all baptized into one body.

It is this wider context that we see the Spirit as the leader of mission. Each aspect of the Son's incarnate ministry was animated by the Spirit – his conception (Luke 1.35), his intimacy with the Father (Luke 3.22), the empowering of his ministry (Luke 4.18–21; Acts 10.38), his sacrificial death (Heb. 9.14) and his resurrection (Rom. 8.11). His ministry then continues through the Church in the power of the Spirit (John 20.21f.).

The moment we turn from the Gospels to the mission of the church in the Acts of the Apostles, it is the Holy Spirit who takes central place, but the Spirit's fundamental purpose is to point to Jesus. 'Acts narrates the journey of the Spirit even more deeply into the way of Jesus and the journey of Jesus more deeply into the way of the Spirit' (Jennings, *Acts*, p. 16). St Luke's second volume begins, 'In my former book, Theophilus, I wrote about all that Jesus began to do and to teach until the day he was taken up to heaven' (1.1–2, NIV). This could imply that the second volume told what the risen Jesus continued to do, by the Spirit (though some translations read 'from the beginning' rather than 'began to do'). But either way, Jesus is active in the book of Acts, sometimes explicitly, intervening with Paul on the road to Damascus: 'I am Jesus' (9.5), sometimes by the power of his name (2.38; 3.6; 4.30; 19.13; 21.13), occasionally by an angel (for example, 11.12–17) and mostly through the agency of the Holy Spirit. John V. Taylor wrote, 'The chief actor in the historic mission of the Christian church is the Holy Spirit. He is the director of the whole enterprise. The mission consists of the things that he is doing in the world. In a special way it consists of the light that he is focussing upon Jesus Christ' (*The Go-Between God*, p. 3).

In the closing passage of Luke's Gospel, Jesus opened his disciples' minds to understand everything written about him in the scripture and then promised them the Holy Spirit as power from on high. When Acts opens Jesus has been instructing the disciples about the kingdom and promises the Spirit. The two passages dovetail into one another. These scripture-informed and Spirit-filled disciples will be witnesses to Jesus. As he had said in John's Gospel, 'When the Advocate comes, whom I will send to you from the Father, he will testify on my behalf. You also are to testify' (John 15.26–27).

Early in each of Luke's volumes comes a programmatic Old Testament text which gives advance warning of what is to come. In the Gospel the passage from Isaiah 61 shows the ministry that Jesus, the anointed one, will fulfil. In Acts the passage from Joel shows that this anointing is now poured out on 'all flesh', on the whole church. Jesus' mission with his disciples was in the power of the Spirit and is now to continue by the Spirit.

Following the missionary spirit

The book of Acts provides a series of examples where the current default setting of the church is changed by the missionary initiatives of the Holy Spirit. 'The narrative of Acts suggests that a community truly led by the Spirit will be led in new and surprising directions' (Johnson, *Prophetic Jesus*, p. 71). Over-familiarity can blind us to scripture, whether that be from preaching similar sermons on Acts 2 every Pentecost, or from memories of drawing maps of Paul's missionary journeys in Sunday school. At conferences I frequently invite readers to engage the text again from the beginning, to read each incident as though it were new rather than over-familiar, and each time to ask the question, 'Do you think they expected that?'

Waiting in Jerusalem

The apostles, and the rest of the 120, waited obediently and prayerfully in Jerusalem, having received Jesus' promise of power to witness, when the Holy Spirit came upon them (1.8). '"Witness" and its cognates occur no less than twenty-three times in Acts' (Rowe, *World Turned Upside Down*, p. 120). It is one of Luke's core terms. The apostles' witness will have two elements, they 'will speak of when they walked with Jesus' and are the story keepers of 'the real history of life with Jesus' (Jennings, *Acts*, p. 18), a process that will eventually result in the composition of the four Gospels, so that it can be a part of all of our witness today. Then there will be their continuing testimony of the presence of the risen Jesus by the Spirit.

The risen Lord's promise was not merely about what they would say, in bearing witness to Jesus, but what they would become: 'You will *be* my witnesses.' The Holy Spirit is a gift for transformation, empowering a way of life, and a capacity for sacrifice, which is all coherent with the message about Christ. 'Acts does not construe "witness" monothematically as the proclamation of Jesus' resurrection – preaching the word, as it were – but more comprehensively as living out the pattern of life that culminates in resurrection' (Rowe, *World Turned Upside Down*, ch. 5).

This empowered witness, according to Jesus, would be 'in Jerusalem, in all Judea and Samaria, and to the ends of the earth'. I had always taken this to be a programmatic anticipation of what would take place in the following chapters. In one sense it is. Acts portrays the geographical expansion of the gospel message and of the church which it creates. To a devout Jew, Jerusalem with its temple was the centre of the earth and Rome, where the Acts narrative ends, was at 'the ends of the earth'. But I am now convinced there is more to this gift of the

Spirit than that. For the gospel to expand territorially it also has to expand cross-culturally. The empowering promised by Jesus is a power to impact imagination, to reset default settings, and to result in mission beyond the familiar, and beyond existing comfort zones. The apostles default setting was limited to the restoration of Israel. Their imagination was captured by heritage restored (as it often is still for parts of the church today); as yet it had no place for what St Paul would later call the 'grafting in' of the Gentiles. There is an unsettling element to the gift of the Spirit. The apostles could not fully understand what they were waiting for, or know what it would lead to. But they knew they should pray.

Pentecost

When it came, the filling of the Holy Spirit was a sudden and powerful experience. Whether or not the 120 had any advance perception of what it would be like, they recognized it as the fulfilment of Jesus' promise. There were two pieces of evidence. First the encounter led directly to worship and to the witness, which Jesus had said was its purpose. Acts 2 begins with a group indoors, responding to the Spirit's arrival with praise in tongues. Before we know, and without our being told, they are outdoors, a large crowd has gathered and the tongues are recognized as 'speaking about God's deeds of power'. Peter's sermon, which follows, results in 3,000 baptisms: clear evidence of the Spirit's work.

But there is a second source of evidence. The experience is understood as the fulfilment of scripture and interpreted accordingly. Following his resurrection Jesus had 'opened their minds to understand the scriptures, and he said to them, "Thus it is written, that the Messiah is to suffer and to rise from the dead"' (Luke 24.44–45). Over 40 days he had been speaking with the disciples 'about the kingdom of God'. The fruit of this instruction is seen in Peter's speech, which is full of references to scripture and its fulfilment by Jesus. Scripture is always key to recognizing the initiatives of the Spirit.

FOLLOWING THE SPIRIT

Throughout his ministry, Jesus' teaching about the kingdom had a 'now and not yet' character (see Beasley-Murray, *Jesus and the Kingdom of God*). In his post-resurrection instruction he taught them about the kingdom and promised the Spirit. The Spirit is the foretaste and the guarantee of the future kingdom in its fullness. In many other parts of the New Testament the work of the Holy Spirit has this now-and-not-yet, or foretaste-and-guarantee character (see Fee, *God's Empowering Presence*, chapter 12). In Acts 2 the events of Pentecost are seen as the continuing ministry of Jesus. He has poured out the Spirit. The significance of his outpouring is interpreted via Joel 2.28ff.

1 The gift of the Spirit would no longer be restricted to prophets, priests and kings. The Spirit would be continually poured out on all who believe, irrespective of age, gender or status.
2 This was an era-shifting event. Peter says the event of Pentecost is the fulfilment of Joel's prophecy. So the 'portents in the heaven above and signs on the earth below, blood, and fire, and smoky mist. The sun shall be turned to darkness and the moon to blood' (Acts 2.10–20) are not literal cosmic phenomena to be seen just before Jesus returns. They are typical imagery used by the prophets to show the spiritual significance of events on earth, particularly during times of spiritual and social upheaval (for example, Isaiah 13.9ff.; 34.1ff.; Ezekiel 32.7–8; Amos 8.9). In particular, Peter is saying this pouring out of the Spirit by the risen and ascended Jesus is an event of Exodus proportion. Blood, fire, smoke, darkness are all Exodus motifs. Wonders and signs were associated with the Exodus. On the mount of Transfiguration, Moses and Elijah spoke with Jesus about the 'exodus' he was to achieve in Jerusalem (Luke 9.30–31). The initial outpouring of the Spirit was in one sense unique, but it is also for the whole era from Pentecost to the return of Christ. Quoting Joel, Peter defines this era as 'the last days' which 'last' until 'the coming of the Lord's great and glorious day' (Acts 2.17, 20).
3 The characteristic of this era will be that what the church does on earth is to be is derived from and backed up by

heaven. It is a partnership between 'heaven above and earth below'. For this reason the manifestation of the Spirit's filling will be prophecy, dreams and visions. Prophecy in Luke is a broad theme, includes Spirit-filled praise and prayer, guidance from the Spirit and empowered witness. The Spirit's filling is a sensitizing for recognizing the Spirit's voice. Dreams and visions enable the church to imagine a future that is not based on past experience, but is an anticipation of the future Christ has secured.

However powerful Pentecost may have been as an intense experience, its consequence was the creation of a disciplined community around Christ, devoting itself to 'the apostles' teaching and fellowship, to the breaking of bread and the prayers'. Authentic encounters with God lead to disciplined lives in a community which practises and supports those disciplines. And Jesus continued his mission through them: 'day by day the Lord added to their number those who were being saved'. 'The Lord himself [the ascended Lord of verse 36] was continuing to draw people into the fellowship of his church' (Acts 2.42–47; Peterson, p. 164). Whatever the apostles, and the rest of the 120, had or had not expected, Pentecost was more than an empowering for witness, it was an equipping for following the missionary Spirit. Reflecting on Peter's speech one commentator wrote, 'Before the Spirit came Peter had little to say. His words will now and forever be only commentary on what the Spirit is doing, and what God has done for us in Jesus' (Jennings, *Acts*, p. 34).

As the Acts narrative unfolds, Jesus continues his ministry through a church empowered and guided by his Spirit and acting in his name. A man lame from birth is healed 'in the name of Jesus'. The apostles are brought before the Council and Peter gives a Spirit-inspired speech. The church prays for boldness and is filled again by the Spirit. The seriousness of putting the Spirit 'to the test' is shown by the deaths of Ananias and Sapphira. As the church grows, a racial injustice is recognized about food provided for widows. It is solved by being entrusted to seven members of the minority group, who are 'full of the Spirit and of wisdom'. Two of these men, Stephen and Philip, soon prove to be powerful preachers as well as wise administrators. In all of this the Spirit is active, but it all takes place in Jerusalem. There is no hint of a move elsewhere until an enforced one, when the martyrdom of Stephen leads to a persecution which scatters the church into Judea and Samaria (well, well!). Only the apostles, who had been the leaders and preachers up to this point, remain in Jerusalem. Now, ordinary disciples proclaim the word wherever they go. The Spirit had truly been poured out on all, not just on the leaders.

News of Philip's powerful ministry in Samaria gets back to the apostles, who sent Peter and John to check it out. The only times they had been in Samaritan territory were with Jesus, because 'Jews have no dealings with Samaritans' and devout Jews normally took a diversion to avoid a route through Samaritan territory. On one occasion, Luke tells us that John and his brother suggested calling down fire from heaven on a village that would not receive them (Luke 9.54). The confirmation that this really was a work of the Spirit comes when the newly baptized disciples receive the Holy Spirit through the laying on of hands by Peter and John. A different kind of fire was called down from heaven! The witness to Jesus had now crossed its first significant cultural barrier, and on their way home, Peter and John preach in Samaritan villages. They had learned from the Holy Spirit's missionary initiatives. But Philip was given no time to nurture the new church he had planted. An angel directed him to the wilderness road, the Spirit told him to approach a chariot, and an Ethiopian official is led to faith and baptized. Before he can breathe, Philip is snatched away by the Spirit of God. There is no question about who was leading the mission, while the church played catch-up!

The next incident is the most surprising. It was the direct initiative of the risen Lord. Saul, the lead persecutor, is encountered by the risen Jesus on the road to Damascus and the Lord directs an ordinary disciple called Ananias to him. It is a pivotal moment in the Acts narrative. Saul was left in no doubt about the identity of the one he was encountering – 'I am Jesus' – or of the Lord's total identification with his church, 'whom you are persecuting' (9.5). I wonder if this gave Paul his first inkling that the church was the body of Christ. Certainly to persecute it was to persecute him. Paul would later describe his encounter with the risen Lord as 'Last of all, as to someone untimely born, he appeared also to me' (1 Cor. 15.8). Ananias tells him, 'The God of our ancestors has chosen you to know his will, to see the Righteous One and to hear his own voice' (22.14). N. T. Wright says:

> Paul was adamant that he really had seen Jesus. He was aware that the other apostles had seen Jesus alive after his death in what might be termed the 'ordinary' sequence of resurrection appearances, and that he had had the same sighting of Jesus but at a time when the others had ceased to see Jesus ... The language he uses is not that of mystical vision, of spiritual or religious experiences without any objective, definitive referent. Paul did not think he went on seeing Jesus in this way in his subsequent continuing Christian experience, though he remained intensely conscious of his presence, love and sustaining power. He uses the language of actual seeing. (*What St Paul Really Said*, p. 35f.)

Having taken this initiative, the Lord then directs a disciple to go to Saul. Three times Luke tells us: '*The Lord said* to him in a vision, "Ananias"' (9.10); '*The Lord said* to him, "Get up and go to the street called Straight, and at the house of Judas look for a man of Tarsus named Saul"' (9.11); 'But *the Lord said* to him, "Go, for he is an instrument whom I have chosen"' (9.15). He is called by name and instantly recognizes God's voice and responds, 'Here I am Lord.' It sounds like the experience of an Old Testament prophet: and why not, for the Spirit had been poured out on all believers and all may now 'prophesy'. The clarity of the Lord's message and Ananias's capacity to receive it is striking. Here is the address, here is the owner's name, and this is the one you are looking for (9.11). Ananias' response is not 'I wonder if that was really God or was it just my imagination?' It is to argue! Do you know who this guy is, Lord? 'But Ananias answered, "Lord, I have heard from many about this man, how much evil he has done to your saints in Jerusalem; and here he has authority from the chief priests to bind all who invoke your name'" (9.13–14). Hearing was not the problem! What he heard was the problem. Despite his history so far Saul was 'an instrument whom I (Jesus) have chosen to bring my name before Gentiles and kings and before the people of Israel'. And Jesus had prepared the way: Saul of Tarsus 'has seen in a vision a man named Ananias come in and lay his hands on him so that he might regain his sight' (Acts 9.12). Ananias goes obediently. He tells him, 'Jesus – even the Lord' has sent him. He calls the persecutor 'brother Saul', prays for the restoration of his sight, prays that he will be filled with the Holy Spirit and urges him to seal his new faith and receive God's forgiveness in baptism (22.16). Saul had already been told on the Damascus road that it was in Damascus that he would be shown what he was to do (22.10). Ananias tells him 'You will be his witness to all the world of what you have seen and heard' (22.15). The church was in no way expecting anything like this and it would take the later intervention of Barnabas for them to accept it as it really was (9.26–27). Jesus is the leader of the church's mission. He chooses the part we are play. He directs and equips his servants. Often the direction is surprising, and we only grasp God's purpose in retrospect.

It seems that God has no difficulty reaching directly to the person he wishes to bring to faith – whether it is on the Damascus Road, in Judas' house in Straight Street (verse 11b–12) or, as we shall see in a moment, in a Gentile household in Caesarea. He is the one who takes the initiative. It is getting believers where he wants them to be as witnesses that seems to take longer!

Cornelius

One surprise follows another as Peter's itinerant ministry takes him to Caesarea, to people and a place he could not have previously imagined wanting to visit. The Cornelius story is 'a response to divine initiative from beginning to end' (Johnson, *The Acts of the Apostles*, p. 200). Caesarea was a Hellenistic-style city with a dominant population of Gentiles. It was the provincial capital, and the main place of residence of the governor. There had been considerable friction between Jews and the much larger Gentile population. It was a 'Rome away from Rome', the set piece of Romanization in Palestine. The spiritual and cultural distance between this and Peter's devout familiar world was substantial. So God worked on both sides of the divide. Each had a vision and each received a divine message. 'No doubt must be left that this initial step was directly at God's bidding' (Dunn, *The Acts of the Apostles*, p. 134). Cornelius, who sends his servants to invite Peter, is the doorkeeper to a whole network, his (Cornelius') relatives and close friends (Acts 10.24). Through him a whole new front for mission can open up.

Cornelius is a 'God fearer', a Gentile worshipper of the God of Israel, but not a proselyte, a full convert. God fearers 'had not taken the final steps of full conversion; those who belonged to this category, although they honoured the God of Israel, had no part in the Covenant on the basis of baptism, circumcision and offerings' (Van Unnik, *Sparsa collecta*, p. 249). He performs two of the three main acts of Jewish piety – prayer and almsgiving (Acts 10.2) and keeps one of the three traditional Jewish times of prayer at 3 p.m. The Rabbis distinguished between 'proselytes' and 'sojourners', who were to be well treated but not within the Covenant. Because he was in the military, he would have been unable to observe Torah, even had he wished to do so. He remained technically a heathen!

If this was Peter's understanding, he would have believed that Cornelius could expect some blessing in this life but had no part in the age to come. His prayers were admirable but insufficient. But God appeared to have a different view. Cornelius' prayers had been received as 'a memorial before God' (verse 4). Peter's attitude would count out someone whom God was about to count in! It seemed that if Cornelius was to be converted to Christ then Peter would need to be converted to Cornelius! 'The first part in the process is the conversion of Peter himself ... a conversion from traditional and deeply rooted convictions which had completely governed his life till that moment' (Dunn, *Acts*, p. 132).

This unfolds like a drama with a number of acts. It begins at the house of Simon the Tanner – an unclean occupation. Peter is staying with a socially marginal Jew. Peter had not been brought up as a Pharisee, and had witnessed Jesus' conflicts with them, and did not share their strict purity codes. It was a short step in the journey he did not know he was about to take. Then he has a vision. Seeing heaven open implies receiving a revelation from God. But it is disturbing, as the vision is of a mixture of clean and unclean animals according to the Old Testament food laws. But nothing unclean descends from heaven. Peter is hungry and is told to kill and eat. His answer is 'No Lord'! (a prayer used often down the centuries!), 'By no means, Lord; for I have never eaten anything that is profane or unclean.' Peter is faced with a challenge of both obedience and imagination. Obedience because he was seeking to remain faithful to his understanding of scripture and God's will, and the traditions which expressed them, yet the voice from heaven seemed to be calling him to break from them. Imagination because he could not yet imagine this part of the transformation between human cultures which Christ had made possible. In one way his experience is unique. This is a key point in salvation history as the door to the Gentiles is opened. But we, like Peter, also need to be open to the Spirit's challenges to our assumptions, interpretations and traditions. The Spirit frees our imagination and gives fresh visions. Ultimately, as here eventually, there will be no conflict between the Spirit and scripture. But such challenges can be as disturbing for us as this was for Peter. 'The voice said to him again, a second time, "What God has made clean, you must not call profane."' But Peter has no time to reflect as the Spirit tells him to receive the men who are arriving looking for him, 'without hesitation' or 'without discrimination' as the Spirit has sent them.

Peter is obedient and (presumably with Simon's blessing) offers his Gentile visitors hospitality. 'That Peter should provide them with bed and board was in itself a liberal gesture towards Gentiles, though it did not involve the same risk of ceremonial pollution as his acceptance of hospitality would involve' (Bruce, *Acts*). Having heard his visitors' account of the angelic message, and of Cornelius' obedience to it, Peter is equally obedient and, fully aware of the break he is making with his traditions, returns with them. Now he understands that the vision he was given was not just about food, but about people (10.28).

The underlying issue was about the boundaries and identity markers of God's people: the practices which publicly marked them out as distinct. Central to this were the biblical food laws (see Lev. 20.24b–26; Lev. 11.2–47; Deut. 14.3–21; Dan. 1.8, 12–16; Mark 7.14–23).

> Although Jews were happy to mix with Gentiles in synagogues or possibly even in market places or streets, eating with them was a very different matter. Eating was an occasion fraught with the possibility of breaching the purity code, one of the most crucial aspects of the mosaic law for the maintenance of the separate identity of the Jewish ethnos. (Esler, *Community and Gospel in Luke–Acts*, p. 84)

Circumcision, the other distinctive mark of Jesus' faith, was a private matter and for males only, but the food laws made Jewish faith a public affair. The ban on eating with Gentiles was not a specific prohibition of the Torah, but the logical consequence of the food and purity laws. To abandon them was to abandon the faith.

> Those Jews who permanently gave up the prohibitions which distinguished them from the Gentiles ceased to be Jews. One must assume that those Jews who did fudge the boundaries between Jew and Gentile were rightly regarded as endangering the ethnic identity of the Jewish people and came under heavy pressure to conform or to abandon Judaism altogether. (Esler, *Community*, p. 86)

The challenge for the church's mission was that hospitality was central to ancient cultures. 'It is simply not possible to fully accept someone with whom you are unwilling to share in the intimacy of table fellowship. The early church had to solve the problem of kosher food laws in order to launch a mission to the Gentiles' (Polhill, *Acts*, p. 256). But table fellowship lay at the heart of the lifestyle of the young church (2.46), and the household was to become the usual meeting place of the churches. The church's vocation was to bear witness to Jesus 'to the ends of the earth'. But this problem would stop Jewish missionaries from entering the culture of those they were called to win. It was a struggle. On one occasion Peter himself reverted under pressure (Gal. 2.11–13). The church had to be converted to the Gentiles for the Gentiles to be converted to Christ.

> By means of the issue of hospitality, Luke demonstrates that the conversion of the first Gentile required the conversion of the church as well. Indeed, in Luke's account, Peter and company undergo a change that is more wrenching by far than the change experienced by Cornelius. (Gaventa, *From Darkness to Light*, p. 109)

An even greater danger was that there could be two churches each racially defined in contrast to the other.

Cornelius has been told to expect 'a message by which you and your entire household will be saved' (11.14). Peter had been invited to preach and preach he does. 'Jesus Christ ... is Lord of all' (11.36), irrespective of race or culture. His sermon refers to those 'who ate and drank with him (Jesus) after he rose from the dead' (11.41) as he preaches. Peter knows he has to eat and drink with Gentiles who will become disciples. The sermon is interrupted as the Spirit falls on the whole group. The Spirit who initiated this vital missional transition left no opportunity for misunderstanding. One of those who received the Spirit's anointing at Pentecost now watches as Gentiles receive it 'just as we have', 'just as it had upon us at the beginning' (11.15–17), 'the same gift that he gave us' (15.8), 'just as he did to us'. The confirmation of the rightness of this crossing of cultural borders was the outpouring of the Spirit in a way recognizably the same as that experienced by the missionaries, but in a quite different cultural context. The baptisms which followed were a direct response to this sovereign filling by the Spirit. 'Can anyone withhold the water for baptizing these people who have received the Holy Spirit just as we have?' (10.47).

The problem was that when Peter and his companions returned to their home church in Jerusalem, none there had seen the vision, heard the Spirit's voice or seen the Spirit fall. Quite reasonably they are exactly where Peter was, when the vision was given. So the question asked was not 'Why did you baptize Gentiles?' or 'Why did you preach to Gentiles?' but 'Why did you eat with Gentiles?' They had stayed in Cornelius' home for several days so at this point the question was reasonable. The story had to be retold so that the whole church could own it. Significant initiatives by the Spirit are not private experiences but need to be grasped by the church as a whole. Without this the process of discernment is incomplete. 'The struggle Luke seeks to communicate to the reader is the process of human decision-making as the Church tries to catch up with God's initiative' (Johnson, *Acts*, pp. 106–7). But note that to take new initiatives can get you in trouble in your church!

That the gospel was for the Gentiles had been established. What was required of them when they turned to Christ remained a matter of dispute until the Jerusalem Council, when the story was told briefly for a third time. The issue was resolved on the basis of scripture (the Old Testament and the words of Jesus). But the initiative of the Spirit enabled them to see scripture from a new perspective. The process began in Cornelius' house. Peter receives an enlarged understanding of the scope of the prophets' message (10.43) and of Jesus' promise of the Spirit:

> The experience of the Spirit among Gentiles deepens Peter's understanding of Jesus words (11.16): it is when he sees the Gentiles speaking in tongues and praising God that he 'remembers' the saying of the risen Lord about baptism in the Spirit (1.5). What is most fascinating about this remembrance is that Jesus spoke the words to a small band of Jewish followers. The words of Jesus are given a new understanding because of the continuing work of the Spirit. (Johnson, *Acts*, p. 201)

At the Jerusalem Council, Peter, Paul and Barnabas tell of the activity of the Spirit. James then turns to scripture, quoting Amos 9.12 together with allusions to a number of other texts from the prophets.[1] The concluding judgement is 'It has seemed good to the Holy Spirit and to us' (9.28). The way ahead had been confirmed through scripture understood in the light of the action of the Spirit. Word and Spirit had come together. If the Holy Spirit is both the inspirer of scripture and the leader of mission, ultimately there will be no conflict between the two. Word and Spirit go hand in hand. But the process can take time and is no guarantee that our previous interpretations and assumptions were right. Sometimes we discover that we had misinterpreted. Sometimes we see what we had been unable to see before. 'God is already ahead of all evangelism, carrying on his mission to the world ... More often than not respectful discernment will demand drastic changes of heart and mind, as for Peter with his own traditions' (Ford and Hardy, *Knowing and Praising God*, p. 151).

The events around Cornelius are just one example of the importance of Spirit inspired interpretation of scripture in Acts. We have already seen this at Pentecost and in the resolution of the questions raised by the conversion of Cornelius. But Levison claims that:

> Throughout the book of Acts, however, spectacular events take second place to the sanity of the inspired interpretation of scripture ... The inspired interpretation of scripture, more than mission in a general sense, or miracles or speaking in incomprehensible tongues, is the principal effect of the holy spirit in the book of Acts. (Levison, *Inspired*, p. 152)

Mission is founded on the central place of the role of scripture, understood Christologically and interpreted through the Spirit contextually. Luke places a programmatic prophecy about the Spirit near the beginning of both his volumes (Luke 4.17–19; Acts 2.16–21). Jesus spent the weeks between his resurrection and ascension 'opening their minds to understand the scriptures' concerning himself, and directly linked this with the coming of the Spirit (Luke 24.44–49). From then on, the Holy Spirit inspired interpretation of scripture takes a key role in the missionary endeavour, for example Peter's speech at Pentecost; the church's prayer for boldness in Acts 4; Stephen's speech at his trial; Philip with the Ethiopian; and so on.

Prayerful disciplined corporate reflection on scripture is an essential tool for a church seeking to follow Jesus in his continuing mission. Levison reflects on Peter's defence in Acts 4.7–13, which is based on Psalm 118.22:

> In this abbreviated speech, Luke combines a quintessential expression of inspiration, filled with 'the holy spirit', with a scriptural text that had wide currency in the early church's memory bank. This little speech, perhaps more than any other portion of the New Testament, demonstrates clearly that inspiration, filling with the holy spirit, need not be spontaneous ... the holy spirit brings out the meaning of ancient scriptures – texts known already to the speaker – for contemporary contexts. This sort of inspiration takes place when speakers are already familiar, through sustained study, with those scriptures. (Levison, *Inspired*, p. 153)

The consequence is that the disciples are recognized as 'companions of Jesus' though they are uneducated and ordinary men. Levison suggests that this is:

> because Peter cites the same text Jesus cited in his parable of the wicked tenants, who murdered the owner's son when he came to collect rent. In all three synoptic gospels (Mark 12.10–11; Matt. 21.42; Luke 20.17), Jesus cites Psalm 118.22. Why then did the Jewish leaders realize that Peter had been with Jesus? He cited the same scripture as Jesus – and in the same way. In short, he learned this from Jesus. Once again, the presence of the holy spirit and the study of scripture go hand in hand. (*Inspired*, p. 155)

Those who follow the unexpected initiatives of the missionary Spirit, need also to immerse themselves in the scriptures.

Through the events at Caesarea, the foundation had been laid for more adventurous mission. Despite all the disturbance it caused, the breakthrough with Cornelius was with a Gentile who was 'a devout man who feared God with all his household; he gave alms generously to the people and prayed constantly to God.' Much more would be needed to win Gentiles who had no knowledge of the Jewish faith. But the way was now open. 'The conversion of Cornelius ... is a breakthrough not simply because Peter and the Jerusalem church now accept Gentiles for baptism but also because they recognize the right of Jewish Christians to freely associate with Gentiles in the course of their mission' (Tannehill, *The Narrative Unity of Luke–Acts*, p. 137).

Luke immediately follows his Cornelius account with a report on the sharing of the gospel with Gentiles in Antioch and of Barnabas and Saul's investment in teaching the church (11.19–26). The stage is set for the next divine intervention. 'The Holy Spirit said, "Set apart for me Barnabas and Saul for the work to which I have called them."' Barnabas and Saul are duly commissioned by their fellow leaders and 'sent out by the Holy Spirit' (11.4). There follows a pattern of intentional missionary journeys from town to town, with Spirit empowered ministry in the name of Jesus, conversions, and opposition, which continues until it is interrupted by the Holy Spirit who had initiated it.

Christian mission is not intended to be blind or random. Consistent patterns will emerge as the church follows the Spirit's guidance. Just as a disciplined community emerged out of the tongues and fire of Pentecost. But there must be continual openness to the Spirit's often surprising interventions. Following the Jerusalem council Paul, now with Silas and Timothy, sets out again, this time through Phrygia and Galatia, but the Spirit had forbidden them 'to speak the word in (the province of) Asia'. Then 'the Spirit of Jesus' did not allow them to enter Bithynia – these regions would be evangelized later (chs 18—19). The only guidance from the Spirit was negative. There follows a long period of frustration and a silent heaven as they make the long journey towards the coast, to Troas, as the only option left open to them. But the Spirit was equally present in the silence and frustration as when giving positive direction. 'The Spirit is shepherding Paul and his companions to Troas, in order there to grant them a new vision' (González, *Acts*, p. 187). 'Jesus' witnesses must patiently endure the frustration of their own plans, in order to discover the opportunity which God holds open' (Peterson, *Acts*, p. 454). Only when they get to Troas does the Spirit give positive direction. 'During the night Paul had a vision: there stood a man of Macedonia pleading with him and saying, "Come over to Macedonia and help us"' (Acts 16.9). Macedonia had not been part of their plan or in their imagination.

> Paul's ministry in Macedonia and Greece simply does not fit into the world-map of Acts 2: his crossing of the Bosporus marks a breaking out of the known world, a new step carefully signalled in the narrative by a series of false moves successively blocked by the Spirit. It is hardly surprising that the decisive move requires the explicit guidance of a dream. (Alexander, *Acts in its Ancient Literary Context*, p. 90)

Although Paul received the vision, the whole group discerns the call of God. Note the 'we'. When he had seen the vision, we immediately tried to cross over to Macedonia, being convinced that God had called us to proclaim the good news to them (verse 10).

Arriving in Phillipi they have travelled beyond the culturally familiar. The city was a Roman colony and has been described as 'a piece of Rome transplanted abroad', 'Rome in microcosm' (Witherington, *Acts*, p. 488). The citizens had full Roman citizenship. The primary language was Latin, not Greek. This was the mission's encounter with the Roman world. The apostolic team are also beyond their missional experience. Their normal practice was to begin at the synagogue. But there is no synagogue. The only alternative is a place of prayer, a marginal place outside the gate. If they are looking for a man from Greece (as we would say), what they find is a woman from Turkey. Then God the evangelist gets to work. Just as the 'Spirit of Jesus' had led them there, so 'The Lord opened her heart to listen eagerly to what was said by Paul. She and her household were baptized.' Jesus is still on mission. Her home becomes the base for the team (verse 15) and the meeting place for the church as it is founded (verse 40). Welcomed into a home they were less likely to be seen as a dangerous foreign cult. Whatever their plans had been the church is founded on a foreign business woman in a male dominated society, a slave girl delivered from demons and a suicidal jailor. 'In the forming of diverse churches, the Spirit blows and leads creatively' (Dehmlow-Dreier, 'Planting Missional Congregations', p. 5). The founding missionaries had to leave almost immediately. But the very positive letter Paul would later write to this church shows how it grew and developed.

The greater wisdom of the Spirit had opened up new possibilities. Now they knew that the gospel crosses boundaries and could take root in Roman culture. They were on the boundary between two provinces which could then be evangelized, and Paul did not know it but he was being prepared for Rome itself. God's plans are always better. 'The Holy Spirit is not tame – and therefore he is not completely predictable. However, the Holy Spirit is the Spirit of Jesus Christ, and therefore he does bring wisdom, truth and power' (Sunquist, *Understanding Christian Mission*, p. 234).

The text of Acts makes clear that Jesus continues to lead the mission of the church, chiefly by the agency of the Holy Spirit. 'In their view, the Christians were subject to the freedom and initiative of the Holy Spirit and would go where the Spirit led; indeed, the Spirit could even directly contravene their own intentions and plans' (Rowe, *World Turned Upside Down*, p. 119). As Peter said, 'We are witnesses to these things, and so is the Holy Spirit whom God has given to those who obey him' (Acts 5.32). 'They were not invited to deploy their resources or plan their strategy' (Taylor, *The Go-Between God*, p. 2). As with them so it is with us: 'the Breath of God has always played a more decisive part than our human strategy' (Taylor, *The Go-Between God*, p. 53).

The church may be led in surprising and unexpected ways, but the consequence is a distinctive, contextually appropriate Christian way of life, in community.

A community of disciples on the way

The Jesus movement was known as 'the Way' from as early as the first major persecutions (9.2; 22.4). Apollos is instructed in 'the way of the Lord' (18.25) or 'the way of God' (18.26). In Ephesus evil is spoken against the Way (19.9) and there is a riot as it impacts the economy of the city (19.23). When defending himself before Felix, Paul identifies his faith as 'according to the Way' (24.14) and Luke tells us the governor was 'rather well informed about the Way' (24.22).

Throughout Acts (1.15; 4.32; 5.14; 9.30, 32; 10.23; 11.21; and so on), believers in Jesus are also called disciples (11.29), just as were those who followed him physically in Galilee. The church is 'the community of disciples' (6.2). Frequently the local church is described as 'the disciples' (6.1; 9.26, 38; 11.29; 13.52; 14.20, 28; 18.27; 19.9; 20.1; 21.4, 21.16). Disciples are 'made' through the proclamation of the gospel (14.21). They are baptized in the name of Jesus (2.38; 8.12; 10.48) into his salvation, his community and his continuing ministry, and act in his name (3.6; 4.10, 18; 9.27; 16.18). They are to be available to their Lord (9.10; 13.2). Their numbers increase (6.1, 7). They need the power of the Holy Spirit (13.52; 19.6). They need to be strengthened and encouraged (14.22; 18.23; 20.1). They need teaching (2.42) and can be led astray by false teachers (2.30). Barnabas and Saul spent a year teaching the young church at Antioch, with its new mixture of Jews and Gentiles (11.25–26).

> Luke believes the first sizable Christian community to include gentiles needs an entire year of instruction. The new converts in Antioch are to be ... resocialized – in the common practices that constitute their life as a community of repentance and salvation ... according to Acts, the distinctive life of Jews and gentiles together in the Antiochene community forms the public witness that calls forth the label Christianos. (Rowe, *World Turned Upside Down*, pp. 129–30)

'Christian' was a nickname given to disciples of Jesus the Christ. Faithful discipleship was sure to create some conflict with the predominant Roman culture. Jesus had promised, 'When they bring you before the synagogues, the rulers, and the authorities, do not worry about how you are to defend yourselves or what you are to say; for the Holy Spirit will teach you at that very hour what you ought to say' (Luke 12.11–12). Kavin Rowe's important study *World Turned Upside Down* focuses on the scenes and speeches in Acts where Christians appear before Roman officials. His thesis is:

> On the one hand, the Christian mission into the gentile world entails a collision with culture-constructing aspects of that world. In this way, Christianity and pagan culture are competing realities. Precisely because the Christian call to repentance necessarily involves a different way of life, basic patterns of Graeco Roman culture are disrupted and face collapse. The pagans are justifiably incensed: the Christians embody cultural peril. On the other hand, the attempt to read this cultural peril as a bid for governmental power is roundly rejected. The upheaval that inevitably attends the arrival of Christian missionaries has nothing whatever to do with sedition and treason. ... new culture, yes – coup, no. (p. 149)

Becoming a disciple implied a substantial change in personal and public behaviour. In the ancient world, 'religion' was not a separate compartment of life (that is an Enlightenment construct) but pervaded the whole. Christian conversion, the call to turn to God, carries with it 'an entire pattern of life' (Rowe, *World Turned Upside Down*, p. 142). It involves withdrawing from sacrifice to the gods and being identified with the others who did the same (on this see Hurtado, *Destroyer of the Gods*). 'The accounts of the Christian mission in Lystra (Acts 14), Philippi (Acts 16), Athens (Acts 17), and Ephesus (Acts 19) do not merely target one particular aspect of pagan religion but display narratively the collision between two different ways of life' (Rowe, *World Turned Upside Down*, p. 50). The missionary initiatives of the Spirit do not shortcut the necessity for disciple making practices, rather they create the necessity for them, and empower them. The Spirit creates Christlike communities.

These communities combine local character with shared recognizable qualities. Paul and his colleagues can recognize the family likeness of groups of disciples in very different contexts (21.4, 16; 28.14–15) and also recognize when something is not right, as in Ephesus (19.1–6). The communities are connected (18.27). The boundary-crossing ministry of Jesus by the Spirit creates both unity and diversity. Loveday Alexander has described this as 'extensivity' and 'intensivity' (*Church* 3.4.2 to 3.5.6). Extensivity leads to '*diversity*: geographical diversity; ethnic diversity; diversity of proclamation; and diversity of liturgical space'. Intensivity is provided by the role of the apostles, who are 'sent out in mission, but in following their calling they also provide the growing Church with a constant connection back to its single point of origin' and by the practice which the churches share in common (Acts 2.42).

Conclusion

To be on mission with Jesus is to follow the Spirit. Max Warren, then General Secretary of CMS, wrote, 'Unless the missionary movement can be responsive to the unpredictability of the Holy Spirit, it will cease to be a movement' (Warren, 'The Fusion of IMC and WCC', p. 194). His successor, John V. Taylor, advised that 'Our theology would improve if we thought more of the church being given to the Spirit than of the Spirit being given to the church' (*The Go-Between God*, p. 133).

Notes

1 See Richard Bauckham, 'All the variations of the text of Acts 15.16–18 from that of Amos 9.11–12 LXX belong to a consistent interpretation of the text with the help of related texts which refer to the building of the eschatological temple (Hos. 3.4–5; Jer. 12.15–16) and the conversion of the nations (Jer. 12.15–16; Zech. 8.22; Isa. 45.20–23) in the messianic age' ('James and the Gentiles', p. 165). Also Ben Witherington III, 'The events that happened when Peter visited Cornelius are said in v15 to agree with the words of the prophets, indicating that what follows will be a composite text' (*The Acts of the Apostles*, p. 459).

5

On Mission With Jesus: Shaping the Church

> Mission is 'the good news of God's love, incarnated in the witness of a community, for the sake of the world'. (Bosch, *Transforming Mission*, p. 519)

We have seen that the ongoing mission of Christ through the Spirit often takes surprising turns, but results in stable local communities of disciples. The question remains: 'What principles can we learn about the forming and shaping of those communities from this mission and from Paul's letters to churches, many of which he planted?'

Two-handed mission

St Irenaeus famously called the Son and the Spirit 'the hands of the Father', often referred to as 'the two hands of God' (*Against Heresies* Book 5 ch. 6). 'The Church is the creation of both the Spirit and the Son' (Wolfhart Pannenberg in Pickard pp. 18–19). It is the Spirit who baptizes us into the body of the Son (1 Cor. 12.13), not just universally, but also locally and contextually, as the body of Christ in Corinth, or Rome, or Leeds or Sheffield or Barnsley and so on.

The establishment of new ecclesial communities, whether fresh expressions or other kinds of church plants, needs to be a two-handed process! Both Christology (the doctrine of Christ) and pneumatology (the doctrine of the Holy Spirit) need to be brought to bear. The Orthodox theologian, Metropolitan John Zizioulas wrote:

> Christ in-stitutes (the Church) and the Spirit con-stitutes. 'The in-stitution' is something presented to us, more or less a fait-accompli ... The 'con-stitution' is something that involves us in its very being, something that we accept freely because we take part in its very emergence. (*Being as Communion*, p. 130)

In other words, the person and work of Christ is the given of the gospel. Any attempt at translation or embodiment of the gospel has to be faithful to that which is given. The church is only 'the body of Christ', as in 1 Corinthians 12, if it is the Christ of the scriptures, as in 1 Corinthians 15, who is being embodied. The body of Christ is called to bear the image of the biblical Christ.

But translatability is also of the essence of the gospel. 'Christianity is culturally infinitely translatable' (Walls, *The Cross-Cultural Process*, p. 29). The early church quickly dispensed with the culture and language of its founder and opened up other languages and cultures (see Lamin Sanneh, *Translating the Message*). Our Gospels are missionary documents in which the original words of Jesus have been translated into Greek, as the primary first-century language of mission. The translation was not of words alone but from one culture to many. The Holy Spirit was and is the chief translator and interpreter. The Spirit works 'with' the church to enable it to take Christlike shape, appropriate to its context. Translation is 'a fundamental aspect of the Church's missionary being' (Radner, *Church*, p. 158).

Tom Smail wrote:

> It is helpful to think of the Spirit ... as an artist whose one subject is the Son, and who is concerned to paint countless portraits of that subject on countless human canvases using the paints and brushes provided by countless human cultures and historical situations. (*The Giving Gift*, p. 77)

The church in each context is to be both *incarnational* (the body of Christ as it needs to be for this place, now) and *prophetic* – a genuine foretaste of the new heaven and earth for this place now: a gateway to God's future for that context. The two belong together, because Jesus embodied both. He was, in his incarnation, a first-century Palestinian Jew appropriately addressing his contemporaries, while simultaneously bringing the foretaste of the kingdom of God into his context. All of this was by the Holy Spirit. And so with us, an emphasis on incarnation alone can reduce contextual ministry to an attempt just to be 'relevant', while an exclusive emphasis on the prophetic can easily lose touched with the lived reality of the community it seeks to address. Both are ministries led and empowered by the Holy Spirit.

- Incarnational: John Taylor wrote, 'Every unit of Christian presence in the world should find its identity primarily in its missionary concern for that area of life towards which its members are immediately responsible' (quoted in Baker and Ross, *Imagining Mission with John V. Taylor*, p. 11).
- Prophetic: Lesslie Newbigin wrote, 'the Church in any place is not rightly understood unless it is understood as sign, first-fruit and instrument of God's purpose in Christ *for that place*' (*A Local Church Truly United*, p. 2).

Note in both the stress laid on local place, and that it is not necessarily the local community's understanding of its needs which is to shape the culture of the church, but the future which Christ has secured for that place, when the heavens and earth are made new.

The practice of discernment is focused in two key questions. The incarnational one – 'What shape should the body of Christ take here?' – and the prophetic one – 'How is the missionary Spirit anticipating the future Christ has secured here?' – which we will examine further in the next chapter.

Christology and incarnational mission

Mission is 'the good news of God's love, incarnated in the witness of a community, for the sake of the world' (Bosch,

Transforming Mission, p. 519). 'We are to be the tangible presence of Christ in the world – a body' (Williams, *On Christian Theology*, p. 172). 'Mission is ... a task for the whole church, since the Church, as the body of Christ in the world, represents to the world what Christ is' (Hooker and Young, *Be Holy As I Am Holy*, p. 18). Before examining the New Testament texts on this issue it will be necessary to explore the relationship between mission and an incarnational approach to ecclesiology.

'The Church is a kind of historical image of the figure of Jesus', says Ephraim Radner (*Church*, p. 10), leading to the question of how that image should be established in this particular time in history. 'Inculturation is a necessity for the continuation of Christ's mission', wrote Aylward Shorter (*Towards a Theology of Inculturation*, p. 80), implying that Christ's mission cannot be continued adequately if the church does not adequately engage with culture. 'It is only successful enculturation that makes possible the successful mission of the church', says Miroslav Volf (*After Our Likeness*, p. 255), opening the question of what successful enculturation looks like and how it is achieved. In fact, every church is embodied in a culture. Andrew Walls writes, 'Christian faith is embodied faith; Christ takes flesh among those who respond to him in faith. But there is no generalized humanity; incarnation has always to be culture specific' (*The Missionary Movement*, p. 47). The question is whether that embodiment appropriately displays and offers Christ in and for the culture/s where it is located.

Many of us have got used to the idea that the mission of the church has taken different and distinctive shape as it has crossed new cultural frontiers or entered new eras of culture. As we have seen in an earlier chapter, David Bosch identified different historical missionary paradigms. Bevans and Schroeder demonstrated different combinations of 'constants in context'. From Lesslie Newbigin we learned that contemporary western culture is a challenging mission field in its own right (see Newbigin, *The Gospel in a Pluralist Society*). But these insights have had little impact on ecclesiology, because centuries of Christendom treated mission as an overseas issue, and in the colonial years it was self-evident for missionaries to take their western forms of church with them. On my first visit to Madagascar, it was a culture shock to see the Anglican theological college chapel – a very British mock gothic church with Victorian white Jesus stations of the cross along the inside walls. The task of inculturation is not easy. One church leader in Madagascar commissioned some Malagasy art for his church, only to discover he had chosen art from the wrong tribe! Overall missiology has had little involvement in the shaping of ecclesiology until comparatively recently. The standard texts on Anglican ecclesiology hardly engage with it. The focus, according to Ephraim Radner, has been mostly on ecumenical dialogue or internal disputes, so that 'Defending this or that version of the Church has in fact defined our thinking about the Church almost exhaustively until relatively recently' (Radner, *Church*, p. 14).

The term 'incarnational' has been used by missiologists to explore what it means to be a missionary or missional church. It has been used, with a variety of emphases and interpretations, in a wide variety of Christian traditions, most of which cannot be explored here. It has been used to mean 'following Jesus as the pattern for mission', 'participating in Christ's risen presence as the power of mission' and 'joining God's cosmic mission of enfleshment' (Langmead, *The Word Made Flesh*, p. 8). The most important for our purposes are developments in Roman Catholic missiology after Vatican II, and Newbigin's influence on the World Council of Churches. Vatican II, with its emphasis on the Church as the people of God, and its move from Latin liturgy to the vernacular, opened up a new missional engagement with a wide range of cultures, the best known of which is described in Vincent Donovan's *Christianity Rediscovered*. Theological reflection on this development centred on the incarnation, although, as shall see, the main term became 'inculturation'.[1] So Pope John Paul II in *Redemptorist Missio*: 'Through inculturation the Church makes the Gospel incarnate in different cultures, and at the same time introduces peoples, together with their cultures into her own community.'

The papal encyclical *Ad Gentes* makes the same connection between the mission of the Church and Christ's incarnation.

The Church, in order to be able to offer all of them the mystery of salvation and the life brought by God, must implant herself into these groups for the same motive which led Christ to bind Himself, in virtue of His Incarnation, to certain social and cultural conditions of those human beings among whom He dwelt. The Church must be present in these groups through her children, who dwell among them or who are sent to them. (Vatican Council, 1965, '*Ad Gentes*: On the Mission Activity of the Church', sections 10 and 11)

For the World Council of Churches, Lesslie Newbigin wrote Bible studies on the theme 'Mission in Christ's Way', drawing on John 20.21, 'As the Father has sent me so I send you', as preparatory material for a 1989 conference of the same name.

Traditional Christology had paid little attention to the earthly ministry of Jesus. His ministry was seen as providing evidence for his full humanity as well as deity, but was not treated as significant in other ways by many doctrinal theologians. This is by contrast to New Testament scholars, for whom the various quests for the historical Jesus have proved a central concern. Tom Wright points out the absence of reference to Christ's adult incarnate life, in the creeds and even from an early canticle like the *Te Deum*. 'When you took our flesh to set us free you humbly chose the Virgin's womb. You overcame the sting of death and opened the kingdom of heaven to all believers' (*How God Became King*, pp. 10–20). But an incarnational approach to ecclesiology must take seriously the earthly life of Jesus, if we are to share in his mission in his way:

> Jesus was sent to walk in and with people of a particular culture and time. Jesus did not provide esoteric teachings from a distant mountain or from deep in the desert; he walked with people, spoke their language, touched their sores and gave them hope now and for the future. He held their children and was held, as a child, by his own mother. (Sunquist, *Understanding Christian Mission*, p. 219)

Christ's mission in Christ's way means we are called to the same.

An incarnational approach is not alien territory for the Church of England. The parochial system is based on an incarnational understanding. There has been and remains a strong incarnational emphasis underlying Anglo-Catholic ecclesiology. Recently Samuel Wells has written insightfully of 'incarnational ministry' and 'incarnational mission' as 'being with', as in Emmanuel – God with us. As part of this heritage, incarnational mission was key to the writing of the *Mission-Shaped Church* report. In the Chairman's introduction, I wrote:

> One of the central features of this report is the recognition that the changing nature of our missionary context requires a new inculturation of the gospel within our society. The theology and practice of inculturation or contextualization is well established in the world Church, but has received little attention for mission in the West. We have drawn on this tradition as a major resource for the Church of England. Inculturation is central to this report because it provides a principled basis for the costly crossing of cultural barriers and the planting of the church into a changed social context ... At the same time, any principle based on Christ's incarnation is inherently counter-cultural, in that it aims at faithful Christian discipleship within the new context, rather than cultural conformity. The gospel has to be heard within the culture of the day, but it always has to be heard as a call to appropriate repentance. It is the incarnation of the gospel, within a dominantly consumer society, that provides the Church of England with its major missionary challenge. (pp. xi–xii)

Challenges

This missional application of the incarnation has not gone unchallenged. Good questions have been asked about the meaning and appropriateness of 'incarnational'.

1. There is a proper concern to protect the once for all uniqueness of Christ's incarnation, believing that the use of the adjective incarnational blurs a clear understanding of that unique act. This need not be the case. The clearest statement comes from Darrell Guder:

   > When we expound both the what and the how of mission incarnationally, we need to be careful always to emphasize that the incarnation is the unique event that founds and forms the church's witness. The event defines how it is to be embodied and thus communicated. (*Incarnation and the Church's Witness*, p. 15)

   The unique status of the incarnation of our Lord must be maintained, but it has missional consequences. 'The event defines how it is to be embodied and thus communicated.' The pattern of God's unique, once for all, saving act, also provides the pattern for mission: as Newbigin wrote, it is 'Christ's mission in Christ's way'.

2. A further criticism is based on the perfection of Christ's incarnation. But that would disallow any imitation of Christ. As in Paul's exhortation: 'Be imitators of me, as I am of Christ' (1 Cor. 11.1). All our attempts to become Christlike are inevitably imperfect in this life, but that does not mean they should not be our aspiration, trusting in God's grace.

3. Finally, it is important that the application of the incarnation as Christ's mission in Christ's way is not restricted to his condescension in taking flesh and entering our world. That is a vital part, but the Word who became flesh lived a full human life, ministered the kingdom of God, opposed evil, suffered and died on the cross in sacrificial love, rose from the dead in transformed flesh and ascended to the Father in his full humanity. Every part of that unique work for us, shapes incarnational mission for others, as we partake in Christ's ongoing mission, from the Father to the world in all its diversity, by the Spirit.

The Roman Catholic missiologist Aylward Shorter clarified the issues involved. He affirmed the use of 'the analogy of the incarnation' as 'a necessary concomitant of his (Christ's) human nature', that Christ 'accepts human cultures and expresses himself through them. He lives their way of life' (*Towards a Theology of Inculturation*, p. 80). He also acknowledged: 'Christ's need of cultures in order to spread his Good News of the Kingdom and to share his life with humanity.' And most significantly, 'There could have been no earthly ministry for Jesus if he had not adopted the cultural concepts, symbols and behaviour of his hearers. The same is true of the church in every age and place.' He also recognized that Christ's 'adoption of a specific human culture, inserted him into the whole historical process of communication between cultures', saying, 'Cultures do not stand alone, they interact as a matter of course ... Jesus accepted the intercultural process as a consequence of his own enculturation, and this should be a sufficient precedent for the Church that continues his mission.' But Shorter then criticized the use of the analogy where it is limited to Christ's entry into a human culture, rather than including his whole work. This is inadequate, because it can be 'equated with the first insertion of the gospel into a culture', whereas inculturation is 'an on-going dialogue between Gospel and culture' (pp. 80–2).

For Shorter it is at this point that some uses of the analogy break down. It can be seen as 'a one-way view of inculturation'. This is because it is 'a Christology from above ... a unique and unrepeatable act ... Today in the process of inculturation, there is no virginal conception, no "coming down from heaven". Once inaugurated, the Incarnation continues upon earth to recruit culture after culture through the ordinary processes of history and human communication.' Accordingly, 'The incarnation-model may encourage people to succumb to the temptation of culturalism. In concentrating on the enculturation of Jesus, about how he accepted and identified with a particular culture, we may forget to ask how he himself challenged the culture of his adoption.' Even the shallowest reading of the Gospels shows that our Lord's incarnation involved him in making profound challenges to the culture in which he ministered. These challenges led to the cross.

But, says Shorter:

> All of these defects in the incarnation-model are remedied when a more inclusive approach is taken to the mystery of the Word made flesh ... One cannot use only one aspect of the Christ-event to illuminate the dialogue between Gospel and culture. The whole mystery of Christ, passion, death and resurrection, has to be applied analogically to the process of inculturation. (p. 82)

Shorter call this 'the Paschal Mystery' through which the cross and the resurrection are key to a proper understanding of inculturation. 'The Resurrection enabled Christ to transcend the physical limitations of an earthly life bounded by time, space and, of course culture. The Resurrection made it possible for him to identify explicitly with the cultures of every time and place.' Christ died and rose again. Shorter asked: 'Can it be said that a culture dies and rises again when it is confronted with the Risen Christ?' (p. 83). In one sense, he says, the answer is yes. 'Cultures are called upon by Christ to "die" to everything that is opposed to the ultimate good of humanity. They are to be purified and made to submit to the test of the cross ... It is only in the light of the "doctrine of the cross" (Newman) that the real worth of human culture can be seen' (p. 84).

In *Mission-Shaped Church* (pp. 30 and 88–9), and in harmony with Shorter's emphasis on 'the paschal mystery', we proposed a particular application of the cross to the process of inculturation or incarnational mission. We used the term 'dying to live' to indicate that the initial price of contextual or incarnational mission is to be paid by the person or team taking the initiative. Following Jesus' analogy of a seed in John 12.23ff., we wrote:

> Seeds must be taken out of the packet and placed in the soil of the mission context, where the seed itself (in this context the planting team) dies to its original life. The seed loses its previous identity, which was to be part of the sending church with its particular manifestation and culture. It will become something different from what it was before. Dying to live is inherent in the planting process. (p. 30)

This sacrificial approach to cross-cultural mission guards against the 'culturalism' which Shorter warned against. So it all depends what is meant by incarnational. Guder, whose little book I strongly recommend, uses 'incarnational' for what Shorter calls 'the Paschal Mystery': 'By incarnational mission I mean the understanding and practice of Christian mission that is rooted in and shaped by the life, ministry, suffering, death and resurrection of Jesus' (*Incarnation and the Church's Witness*, p. xii).

The health warning is that the term 'incarnational' is used differently by different writers, some referring to the Word's becoming flesh in a particular culture, and others to the whole work of the incarnate Lord. Nor are writers always consistent. I own up to such unintended inconsistency in one place in *Mission-Shaped Church*, as spotted by Michael Moynagh (*Church in Life*, p. 160).

To summarize, the whole work of the incarnate Lord shapes the mission of the church in three ways (*Mission-Shaped Church*, pp. 87–9):

1 There is a world to enter. 'Our mission is to be contextual. We do this as we join in the mission of the Messiah. In the incarnation, Jesus took on human flesh and dwelt among us. He incarnated and contextualized' (Hill, *Salt, Light and a City*, p. 130). Although the gospel calls people out of the world, in the Pauline sense, where the world is the whole of society living apart from God, and the appropriate response is repentance. There is a prior need to enter the actual cultural, flesh and blood world of a community, before that call to repentance can make any sense. This is analogous to our Lord's incarnation, as described by Andrew Walls:

> Mission involves moving out of oneself and one's accustomed terrain, and taking the risk of entering another world. It means living on someone else's terms, as the Gospel itself is about God living on someone else's terms, the Word becoming flesh, divinity being expressed in terms of humanity. And the transmission of the Gospel requires a process analogous, however distantly, to that great act

on which the Christian faith depends. (*Christian Scholarship and the Demographic Transformation of the Church*, pp. 170–1)

2 But there is also a world to counter from within. 'Christianity is a way of seeing the world which may go against the grain. This is what Jesus offers us – an upside down kingdom, an alternative reality, a remedial perspective ... This approach is what Jesus modelled to us in his incarnation' (Ross, *Seeing Afresh*, pp. 30–1). Shorter emphasized Christ's challenges to the culture he adopted. There is no call to 'deny yourself, take up your cross and follow me' in a culture which only needs to be affirmed. Volf warns that, 'The incarnation of divine love in a world of sin led inevitably to the cross' (*Exclusion and Embrace*, p. 25). The gospel offers the better way, but it can only be found by turning from a worse way. In the communities where the gospel was proclaimed in Acts, 'the "good news" seemed far from good to many it encountered; instead it entailed a deep threat to pre-existing, foundational ways of life in the Mediterranean world' (Rowe, *World Turned Upside Down*, p. 141). Those who make such a call to repentance are first called to deeper discipleship themselves. 'The continuing conversion of the church to incarnational witness does not mean selling out to the ... cultures that form our context. Our conversion is to more faithful witness, to more loving and creative translation of the gospel.' Guder adds that 'God's Spirit is promised to us for precisely this continuing task' (*Incarnation and the Church's Witness*, p. 55).

3 Finally, there is a world to anticipate. New creation is birthed in the midst of the old, rather than replacing it. Both the resurrection and the gift of the Spirit are described as 'first fruits' of the harvest which is to come. This role of the church as foretaste of the kingdom will be developed further in the next chapter.

So there is a debate about the use of the 'incarnation' as a model for the church's mission – with some recommending using the terms contextual, representational, or inculturational instead of incarnational – but whichever term we choose, missional ecclesiology values contextual mission and ministry. It understands that the church participates contextually in the mission of Christ Jesus, who showed us what it means to enter the world of others for their sake. He did this in a contextualized, self-giving, and missional way. 'The "messianic mission of Jesus" is basic to the nature, structures, ministries, and mission of the church. Every generation must contextualize the gospel. Every group must pursue the mission of Christ in contextual and transformative ways' (Hill, *Salt, Light and a City*, p. 230).

New Testament evidence

Paul's explanation of his own missionary practice of evangelism and church planting in 1 Corinthians 9 gives biblical warrant. 1 Cor. 8.1—11.1 is a unit. Paul addresses a number of discipleship issues precisely about the tension between being both involved in culture and maintaining Christian identity (meat offered to idols, and invitations to social issues in pagan temples), and about the nature of freedom and a Christian understanding that love takes priority over our rights. In the midst of these issues he uses his own practice as an evangelist as an example. Although the original context of a Jewish evangelist with a Gentile mission is not identical to ours, it has a great deal to say to our context, where we urgently need to find ways to evangelize people who are culturally very different from either ourselves or certainly from the culture of our churches:

> we endure anything rather than put an obstacle in the way of the gospel of Christ ... If I proclaim the gospel, this gives me no ground for boasting, for an obligation is laid on me, and woe to me if I do not proclaim the gospel! For if I do this of my own will, I have a reward; but if not of my own will, I am entrusted with a commission. What then is my reward? Just this: that in my proclamation I may make the gospel free of charge, so as not to make full use of my rights in the gospel.

> For though I am free with respect to all, I have made myself a slave to all, so that I might win more of them. To the Jews I became as a Jew, in order to win Jews. To those under the law I became as one under the law (though I myself am not under the law) so that I might win those under the law. To those outside the law I became as one outside the law (though I am not free from God's law but am under Christ's law) so that I might win those outside the law. To the weak I became weak, so that I might win the weak. I have become all things to all people, that I might by all means save some. I do it all for the sake of the gospel, so that I may share in its blessings. (1 Cor. 9.12–23)

This passage, in its context, is the nearest thing we have in the Pauline letters to a Great Commission. Just as the eleven are addressed as representative disciples in Matthew 28, so Paul, who is very aware of his distinctive calling as an apostle, and an 'apostle to the Gentiles' (Rom. 11.13), uses his own practice as an example for the disciples in Corinth to follow. The whole sections ends with, 'Be imitators of me, as I am of Christ' (11.1). The passage deserves close attention, noting Paul's commitment to 'endure anything rather than put an obstacle in the way of the gospel of Christ'. He has already said that the proclamation of Christ crucified is 'a stumbling-block to Jews and foolishness to Gentiles' (1.23). In the verses which follow he demonstrates his determination to allow no other obstacle to be in the way of these people groups as they engage with the gospel.

For Paul, to receive the gift of salvation in Jesus Christ is a great privilege, but the nature of the gift, freely given to those who have done nothing to deserve it, make it a gift to be given away. Receiving this gift carries an obligation, so 'woe to me if I do not preach the gospel'. This is not a matter of duty, but of trust. The Lord Jesus had not only saved him but entrusted him with a commission. Paul would never understand a gospel received but not shared. This would be to misunderstand the gift that had been given. Rather he says it is a matter of partnership. Morna Hooker proposes that verse 23 should be translated as, 'I do it all for the sake of the gospel in order to be *a partner* in it, meaning that Paul is a partner in the gospel in the sense that he and the gospel are "partners" in a common enterprise ... the receiving and the sharing cannot be separated ... he is surely saying here that the only way to receive those benefits is to share in *ministry* – to be a *partner* in the Gospel in every sense of the term' (Hooker, 'A Partner in the Gospel', p. 89). The risen Lord not only commissions but trusts his servants to participate as partners in his continuing ministry.

This obligation is because all men and women need the salvation which Christ has secured. In verses 19–23, he uses 'win' 5 times – 'all' (broken down into Jews, those under the law, those outside the law, and the weak) need to be won. Because all need to be saved, not just convinced (verse 22 and 10.33). This is why the cross lies at the heart of his message (1 Cor. 1.17–18 and 2.2) despite this seeming so counter-intuitive. 'For the message about the cross is foolishness to those who are perishing, but to us who are being saved it is the power of God' (1.18). For Paul, cultures are relative in a way that the gospel is not. His summary verse is verse 23: 'I have become all things to all people, that I might by all means save some. I do it all for the sake of the gospel.' There is a core message about what God has done in Christ, that is to be communicated irrespective of the cultural context. Paul summarizes this in 1 Cor. 15: 'For I handed on to you as of first importance what I in turn had received: that Christ died for our sins in accordance with the scriptures, and that he was buried, and that he was raised on the third day in accordance with the scriptures' (verses 3ff.). This Jewish biblical message becomes a message for all peoples and cultures. Tom Wright says:

> Paul did not have to make the Jewish message into an essentially Gentile message for it to be audible or comprehensible to his pagan hearers. What the Gentiles needed was precisely the Jewish message, or rather the Jewish message *as fulfilled in Jesus the messiah* ... The message paradoxically *had* to remain essentially Jewish if it was to have its proper relevance to the pagans. (*Paul*, pp. 82–3 and 43)

The one story is for all peoples, but this does not mean that we use identical language in all situations – like Paul we need to become skilled translators and appliers. In this passage he demonstrates how he engages different cultural groups. But there are clear doctrinal limits to the translation and communication of the gospel, if it is to remain a gospel of salvation.

For this cross-cultural engagement to be authentic, the identity of the ones who share the gospel must be rooted in the gospel. He uses the word 'as' in verses 20–21. For each of three named groups he becomes 'as' one of them. At first, his statement 'to the Jews I became as a Jew' seems very odd, because he was one and proud of it (Rom. 9.4–5); but he has a new identity in the Messiah. In his missionary activities, he identifies himself with each group as he engages with it and accommodates his lifestyle to theirs, as far as is possible with Christian conscience, but both rooted in and governed by his new identity in Christ.[2] Bringing the one gospel to different cultural groups requires a deep sense of identity in Christ, where belonging to him has a stronger claim than those of any culture, even and most particularly the one Christ's witnesses and ambassadors were raised in. This form of incarnational ministry requires a measure of detachment from one's own culture, before engagement with a different one, or we become bearers of our culture to another, without our starting point being refined by the gospel. Douglas Campbell says that Paul 'adopted the practices of the people he was befriending, so he lived and worked alongside them. He assumed their identities, thereby extending the incarnational principle already evident in his missionary activity' (*Pauline Dynamics*, p. 450). At the heart of Paul's statement is an incarnational principle, not just of accommodation to different cultures, but of an exchange. If the cross is the heart of the message of evangelism, the incarnation provides the model for the praxis.

Morna Hooker says, 'Five times over Paul spells out the same theme: he became what others were, in order to win them for the gospel. Five times over he uses the word to gain or win, introduced each time by 'in order that' ('A Partner in the Gospel', p. 84).

1 He is 'free with respect to all' but chooses to become 'a slave to all'. This is the underlying principle.
2 'Jews'   'as a Jew'
3 'under the law'   'as one under the law' but 'myself not under the law'
4 'outside the law'   'as one outside the law' but still 'under Christ's law'
5 'the weak'   'became weak'

Summing it up as being 'all things to all people' (all the above) in order to 'save some'. 'As far as possible he has deliberately identified himself with those whom he has sought to win for the gospel' ('A Partner in the Gospel', p. 85).

Paul has no illusions about the range of responses to the gospel. His experiences recorded in Acts included plenty of rejection. This is not an effective method, which can be discarded when it no longer seems to work. It is a principle required by the gospel itself. Hooker points out that this Pauline vocabulary is familiar from other parts of his letters. It is the language of exchange he uses when he describes what Christ has done for us (2 Cor. 5.21; 8.9; Gal. 3.13–14; 4.4–5; Rom. 8.3–4; Phil. 2.6–8). The one who knew no sin is made sin, so that we become the righteousness of God. The one who was rich became poor, so that by his poverty we might become rich. He became a curse that we might receive the Spirit. God's Son is born that we might receive adoption as God's children. God sends his own Son in the likeness of sinful flesh, and to deal with sin, so that the just requirement of the law might be fulfilled in us, and so on. Though he was in the form of God, he was born in human likeness and found in human form. In each case he acts 'so that' we benefit. He enters our lost and sinful condition so that we can share his purity, his freedom and his relationship with the Father. 'What Paul describes is the self-identification of Christ with men and women which, in turn, results in their sharing in what he is' ('A Partner in the Gospel', p. 90). Significantly, God's Son does not become 'less' through his self-emptying and incarnation (Phil. 2.6–8); rather, he reveals more fully the nature of his sacrificial love.[3] So it is with us. It is this dimension of Christ's incarnation for us which provides Paul's sacrificial model of mission. He summarizes the whole of chapters 8—10 as 'be imitators of me as I am of Christ' (11.1). 'Paul, in turn, became what the men and women to whom he proclaimed the Gospel were, in order that he might gain them for the Gospel' ('A Partner in the Gospel', pp. 9–10). The surest foundation of a church is Christ's gospel proclaimed in Christ's way.

For this incarnational approach to be truly in Christ's way, there have to be some qualifications. To return to the texts about Christ, they have essential qualifications. He became sin, though he knew no sin. He came in the likeness of sinful flesh, as we are not to think of him as sinful. So Paul, in imitation of his Lord came under the law, 'even though he was not under the law'. At various points in Acts, Paul is seen adopting Jewish practices in Jewish contexts (Campbell, *Pauline Dynamics*, p. 451), for example, in Acts 21.23ff. Then he became as one without law, 'even though he was not without God's law'. There are ethical, as well as doctrinal, limitations to 'accommodation'. 'It is difficult to conceive of Paul saying, "to the adulterer I became an adulterer in order that I might win the adulterer"' (Carson, 'Pauline Inconsistency', p. 13). In Paul's statements about Christ we benefit from Christ's actions. In the statements about his ministry others benefit through our actions in Christ, as, following Paul's identification with them they are won for Christ. In this sense Paul acts as a partner in the gospel.

Contrary to so much missionary practice in the colonial era and since, we learn that disciples who share in Christ's continuing mission are not to impose their culture upon those they are trying to win. 'Paul's principle of accommodation is ... a servant's role that asks, "How can I most effectively gain men and women for Christ?"' (Carson, 'Pauline Inconsistency', p. 13).

His cultural, religious and educational background, his preferred forms of worship and spirituality are relativized in Christ (Phil. 3.4–11) and were secondary to the need to enter the various cultures of his hearers – so that they would hear the gospel in terms they could understand and consequently engage it with their own culture, rather than be drawn out of their culture into his. Campbell says this prevents 'colonizing our potential converts through the inappropriate use of power' (Campbell, *Pauline Dynamics*, p. 450).

The four groups Paul identifies are the Jews, which we can apply to those of our own culture and upbringing. Then those 'under the law', which expanded the first category to include Gentile converts to Judaism proselytes and perhaps the 'God-fearers' like Cornelius who were attracted to the piety and moral dimensions of the Law. We might apply that to people who are attracted to the teaching of Jesus but do not engage with the church. Next come 'those outside the law', the great majority of Gentiles who had no knowledge of or interest in the Jewish faith. The majority then and increasingly their equivalents are the majority in the West today. The final group, 'the weak', is of a different sort. Within this section of 1 Corinthians it could well refer to 'Christians whose consciences trouble them about matters not in themselves wrong (as in 1 Cor. 8)' (Carson, 'Pauline Inconsistency', p. 14). This would clearly mean that for Paul to 'win' people for Christ meant far more than initial conversion but growth to mature discipleship. But this is Paul's intent anyway. He has already told the Corinthian church that, to his distress, they are still 'infants in Christ' (3.1–2), 'not ready for solid food'. In his letter to the Galatian church he says he is in the pain of childbirth until Christ is formed in them (4.19). So the weak may well include those with an untutored conscience, but much more likely it refers to those who are objectively weak, socially or culturally weak, the vulnerable whose lives depend on the power and decisions of others (Thiselton, *1 Corinthians*, pp. 705–6). The great majority of the church in Corinth are from this category (1.26). 'God chose what is weak' (1.27). If the gospel is 'good news for the poor' it is not surprising that 'the weak' are a missional priority for Paul. But to reach them he has to identify himself with them, not dazzle them with his education and apparent superiority. It is particularly striking that he opens this statement by saying 'For though I am free with respect to all, I have made myself a slave to all' (verse 19).

This incarnational praxis leaves Christ's witnesses open to accusations of inconsistency. In saying he is 'all things to all people' and that 'I try to please everyone' he inevitably makes himself vulnerable, because he does act differently in different contexts. From a spectator's perspective:

> Like the cuttlefish or the chameleon, he adapts to his surroundings. Versatile, pliant and readily changeable, he can assimilate and accommodate himself to many persons and circumstances. He is a skilled role-player, with a capacity for infinite changes of style to suit changed circumstances and associates with good and bad alike. He is not to be trusted, he is insincere, and a false friend ... Everything he does is for his own gain; he is a charlatan and a coward. (Marshall, *Enmity in Corinth*, pp. 309–10)

Paul took every action he could to avoid misunderstanding. The style of his letters make it clear that he was trained in rhetoric. But he did not use it when he first preached the gospel in Corinth. 'My speech and my proclamation were not with plausible words of wisdom, but with a demonstration of the Spirit and of power' (2.4). He worked as a tentmaker rather than accept patronage from a wealthy family (Acts 18.3). The reason being that public orators were employed by the powerful to promote their aspirations through dramatic speeches. Had he accepted patronage the popular view was that he was being paid to promote what a prominent citizen wanted, and so was not sincere, just selling something. But to win people from different parts of society he had to risk apparent inconsistency. What mattered was the consistency of his motives, in imitation of Christ. Such an imitation is costly, not just in terms of public reputation, but personally. 'This passage is often read as a statement of St Paul's cultural flexibility for the sake of his mission; rightly so, but its deeper point is Paul's willingness to relinquish his own freedom for the sake of the gospel' (Hays, *The Moral Vision of the New Testament*, p. 43). When Paul says he 'puts himself into slavery to all' we need to remember that in the Roman world this was a powerful and emotive metaphor. Paul was a Roman citizen. The thought of becoming a slave was horrific to a Roman citizen. For the sake of the gospel he lays aside all his rights in order to win people, irrespective of their rights or status.[4]

Soon after he says he becomes like 'those without the law'. He uses a term that in the Jewish literature of his period frequently referred to Gentiles. When used in this way, however, it most often carried the negative connotation of 'godless Gentiles'. These were the ones whom, as a former Pharisee, he had once despised! Given his upbringing, when for the first time Paul ate non-kosher meat, from shared dishes in a Gentile home, the former Pharisee must have felt he was denying his heritage. But the apostle knew he was there because Jesus the Messiah had sent him. As it was with Peter and Cornelius, so here with Paul. There sometimes needs to be a deep conversion in us before there can be a conversion among those to whom we are sent!

Paul concludes the whole section in this way: 'So, whether you eat or drink, or whatever you do, do everything for the glory of God. Give no offense to Jews or to Greeks or to the church of God, just as I try to please everyone in everything I do, not seeking my own advantage, but that of many, so that they may be saved. Be imitators of me, as I am of Christ' (10.31—11.1). Clearly, 1 Corinthians 10.32–33 refer back to 9.19–23, so 11.1 must imply that Paul requires Corinthians, in their circumstances, to fulfil the same commission he received, according to the same set of principles. Nor is this teaching unique to the correspondence with Corinth. The earlier letter to the Galatians challenges them similarly to 'become as I am, for I also have become as you are' (4.12). Paul 'is probably referring to the way that he was prepared to live in their midst "in a gentile fashion" (2:14)'. In Galatians this is not just a missionary device. Paul's whole sense of identity and worth, and any sense of worth comparing himself with other identities, 'had been reset by Christ, the source of his new life (2.19–20)' (Barclay, *Paul and the Power of Grace*, p. 75). Christ had changed his perspective on different identities (3.28). As with Galatia and Corinth, so with us. This principle is binding on us also! It sets the standard for Christian mission.

The Body of Christ

The consequence and continuation of such incarnational mission is the church as 'the Body of Christ'. Not 'the continuation of the incarnation', but the consequence of Christ's work carried on incarnationally: in Christ's way. 1 Corinthians goes on to identify the (perhaps) one house church planted, according to the principles in chapter 9, as the body of Christ (1 Cor. 12). In Romans the term is used when addressing a collection of house churches across a city (Rom. 12). In Ephesians (and Colossians 1.18) it is applied to the whole church (Eph. 1 and 4). We are so used to the application of this image of the church in terms of unity, diversity and gifting that we miss its core meaning, the presence of Jesus by the Spirit, continuing his ministry, through the physical presence of a local community of Christians.

The body of Christ is an incarnational term. This is seen most clearly in Ephesians. Ephesians provides the fullest exegesis of the role of the church in God's purposes. 'Colossians expounds on the cosmic role of Christ, whereas Ephesians expounds on the cosmic role of the church' (Bruce, *Colossians*, p. 231). In both Christ is the 'head' of all creation and of the church (Col. 1.18; 2.10, 19; Eph. 1.22; 4.15; 5.23). Ecclesiology is determined and measured by Christology. The body of Christ exists for God's purposes in the world, which are described in Ephesians as 'a plan for the fullness of time, to gather up all things in him (Christ), things in heaven and things on earth'. This is God's great plan, his economy: the macroeconomic plan of salvation, 'the all inclusive purpose of God'. It is a plan for reconciliation, to bring all things together, literally to be 'summed up' or recapitulated in Christ (1.10). 'The cosmos has been plunged into disintegration on account of sin, and it is God's purpose to restore its original harmony in Christ' (Lincoln, *Ephesians*, p. 33). Most of the first chapter of Ephesians describes God's rich provision for his people in Christ, a privilege that contains a calling. As the chapter concludes, Christ is described as 'head over all things for the church, which is his body, the fullness of him who fills all in all' (1.22–23). The link between this and the earlier statement is 'all things'. The church, as Christ's body, is the vehicle by which Christ engages his work of reconciliation with 'all things'. 'Christians are 'members of the group that embody God's purpose for the cosmos' (Lincoln, *Theology of the Later Pauline Letters*, p. 95).

Aspects of verse 23 are difficult to interpret. (See the commentaries for the various readings.) But three things are clear.

- Christ has authority over all creation.
- He fills the church with his presence.
- As his body it is to be present and represent him and his cause in every place.

The theme of 'fullness' is woven through Ephesians. Christ comes in 'the fullness of time' (1.10). The church is his 'fullness' (1.23), but this is a dynamic concept. The church is to aspire to 'be filled with all the fullness of God' (3.19). It is to grow 'to maturity, to the measure of the full stature of Christ' (4.13), for which it needs to be continually 'filled with the Spirit' (5.18). 'Paul is not establishing the church as filling Christ or filling the world. Instead, the church serves the world, as it grows to maturity in Christ' (Cohick, *Ephesians*, p. 240). Only thus it fulfils its vocation as the body of Christ.

According to Marcus Barth, 'The church is the self-manifestation of the crucified and risen Jesus Christ to all powers, all things, all men. "For his own sake" and/or "with his own self" he fills the church in order to reach all creatures. She is proof and manifestation of the living Christ who is "enthroned at God's right hand in the heavens"' (*Ephesians*, p. 119). The gist is caught by Eugene's Peterson's translation *The Message* – 'The church is Christ's body, in which he speaks and acts, by which he fills everything with his presence.'

'Church' in Ephesians is always the universal church, never merely the local assembly, but expressed through the local assembly (Eph. 1.22; 3.10, 21; 5.23–24, 25, 27, 29, 32). The church is made up of individuals reconciled to God (2.1–10) and simultaneously reconciled to one another as the new humanity in Christ (2.11–22); this new unity displays God's wisdom to the 'rulers and authorities in the heavenly places' (3.1–13), and can be filled with all God's fullness (3.14–21). This is Christ's body which he has gifted for its continuing ministry (4.1–16) and which displays to the world the new, transformed way of life in Christ (4.17—6.9). This body dons the armour of God as it does not do battle against people but against evil (6.10–20). A physical (risen and ascended) Christ in heaven has a physical body on earth. The mission of Christ continues by the Spirit in the body of Christ. The call is for a Christ-shaped, Christ-filled community, sharing in his continuing ministry in each place. In chapter 4 we are told that Christ 'ascended far above all the heavens, so that he might fill all things' (which chapter 1 implies he does, in part at least, through his church in each place). Chapter 4 then describes his gifts 'to equip the saints for the work of ministry', the continuing ministry of the ascended Christ in the world. The purpose is 'the measure of the full stature of Christ'.

It is evident from Paul's ministry that the call to 'all things' and all places requires the sort of cross-cultural mission which he described in 1 Corinthians. This makes such mission a voyage of discovery. Rather than impose our conceptions of church we have the privilege of discovering new dimensions and applications of the good news as we see, under the Spirit, how Christ takes shape in his body as he 'fills' each new context.

Of course, no local church can engage with 'all things' in its context. It has to be discerning and allow itself to be led by the missionary Spirit. But this makes its public witness and example particularly important. 'The church ... is the prophetic sign to the world that God has organized all things around the one whom he has enthroned at his right hand' (Farrow, *Ascension and Ecclesia*, p. 32). So the later chapters of Ephesians are as strategically important as the more apparently doctrinal ones. The purpose of Christian community is to form a way of life worthy of the gospel: 'Lead a life worthy of the calling to which you have been called' (4.1), to show the world an alternative way of life. Paul makes a strong contrast between the believers' former way of life and the way in which they 'learned Christ' (4.20). They had been taught (disciples) to put off the old way of life and clothe themselves with the new (4.22–24). The contrast is between darkness and light (5.8–14).

Paul wants his readers to realize that the Church is to live by values as radically opposed to that of society's values as light is opposed to and incompatible with darkness. Yet it is interesting to note that this clear sense of being different from others is not meant to lead the church into isolationism or defeatism in relation to the world. Rather than be corrupted by the surrounding darkness, believers are urged to exercise their influence on it. The readers are to be nothing less than the community whose conduct shines as a beacon to others, illuminating how life should be lived. (Lincoln, *Ephesians*, p. 335)

'You do not need a strong community, the church, to support an ethic everyone else already affirms' (Hauerwas and Willimon, *Resident Aliens*, p. 73). The reconciliation described in chapter 2 needs to be lived out in daily relationships of mutual accountability and forgiveness (Eph. 4.2, 25, 32; 5.21). 'The church is marked by community, inter-personal relationships, mutuality and interdependence' (Snyder, *Community of the King*, p. 84). This communal life is possible because it is empowered by the Spirit (5.15–21). The fullness of the Spirit is not as much for anointing and gifts, as for distinctively Christian behaviour. Not so much about individuals, as for community. Even though we can only respond as individuals. Not so much a once for all experience, as an ongoing dependence.

Christ continues his ministry through his body, by the Spirit. It is to be built up by all who belong to it, until all of us come to 'to the measure of the full stature of Christ' (4.13), 'it is specifically Christ who is the standard of maturity, indicating again that for this writer ecclesiology remains determined and measured by Christology. The Church is in Christ and has to grow up toward him' (Lincoln, *Ephesians*, p. 261).

The 'body of Christ' passages in 1 Corinthians (and Romans) fit into this foundational picture and add to it, but are applied to specific local issues, whereas Ephesians seems to be a more general letter. There are problems of unity at Corinth. The church needed reminding the Holy Spirit had put them together, irrespective of race or status. 'In the one Spirit we were all baptized into one body – Jews or Greeks, slaves or free' (12.13). One particular problem was between the strong and the weak, the slave and the free, with one group keen to exercise their 'rights' while others had no rights to exercise (11.22). We must note the deeply countercultural nature of Paul's teaching in this context. The metaphor of a community as a 'body' was much used in Greek and Roman culture, as a device used by the powerful to keep others in their place. But Paul utilizes it by turning it upside down! All are to be honoured equally (12.22–26; see also Horrell, *Solidarity and Difference*, pp. 122–3). All Christian believers constitute a single body (v. 12); to suggest otherwise is to denigrate or tear apart the very limbs of Christ (verse 12b) (see Thiselton, *1 Corinthians*, pp. 992–3). The church is a visible local community in Christ, entered through baptism, and characterized by relational justice.

This comes into particular focus when Paul challenges their behaviour, at the Eucharist, which is celebrated in the context of a community meal (11.17–34). The term 'body' is used with a deliberate double edge. To treat one's fellow believers with contempt (verse 22), is to totally fail to grasp the significance of the cross, to fail to 'discern the body' (verse 29), and how Christ's body is to behave. More generally Christ and the Spirit's gifts are 'for building up the body of Christ' (Ephesians), 'building up the church' (1 Corinthians). But in his letters Paul uses the term 'building up' just as often for the church's ministry to its surrounding society, as for the mutual ministry of its members. And that mutual ministry is ultimately for the sake of ministry to the world (see Cray, *Disciples and Citizens*, chapter 3, in particular pp. 42–3). James Dunn called them 'the living movements of Christ's body' (Dunn, *Jesus and the Spirit*, p. 264). A body which never moves is at best gravely ill. Christ continues his ministry by the Spirit through his body.

The distinguishing characteristic of the body of Christ is love. Just as 'Christ loved (and loves) the church and gave himself up for her' (Eph. 5.25). 'Love is central to Paul's vision of the Christian moral life, in a way that is not true in either Judaism of the Greco-Roman world' (N. T. Wright, *Paul and the Faithfulness of God*, p. 1119). Each reference to the body of

Christ refers to love. The 'members of one another' are to 'let love be genuine' (Rom. 12.4–9). 'The whole body, joined and knitted together by every ligament with which it is equipped, as each part is working properly, promotes the body's growth in building itself up in love' (Eph. 4.15f.). 'Love ... is the means by which the entire Messiah's body holds together' (Wright, *Paul and the Faithfulness of God*, p. 1118); (Col. 3.14–15). 1 Corinthians 13 provides the motivation for all the mutuality described in chapter 12. Love is not merely the characteristic quality of the church on earth, it will endure throughout eternity. 'And now faith, hope, and love abide, these three; and the greatest of these is love' (1 Cor. 13.13). The body of Christ has no meaning if it is not the love of Christ embodied in each place, for each place.

Helen Morris has demonstrated that Paul's understanding of the body of Christ provides a strong foundation for what she calls re-contextual church. Paul first penned the term 'body of Christ' in 1 Corinthians, a context with strong parallels to contemporary Western postmodern society (Morris, *Flexible Church*, p. 65). As we have already seen, he has taken a well-known term and contextualized it for his setting in the light of the gospel, setting an example for contextualization and 'what factors both guide and limit' it. 'Unity and diversity is a marked feature of the motif' (Morris, *Flexible Church*, p. 65). For Morris, serious engagement with this theme addresses some of 'the most contentious areas' of this debate: the role of the sacraments and the relationship between the church's inward life and its outward vocation. It 'brings the motif to the foreground' and aligns with the 'pursuit of a Trinitarian ecclesiology' (p. 66).

The importance and complexity of 'place'

If the church, as Christ's body, is to be present and represent him and his cause in every place. How are we to understand 'place' in our complex modern world, especially as the church is called to bear witness to Christ's purpose of reconciling 'all things'.

In the light of this, Newbigin unpacks the complex missionary calling of a 'local' church. He makes clear that 'place' is not just to be understood geographically, but socially and culturally. 'The "place" of the Church is not thus its situation on the surface of the globe, but its place in the fabric of human society.' A geographically based parish system helps that aspiration but by no means guarantees it. 'A church in every community in the land' is an empty boast if it boils down to there being a church in a given geographical area, without any reference to accessibility or culture (Nazir Ali, *Future Shapes of the Church*). Each local church is called to a deep ongoing process of engagement and discernment in the place or places to which it is called. 'To practice incarnational witness means learning the cultures into which we are *sent*: learning what they think and how they think, what it feels like to be part of their world, and how to communicate on their terms' (Guder, *Incarnation*, p. 54).

Newbigin states that 'place' is not a static: 'Every aspect of it, even its physical configuration, is in process of change.' To be incarnational, the local churches ministry 'means to be making constantly new and difficult decisions in a changing context. The relation of the Church to the place is a dynamic one and not a static one' (*A Local Church Truly United*, p. 3). Furthermore, if place is cultural and social, not just geographical then in modern urban societies most people belong to a complex of 'places'. Ever since the industrial revolution, the home has been separated from the workplace, and from the school and so on. If the church exists to bear witness to Christ's rule over 'all things' simply basing churches where people have their homes is insufficient. Michael Moynagh has emphasized this in his major works *Church for Every Context* and *Church in Life*.

To bring Newbigin's insights up to date, we have to add the impact of globalization. We are living in a complex and unpredictable time of cultural transition – variously described as from modern to postmodern, from Christendom to post-Christendom, from national to global, from monocultural to multicultural, and simultaneously secular, multi-faith and post-secular. Both cultural and global trends influence local contexts but are not the only factors which shape them.

The ugly word 'glocalization' was coined by sociologists in the 1990s to describe the impact of the global on the local. It has become more important as scholars have increasingly recognized that globalization does not simply standardize or homogenize everything and everywhere, because – 'We live in a world partially interconnected and interdependent, but where a multitude of different cultural arrangements coexist with one another' (Roudometof, *Glocalization*, p. 138). So 'glocal' is 'The point of intersection between the global and the local' (Van Hoozer, *One Rule to Rule Them All*, p. 99). It is made even more complex by the massive spread of digital media as a core element of everyday life and community. In their book *The Mediated Construction of Reality*, Couldry and Hepp write, 'As embodied human beings we have no choice but to act *from* a certain locality ... But these localities change their meaning in a world made up of ever more complex translocal connections' (p. 87). Local churches have to be 'glocal' churches.

The relationship of the local church to the communities or networks where God has placed it, or to which it is called, is an essential part of its nature: that is the significance of an incarnational faith, of being the body of Christ. Newbigin states bluntly, 'The Church cannot be described apart from its place. The Church is wrongly described unless it is described as the Church *for that place*' (*A Local Church*, p. 3). But to be 'for' its place with integrity it is to embody Christ and Christ's purpose for that place. Newbigin continues:

> the meaning of the preposition 'for' is determined christologically; that is to say, it is determined by what Jesus Christ has done, is doing and will do with and for the world as its author, redeemer and consummator. The Church in each place is the Church for that place, in the sense in which Christ is for mankind and for the world. (*A Local Church*, p. 3)

However complex culture may be, Newbigin claims, it is the context, rather than the preferences of the congregation, which shape the local church life and ministry:

the character of the local church will not be determined primarily by the character, tastes, dispositions, etc., of its members, but by those of the secular society in which and for which it lives – seen in the light of God's redemptive purpose revealed in Jesus Christ for all men. (*A Local Church*, p. 5)

This is profoundly challenging. Most churches that I have belonged to, or encountered as a bishop, are eventually shaped by the preferences of their members. Often these were established at a time where there was a good connection to the surrounding community, but church life can become ossified even when, to those deeply involved, it continues to sustain them and seems to be vibrant. The test is the degree of connection to and understanding of the current nature of its context.

In *Mission-Shaped Church* we addressed this issue of cultural distance: 'this is also a moment for repentance. We have allowed our culture and the Church to drift apart, without our noticing. We need the grace of the Spirit for repentance if we are to receive a fresh baptism of the Spirit for witness.' We quoted Archdeacon Bob Jackson:

> If the decline of the Church is ultimately caused neither by the irrelevance of Jesus, nor by the indifference of the community, but by the Church's failure to respond fast enough to an evolving culture, to a changing spiritual climate, and to the promptings of the Holy Spirit, then that decline can be addressed by the repentance of the Church. (pp. 13–14)

All of this implies that the local church needs both stability, deep roots in Christ and the Christian tradition, convinced of God's grace in its missionary calling; and flexibility, agility in response to an ever-changing context and the missional initiatives of the Spirit.

Postscript: but what about mission and unity?

The understanding of the church as 'The body of Christ' conveys both its incarnational calling and its essential diversity within unit. This creates a practical tension when cross-cultural planting, to reach sectors of society which are untouched by the existing church can appear to lead to a fragmented church. If we are to address this biblically we should note first of all that in the New Testament cross-cultural or incarnational mission (the mission to the Gentiles) created the need for new discussions about unity (the Jerusalem Council). Unity was never given as a reason to prevent cross-cultural or incarnational mission. Seemingly the missionary Spirit is more than content to create these questions. We have already seen from St Paul's teaching and example that when the mission of the church requires engagement with people 'not like us', it is 'us', not 'they', who pay the price of unity, recognizing that the gospel breaks down racial and cultural barriers. The Spirit-led mission of the church in Acts resulted in churches very different from the one to which Christ's witnesses originally belonged. Compare the church in Antioch in Acts 11.19–26 with the church in Jerusalem in Acts 21.17ff. But note also the care which the church in Antioch had for the church in Jerusalem. The standard and the challenge is set in Ephesians and 1 Corinthians. On the basis of Ephesians 2, 'Two races and two cultures historically separated by the meal table now met at table to share the knowledge of Christ' (Walls, *The Cross-Cultural Process in Christian History*, p. 78). We know from the letter to the Galatians that this ideal was not easily upheld (Gal. 2.11–14). Equally at Corinth there were tensions and disunity. So how can the tension be resolved in local praxis?

Writing from his experience in India, where the gospel had to challenge the caste system, Lesslie Newbigin set out some working principles. In summary his view was that 'Diversity is part of God's gracious purpose for the human family ... Separation and mutual rejection is not.' But 'Separation there must be – for the sake of mission – but separation cannot be the last word.' So in what circumstances did he believe there could be separation for the sake of mission? Through the gospel 'the special gifts and insights that God has given to peoples of different language and culture' could be fulfilled, but this could not happen if this culture was only permitted 'on the margin of a community of another language or culture' (*A Local Church*, p. 6). Hence the need for an expression of church within this group, even though it was in the same geographical area. Clearly Newbigin believed that the gospel could be transformative of culture, and that all such transformed cultural groups had a place in the kingdom of God both now and in the future. In the closing chapters of Revelation, we read of 'the glory and honour of the nations' having a place in the Holy City (Rev. 21.22ff.). This fits fully with the statement in Ephesians that Christ's purpose through his church is not just forgiveness but fullness, the reconciliation of all things. Andrew Walls writes: 'Christ is human, and open to humanity in all its diversity; the fullness of his humanity takes in all its diverse cultural forms' (Walls, *The Cross-Cultural Process*, p. 77).

In the meantime, and as demonstrated by the church in Antioch's gifts to the famine-struck church in Jerusalem (Acts 11.29), there are to be 'bonds of mutual recognition and mutual responsibility' between these local congregations. Newbigin was aware of the realities of imbalances of power between different Christian communities, insisting that the recognition of a congregation with a different cultural ethos should never be on the condition that 'the life-style of another place or time' is insisted on. Mutual recognition is of each church as it is, not as the older of culturally more powerful insists that it should be. Congregational distinctiveness is only for the sake of a more authentic sharing of 'diverse gifts in a Christ-given unity'. All cultures are provisional, only Christ is absolute, so in advance of the day when heaven and earth is made new there must be every possible 'movement in the direction of unity' (*A Local Church*, p. 7).

This leaves no hiding place for the scandal of our disunity. Ancient doctrinal divisions are given no hiding place. The quest for unity must continue, but so must the missional urgency to reach all who are as yet unreached, and to discover fresh riches of the gospel as it engages with their cultural distinctiveness. These two vocations of the church live in a creative tension:

1 The vocation of mission – the full breadth of humanity, not just as individuals recruited for a monocultural church, but as cultures transformed by Christ.
2 The vocation of unity – the reconciliation of all Christians. 'Only in Christ does completeness, fullness, dwell. None of us can reach Christ's completeness on our own' (Walls, *The Cross-Cultural Process*, p. 79).

Following these twin vocations we anticipate the time foreseen in Revelation when 'there was a great multitude that no one could count, from every nation, from all tribes and peoples and languages, standing before the throne and before the Lamb, robed in white, with palm branches in their hands' (7.9).

This praxis is now embodied in the Church of England's national strategy in a commitment to a church where 'mixed ecology is the norm', meaning 'a vision with Jesus Christ at the centre that can be shared by the thousands of parishes, chaplaincies, schools, church plants, religious communities, fresh expressions, mission initiatives, messy churches, food banks and refugee ministries'. Since the publication of *Mission-Shaped Church* and the launch of the Fresh Expressions movement in 2004 there is now considerable experience to guide good practice. We have learned that the planting of these new congregations really does widen the scope of the church's mission. We note that the great majority of fresh expressions of church are new congregations within a parish or benefice, not new totally independent churches. Where a stand-alone congregation is needed it will still remain accountable within deanery of diocesan structures, often through the use of a Bishop's Mission Order. The knitting together of congregations with mutual recognition and responsibility which Newbigin required is perfectly possible within these arrangements. The wide range of models of fresh expression which have been developed also illustrate the rich diversity which he sought.

One caricature has been that fresh expressions are all microcultural churches, leading to further fragmentation. In reality life and culture is much more complicated than that. These fresh expressions which begin by evangelizing a subculture often prove to be beachheads not final destinations as they engage the complex networks within which all cultural groups are embedded.

Conclusion

As a community of disciples on mission with Jesus, the church is his body, each individual part deeply rooted in him ('grown into him who is the head', Eph. 4.15), interconnected with all the others ('joined and knitted together', verse 16) and playing its distinctive part (each part working properly', verse 16). This body is also on the move. A body which never moves is at best paralysed. It moves at the direction of the head, it is adaptable, always seeking to engage with its context with Christian integrity, fulfilling its calling to engage all people and places with Christ's presence. This adaptability is essential because:

> The Church does not really have a single culture. On the other hand, it has a single transformative energy, the Spirit of Christ figured in the Scriptures, which, in the process of time, is constantly assimilating, perhaps strengthening, perhaps re-ordering the multiple cultures of Adam's children. (Radner, *Church*, p. 161)

So the incarnational question, 'What should Jesus look and behave like in this place?' requires careful and prayerful discernment: identifying contact points, opportunities to bless, key local issues for repentance and discipleship, and above all, where the missionary Holy Spirit is already at work and ahead of us in complex, changing, localities.

Notes

1 For the reasons for the move from incarnation to inculturation see Aylward Shorter, *Evangelization and Culture*, pp. 35–6, and *Towards a Theology of Inculturation*, pp. 79–83.

2 'Paul refuses to present himself as a Jew who accommodates himself to Gentiles, rather, whether he "becomes like a Jew" or "becomes like a Gentile" it is in *both* cases an act of accommodation. The use is symmetrical; the apostle occupies a *third* ground. But this third ground is binding on him. He is "under Christ's law" ... Paul's principle of accommodation is limited by his submission to the law of God in Christ as he understands it' (Don Carson, *Pauline Inconsistency*, p. 12).

3 'It is not that Christ changes places with men and women. Though he identifies with them, he remains what he is – without sin, Son of God, in the form of God. And when they become what he is it is because they are now identified with him – or, to use the crucial Pauline expression, because they are "in Christ"' (Morna Hooker, 'A Partner in the Gospel', p. 91).

4 See Peter Marshall: 'Verse 19 suggests a conscious effort on his part to make himself a slave of all. It describes the act of a free man who willingly enslaves himself to all people *without distinction* ... The description is similar to that of a man of free status who contracts himself into slavery ... While he becomes slave of one master Paul is slave of all. The notion of self-imposed servility is inseparably linked with diversity of conduct' (*Enmity in Corinth*, p. 312).

6

On Mission With Jesus: Anticipating the Future

> From first to last, and not merely in the epilogue, Christianity is eschatology, is hope, forward looking and forward moving and therefore also ... transforming the present. (Moltmann, *Hope*, p. 16)

> To be a Christian, a person of faith, is precisely to live as a person for whom God's future shapes the present. (Bauckham and Hart, *Hope Against Hope*, p. 83)

In Chapter 4, we observed the Holy Spirit as the director of the Church's Christ-shaped mission, leading it from the present into the future. Now we reverse the direction and see that the Spirit's ministry in the present is to establish anticipations of the future which Christ has secured. In particular the church is to be a sign, instrument and foretaste of that future, of the kingdom of God in its fullness. Once again we see that the ministry of Jesus continues through his church by his Spirit. Like Jesus, and in the power of the same Spirit, the church is a future in advance community, on the move towards the future kingdom.

Jesus, the Spirit and the kingdom of God

The arrival of the kingdom of God was central to Jesus' self-understanding and ministry. 'Jesus spoke and acted as if God's plan of salvation and justice for Israel and the world was being unveiled through his own presence, his own work, his own fate' (N. T. Wright, *The Challenge of Jesus*, p. 21). His core message

ANTICIPATING THE FUTURE

was 'The time is fulfilled, and the kingdom of God has come near; repent and believe in the good news' (Mark 1.15). This was not intended or heard so much as a new philosophy to consider, but a new reality which required a response. 'It is the announcement of a fact ... Something has happened. There is a new fact to be reckoned with. The kingdom, the reign of God, has come near' (Newbigin, *Christ's Way*, p. 2). Or as one scholar puts it: 'The revolution is here!'[1] In what sense was the kingdom of God present? Above all in the unique person of Jesus. His proclamation centred upon the necessity of a response to himself. 'Follow me' (Mark 1.17). 'Come to me' (Matt. 11.28), 'Blessed is anyone who takes no offence at me' (Luke 7.23). To respond to Jesus was the way to respond to the kingdom.

In Jesus' time the usual Jewish view of the kingdom of God – the climax of history through the coming of the Messiah – was that of one age which replaced the previous one. The unprecedented aspect of Jesus' understanding of the kingdom was that, in him, instead of the new age replacing the old, it had invaded it without totally displacing it. This effected a 'decisive shift in eschatology from the future above to the future in the present' (Beasley-Murray, *Jesus and the Kingdom of God*, p. 338). Jesus still saw human history as divided between two ages, but the critical dividing point (*Kairos*) was not the final judgement, but his own proclamation and ministry. From the time of Jesus' public ministry until the judgement, the ages are in overlap. The kingdom is therefore 'the presence of the future' (see Ladd, *The Presence of the Future*). It still awaits its consummation and thus has to be understood as 'already' and 'not yet'.

Through his presence, his ministry and his death and resurrection Jesus brought both a foretaste and a guarantee of God's promised future into the present. 'Christ has cleft the future in two, and part of it is already present' (Bosch, 'Evangelism and Social Transformation', pp. 277–8). This shapes all Christian life, ministry and mission which follows. This can only be by the presence and power of the Holy Spirit, because Jesus' ministry had been by that same presence and power. The inbreaking of the kingdom required not only a unique person (Luke 1.32–33) but a unique power (Luke 3.21–23; 4.14–21).

The root meaning of the word 'kingdom' was dynamic rule or strength. 'Within the symbolic word of the gospels, its main thrust is dynamic strength, even active intervention' (Chilton and McDonald, *Jesus and the Ethics of the Kingdom*, p. 48). The biblical nouns refer to the *act* of ruling. The word means reign, not realm, and refers to actual dynamic power, effective in ministry. Thus the kingdom invades the old age through the person and ministry of Jesus, and that ministry consists of both proclamation of the kingdom with its accompanying call to follow Jesus, and the effective demonstration of the power and reality of the kingdom. Jesus' reply to the Baptist's messengers was 'Go and tell John what you have seen and heard: the blind receive their sight, the lame walk, the lepers are cleansed, the deaf hear, the dead are raised, the poor have good news brought to them' (Luke 7.22). Jesus' ministry of deliverance was by authoritative command through the power of the Spirit, rather than by the ritual exorcisms of contemporary Judaism, was specific evidence that the kingdom was present (Matt. 12.28).

The Gospels show us the scope of the ministry for which Jesus was anointed. The shortest definition of the agenda of the kingdom is found in the Lord's Prayer. To pray 'Your kingdom come' is in effect to pray, 'Your will be done on earth, as it is in heaven' (Matt. 6.10). The parallel between kingdom and Spirit is seen in an early variant of the Lord's prayer. In the place of 'Your kingdom come', it reads 'Send your Spirit upon us and cleanse us' (Dunn, *Spirit and Kingdom*).

The incident in the synagogue at Nazareth, near the start of Jesus' ministry, is of particular importance, for with his Gentile audience in mind, Luke does not introduce the Jewish theological term 'kingdom of God' (Luke 4.43) before allowing the Isaiah 61 passage which Jesus reads in the synagogue to give it content. This passage (Luke 4.18–19) shows us some aspects of God's will on earth. Many of the words in this quotation have multiple applications. Jesus had been anointed to announce to the poor the good news of God's kingdom. The Old Testament words for 'poor' covered many kinds of deprivation. Preaching is only good news to the poor if it announces God's active intervention on their behalf to restore justice. To preach (*keruxai*) is a word mainly used in the New Testament for evangelistic preaching. The content of this preaching was freedom or release, a word applicable either to the forgiveness of sin or to release in the more physical sense. The word for 'prisoners' most commonly referred to prisoners of war. The blind who are to recover their sight clearly include the physically blind (Luke 7.21–22) but Isaiah also used the term to speak of spiritual blindness (for example, Isa. 6.9–10). The release that is promised to the oppressed can speak of forgiveness or it can speak of a more physical liberation. Without question, the oppressed include those who are physically, politically or economically oppressed. Jesus also released the demonically oppressed, but this word does not come from Isaiah 61, but rather from Isaiah 58.6, where it is found alongside the hungry, the poor wanderer without shelter, and the naked; the context being that of 'loosing the chains of injustice'. The year of the Lord's favour was the year of Jubilee, which involved a massive restoration of justice and opportunity, every 50 years. The age of the Spirit is to be an age of perpetual Jubilee.

However, the anointing of the Spirit was not to bring 'the day of vengeance of our God'. Jesus is soon reminding his nationalistic audience of the way in which God's favour reached out to Gentiles, even under the Old Covenant (Luke 4.24–30). The reason is that this judgement dimension of the kingdom is primarily future (see Matt. 25). The already of the kingdom is the age of grace – for example, all people were to love and forgive their enemies, because God in his kingly power, through his servant Jesus, was willing to forgive them (Matt. 6.12–15; 18.21–35; Mark 2.1–12). In an age of grace, they must have the right to accept or reject forgiveness. The kingdom could not be present in overwhelming force, although to reject it in this life was also to be judged in advance (John 3.18).

So the proclamation and the practice of the kingdom were divisive (Matt. 34—39). They either created faith or provoked opposition. Opposition could be overtly demonic (Matt. 4.1–11) and the overthrow of the demonic was one of the evidences that the kingdom of God was present (Matt. 12.22–28), or opposition came through an apparently human source, whether the ignorance of a friend or the malice of foes (Mark 8.32, 33; Mark 14). If the proclamation and ministry of the kingdom of God could provoke vehement opposition, then self-evidently the kingdom had not reached its consummation. Jesus used future language as well as present language (for example, Matt. 20.1–16; 22.1–14, 24, 25, 26). The kingdom was present, but not with irresistible power. People could and did reject it. Too much happened through the ministry of Jesus to be ignored, but not enough to convince overwhelmingly. For John the Baptist, the conflict was between what Jesus was doing, the ministry of the kingdom; and the fact that he, John, was still in prison and the Gentiles had not been judged (Matt. 11.1–16). Evidently this kingdom had not finally overcome the old age, although it had powerfully assaulted it (Luke 4.31–37; 8.26–39; 10.1–20; 11.21, 22; Acts 10.38).

Jesus' actions could be limited by the lack of response of others (Mark 6.1–6). His words could be misunderstood (Mark 8.1–21) or completely rejected, even by his own followers (Mark 8.31–33). The greater part of his teaching about the kingdom came in the form of parables, which some would understand and some would not (Mark 4.9–12). Likewise Jesus' acts of power were not automatically convincing. He refused to respond to those who demanded overwhelming proof (Luke 11.16, 29–32). His deliverance ministry could be interpreted as being of demonic origin (Luke 11.14–15); his table fellowship with the disreputable as a contradiction of his claims to divine inspiration (Luke 7.36–39). Jesus did not encourage his public reputation as a 'miracle worker' (for example, Mark 2.43–45). His primary concern was for the well-being of those he healed or set free; yet his deeds were signs of the kingdom, in that they were genuine experiences of the transforming power or transformed relationships of the kingdom, which pointed beyond themselves to the future consummated kingdom, and which challenged to faith in the present. If the ministry of Jesus was carried in this liminal and ambiguous context, his church should expect the same. He made it clear that his disciples should expect the same mixed response. 'Remember the word that I said to you, "Servants are not greater than their master."

If they persecuted me, they will persecute you; if they kept my word, they will keep yours also' (John 15.20).

The kingdom community in the Spirit

The arrival of the kingdom, of the future in advance, provoked a challenge and a choice. By his core message 'Repent and believe the gospel', Jesus 'was telling his hearers to give up their own agendas and to trust him for his way of being Israel, his way of bringing the Kingdom, his kingdom agenda'. He was calling into being what he believed to be the true renewed people of God (N. T. Wright, *The Challenge of Jesus*, pp. 25–27). His kingdom proclamation brought into being the community of disciples which we met in chapter 3. Once again the ministry of Jesus is seen to continue through the church by the Spirit. Before his ascension the disciples ask Jesus about restoring the kingdom and in response were promised the power of the Spirit. Peter's sermon, based on Joel's prophecy, makes a distinction between 'the last days' (verse 17) and 'the coming of the Lord's great and glorious day' (verse 20). The overlap of the ages, the kingdom now and not yet, continues in the age of the church. The Spirit still brings anticipations of the kingdom.

> The Spirit, we might say, is the presentness of the coming Kingdom, where he is, the Kingdom is, so that to have the Spirit is to have part and lot in the Kingdom here and now, or to put it another way – the Spirit is the executive, ambassador, or steward of the Kingdom: his power and authority are those of the King; his operation is the exercise of kingly rule. (Dunn, *Spirit and Kingdom*)

So Christian experience of the Spirit has the same already/not yet tension within it. This gives New Testament teaching about the Spirit its primary shape. 'The Spirit as "The *certain evidence* that the future had dawned, and the *absolute guarantee*" of its final consummation' (Fee, *God's Empowering Presence*, p. 806). The Spirit is the first fruits of the harvest which will be reaped at the end of the age (Rom. 8.23). He is the down payment, the first part of what will be received in full when Christ returns (2 Cor. 1.22; 5.5; Eph. 1.14). He is the seal which guarantees 'the day of redemption' (2 Cor. 1.21–22; Eph. 1.13; 4.30). He is the present dynamic power of the future age (Heb. 6.4, 5; Acts 1.8; 1 Cor. 4.4). 'By the Spirit we are the present hope of the future healing of the whole creation' (Rom. 8.19–25). 'The action of the Spirit is to anticipate, in the present and by means of the finite and contingent, the things of the age to com' (Gunton, *The Promise of Trinitarian Theology*, p. 68).

Every action of the Spirit contains this double element of anticipation: a tangible reality now, accompanied by a guarantee for the future. When a person receives the assurance of their salvation (Rom. 8.16) they are being assured in the presence of their salvation on the day of judgement. When there is a healing, partial or complete, it is a foretaste and pointer to the day when there will be no more sickness (Rev. 21.4). When there is deliverance ministry it is a foretaste of the day when the forces of evil will no longer exist. When a victory is gained for social justice it is a foretaste of the new heaven and earth where righteousness and justice are at home. But the kingdom in its fullness is still to come. We do not see everyone to whom we bear witness turn to our Lord. We do not see every sick person we pray for healed. Not every struggle against injustice is successful. But the presence of the Spirit is a guarantee of the kingdom in its ultimate fullness. 'The Spirit is *beyond* history, and when he acts in history he does so in order to bring into history the last days, the eschaton' (Zizioulas, *Being as Communion*, p. 130).

Jesus announced the kingdom as a fact, a new reality. So also the church is to be the demonstration of that fact in its context and generation. 'The gospel is not a statement about some remote future, it is the dawn of that future in the Word' (Moltmann, *The Church in the Power of the Spirit*, p. 77). St Paul uses 'first fruits', the vocabulary of Old Testament harvest festivals, to describe this work of the Spirit (Rom. 8.23). On two occasions each year the Israelites offered the beginnings of their harvest in gratitude to God: the barley harvest (Lev. 23.9–14) and then the wheat harvest (Num. 28.26–31). The latter fell 50 days (Pentecost) before the Feast of Weeks, which celebrated the full harvest: 'All is safely gathered in.' So the Spirit is experienced as the first taste of the full harvest which is promised. The same term is used of Christ's resurrection, which guarantees the resurrection of all who believe in him (1 Cor. 15.20–28) and, by James, of the church: 'In fulfilment of his own purpose he gave us birth by the word of truth, so that we would become a kind of first fruits of his creatures.' Consequently:

> The Church does more than merely point to a reality beyond itself. By virtue of its participation in the life of God, it is not only a sign and instrument, but also a genuine foretaste of God's Kingdom, called to show forth visibly, in the midst of history, God's final purposes for humankind. (General Synod, 'Eucharistic Presidency', 2.12)

The language of sign, instrument or agent, and foretaste comes from Lesslie Newbigin, who connects it directly to the reign of God:

> Thus the Church in each place is to be the sign, instrument and foretaste of the reign of God present in Christ for that place: a sign, planted in the midst of the present realities of the place but pointing beyond them to the future which God has promised; an instrument available for God's use in the doing of his will for that place; a foretaste – manifesting and enjoying already in the midst of the messianic tribulations a genuine foretaste of the peace and joy of God's reign. (*A Local Church*, p. 3)

What then is to be expected of the local church in the power of the Spirit? As a local sign it is to be a consistent and faithful witness pointing its community to Christ and the future he has secured, through its words and actions. As God's local agent, and the instrument available in God's hands, it is to be attentive to every direction given by the Spirit for activity in the name of Jesus. And as foretaste, or first fruits, it can expect the Holy Spirit to act through it to bring about changes which its community can experience as reliable characteristics of the future Christ has secured and is offering to them. The language of foretaste reemphasizes that the kingdom is both already and not yet, both in scale and in response. The foretaste of the peace and joy of God's reign (which does not primarily refer to emotions but relationships) accompanies 'the messianic tribulations'. The church on earth can expect to suffer as its Lord did.

The two elements of the church's life in the Spirit – 'The *certain evidence* that the future had dawned, and the *absolute guarantee* of its final consummation' (Fee, *God's Empowering Presence*, p. 806) – are not separate but interrelated. 'The Spirit is as it were the bridge between the present and the future, between the already and the not yet' (Dunn, *Theology of Paul*, p. 469). They form the basis of a missional spirituality. 'By the Spirit's presence believers tasted of the life to come and became oriented towards its consummation' (Fee, p. 810). This was beautifully put by Peter Hocken: 'The Spirit has given both the first fruits and the hope of full liberation, and we are stretched between the two' (Hocken, *Holy Spirit*). This stretching is another way in which the church, as a community of disciples on mission with Jesus is always on the move. It involves a growing dissatisfaction with the current state of the world when compared with its future. To share in the Holy Spirit is to taste 'the powers of the age to come'. Once we have had that taste we cannot remain satisfied with the way the present age, the world, is panning out. Nor can we withdraw and sit out the time until Jesus returns. 'To live in the Spirit is to be agonizingly *aware of the contrast between what is and what should be*' (Taylor, *The Go-Between God*, p. 96). Moltmann draws an analogy from Jesus' words to Paul on the road to Damascus. 'It hurts you to kick against the goads' (Acts 26.14).

> Faith, wherever it develops into hope, causes not rest but unrest, not patience but impatience. It does not calm the unquiet heart, but is itself this unquiet heart in man. Those who hope in Christ can no longer put up with reality as it is, but begin to suffer under it, to contradict it, peace with God means conflict with the world, for the goad of the promised future stabs inexorably into the flesh of every unfulfilled present. (Moltmann, *Theology of Hope*, p. 21)

The motivation for Christian mission lies not so much in grasping what is wrong in the world as from a vision of the new heaven and earth that will one day be. 'The presence of the Holy Spirit ... stirs up the desire and yearning for the coming kingdom and the full rule of the king. The Spirit of God is always pushing towards the completion of all things' (Hocken, *Holy Spirit*). The church is essentially a people on the move, while at the same time longing for the coming of its Lord. 'The Spirit and the Bride say "Come"' (Rev. 22.17).

Word and Spirit

The church moves forward into the future Christ has won through the partnership of word (scripture) and Spirit. This functions as a twin track. Scripture is a gift from the past to keep the church on course. The Spirit comes, as we have seen, as a foretaste, a gift from the future, bringing the future which Scripture describes into the present. The two meet in each time and context to guide and equip the church on its missional journey. Through the inspiration of the Spirit, scripture serves as the anchor and foundation of the church's life. It is the record of God's action in history for the salvation of the world. It is important as the touchstone for doctrine, but for our purpose most significant in setting out the grand narrative in which the church finds its place:

> The Christian metanarrative is the biblical story of the world from creation to consummation. It is the story of the Trinitarian God's relationship with his creation. It sees God as the beginning and end of all things, their source and their goal, Creator and Lord, Redeemer and Renewer, the one who was and who is and who is to come. It is s story which is not yet completed ... The end of the story is still to come, with the God who is also to come to his creation in the end ... This means that those who live by this story live within it. It gives us our identity, our place in the story, and a part to play in the still-to-be-completed purposes of God for his world. (Bauckham and Hart, *Hope Against Hope*, pp. 35–6)

N. T. Wright has likened this metanarrative to a Shakespeare play most of whose fifth act has been lost, and so required experienced actors to improvise the missing part, in a way that was consistent with and recognized the authority of the existing text (*The New Testament and the People of God*, pp. 140ff.). The five acts being:

> 1 Creation; 2 Fall; 3 Israel; 4: Jesus; 5 The writing of the New Testament would form the first scene of the fifth act, and would simultaneously give hints about how the play is supposed to end ... The church would then live under the 'authority' of the extant story, being required to offer an improvisatory performance of the final act as it leads up to and anticipates the intended conclusion.

This sort of scripture-inspired missional improvisation is essential if the church is to cross boundaries of culture and pass on its gospel from era to era:

> It is not enough for the church to go on repeating in different cultural situations the same words and phrases. New ways have to be found of stating the essential Trinitarian faith, and for this the church in each new cultural situation has to go back to the original biblical source of this faith in order to lay hold on it afresh and to state it afresh in contemporary terms. (Newbigin, *The Open Secret*, p. 27)

'The Holy Spirit brings forward a reality which is grounded in divine promise rather than in human thought or achievement' (Doctrine Commission, *Holy Spirit*, p. 171). The Spirit's role in bringing anticipations of the final kingdom into the present is the other vital component for this praxis. 'The Spirit uses the biblical vision to spur us to view our situation in the light of God's future and to open ourselves and our present to the power of that future already at work among us and in our world' (Grenz, *Theology for the People of God*, p. 510). The church is intended to use scripture wisely, not as a collection of proof texts, or just as a source of personal inspiration, but as the narrative which shapes our world view. It needs a scripture soaked and shaped imagination, as Jesus did, enabling it to discern the initiatives taken by the Holy Spirit, who both moves ahead of the church and brings foretastes of the future into the present.

The temple of the Spirit

The vocation of the church as sign, instrument and foretaste of the kingdom of God is seen most clearly in its identity as the temple of the Spirit. 'As the Church belongs to God, is the body of Christ, the temple of the Holy Spirit, so mission belongs to the very being of the church' (Thompson, *Trinitarian Perspectives*, p. 73). Material about the Jerusalem Temple runs throughout the Bible, but a number of aspects are most relevant for our purposes.

'The point of the Temple ... is that it was where heaven and earth met. It was the place where Israel's God, YHWH, had long ago promised to put his name, to make his glory present' (N. T. Wright, *Paul and the Faithfulness of God*, p. 96). The extraordinary nature of this is seen in Solomon's prayer at the dedication of the first temple:

> But will God indeed reside with mortals on earth? Even heaven and the highest heaven cannot contain you, how much less this house that I have built! Have regard to your servant's prayer and his plea, O LORD my God, heeding the cry and the prayer that your servant prays to you. May your eyes be open day and night towards this house, the place where you promised to set your name, and may you heed the prayer that your servant prays towards this place. And hear the plea of your servant and of your people Israel, when they pray towards this place; may you hear from heaven your dwelling-place; hear and forgive. (2 Chron. 6.18–21)

In response 'the glory of the Lord', the *shekinah*, the tangible presence of God, filled the temple (2 Chron. 7.1). God could not be contained by the temple, but it was the place where he could consistently be encountered. The destruction of Solomon's temple by the Babylonians is told is tragic detail in 2 Kings

25.8–21. But the greatest tragedy is found in Ezekiel's visions of the glory (the tangible presence) of the Lord departing from the temple and from Jerusalem (Ezekiel 10). Once the people had been allowed to return there was great disappointment with the two post exilic temples, despite the grandeur of Herod's architecture. There was no ark of the covenant in either, and there are rabbinic sources which question whether God's *shekinah* glory ever returned at all (Badcock, *The House Where God Lives*, p. 117). The temple was also designed as 'a mini microcosm of the earth being filled with the glory of God'.[2] In other words, it was a foretaste of God's purpose for the whole creation, anticipating the time when the whole healed creation will be the dwelling place of God. In the closing chapters of the book of Revelation there is no temple in the Holy City (verse 22), as God is making his home in her. Until that time the temple was to be the place of sacrifice and renewal of the covenant.

In the Gospels Jesus fulfils the Temple's role. He is the place where heaven and earth meet (John 1.51). 'The Word became flesh and 'tented' – was the tabernacle – among us, and we have seen his glory' (John 1.14). He is Emmanuel (Matt. 1.23), God's presence on earth. He is the one upon whom the Holy Spirit falls and remains (John 1.22). He predicts (Matt. 24.1–2), and symbolically anticipates, the destruction of the Jerusalem temple (Matt. 21.12–14), not its 'cleansing'. He refers to his body as a temple (John 2.19–22).

He is the stone which the builders rejected, which becomes the corner stone (see Ps. 118.22; Matt. 21.42; Acts 4.11; 1 Peter 2.7). Note that it is not the church which replaces the temple, but Jesus himself. As the risen Lord he would no longer be restricted to one geographical location. He tells the Samaritan woman that 'the hour is coming when you will worship the Father neither on this mountain nor in Jerusalem ... But the hour is coming, and is now here, when the true worshippers will worship the Father in spirit and truth, for the Father seeks such as these to worship him' (John 4.21–23). True worship takes place wherever the Spirit of truth is, whose role is to bear witness to Jesus. In the letter to the Hebrews Jesus is both the once for all sacrifice and the high priest for ever on our behalf.

Then, according to Paul, the church is God's temple in the world (Eph. 2.22), each local church being God's temple for its place (1 Cor. 3.16–17; 2 Cor. 6.16). It is the temple because Jesus is present by his Spirit, through his body, carrying on his mission to the world. It is therefore the local place where heaven touches earth, offering a foretaste of God's kingdom. The image is primarily corporate. In three of the four occasions Paul uses it, it is applied to the church as a whole (1 Cor. 3.16–17; 2 Cor. 6.16; Eph. 2.22) as a community publicly bearing witness to Christ's presence by the Spirit among them. On one occasion its application is extended to individual believers (1 Cor. 6.19), each of whom becomes a God-bearer, a heaven-meets-earth person for their context.

There was only one temple in Jerusalem, but once the gospel had created communities in pagan cities which were full of temples, these Christian communities were also to provide a contrasting way of life. So 'As God's temple in Corinth they are intended to be his alternative to Corinth, to both its religions and vices ... and they did not so much have a building, they were a building' (Fee, *God's Empowering Presence*, p. 116). But their distinctiveness was not guaranteed irrespective of their behaviour. When unbelievers encountered their gatherings they might either say, 'Surely God is among you' (1 Cor. 14.24–25) or, 'You are out of your mind' (14.23).

The local temple of the Spirit needed to be built on the right foundations:

> you are ... God's building. According to the grace of God given to me, like a skilled master builder I laid a foundation, and someone else is building on it. Each builder must choose with care how to build on it. For no one can lay any foundation other than the one that has been laid; that foundation is Jesus Christ. Now if anyone builds on the foundation with gold, silver, precious stones, wood, hay, straw – the work of each builder will become visible, for the Day will disclose it, because it will be revealed with fire, and the fire will test what sort of work each has done. If what has been built on the foundation survives, the builder will receive a reward. If the

work is burned, the builder will suffer loss; the builder will be saved, but only as through fire. Do you not know that you are God's temple and that God's Spirit dwells in you? If anyone destroys God's temple, God will destroy that person. For God's temple is holy, and you are that temple. (1 Cor. 3.9–17)

Paul laid the foundation of the church in Corinth by the preaching of the cross in the power of the Spirit (1 Cor. 2.1–5), having engaged the cultures of Corinth in an incarnational manner as an imitation of Christ (9.19–23), in absolute conviction that because of the resurrection he was serving a living Lord and that his efforts would not be in vain (15.1–58). The foundation 'is Jesus Christ' (3.11). Every further development of that (and any) church had to be built on that foundation. Not just to acknowledge it but to be shaped by it rather than by other agendas. If this temple of the Holy Spirit was to be a foretaste of heaven and earth made new, its life and witness needed to be evidence here and now of the transformation which happens when heaven touches earth, qualities which will survive the fire of God's final judgement because they are a first fruit of that harvest in advance of that judgement. Paul sees this as a real possibility: 'Therefore, my beloved, be steadfast, immovable, always excelling in the work of the Lord, because you know that in the Lord your labour is not in vain' (1 Cor. 15.58).

The church is the temple of the Holy Spirit. But the Spirit can be resisted, grieved or quenched. The behaviour Paul addresses in Corinth concerns disunity, holiness (N. T. Wright, *Paul and the Faithfulness of God*, p. 711) and a tendency to put personal rights ahead of the service of others. It is not difficult to see how these areas of behaviour would undermine the church's calling to be a foretaste of the kingdom of God. Every church should ask itself, 'Is our behaviour a fit match for our foundation in Christ and our purpose to show people his kingdom?' Anything else, however urgent it may seem at the time, is wood, hay and stubble rather than gold, silver and precious stones. Or to put it differently, are we working with Jesus as he continues his ministry to the world, or are we following other agendas?

The church's identity as a foretaste of the kingdom has a particular importance and resonance today. Paul describes the role of culture and world view as a veil or blindfold, keeping people from seeing 'the light of the gospel of the glory of Christ': Christ 'who is the image of God'. God made visible for all to see (2 Cor. 4.3–4). The particular form that that blindfold takes in western societies at this time has been called by the philosopher Charles Taylor an 'immanent frame', referred to in Chapter 1. Taylor describes an 'exclusive humanism'. He says, 'A way of putting our present condition is to say that many people are happy living for goals which are purely immanent; they live in a way that takes no account of the transcendent' (*A Secular Age*, p. 143). This can take a variety of forms. 'Exclusive humanism' is not one thing but many things, 'which leave no place for the "vertical" or "transcendent", but which in one way or another close these off, render them inaccessible, or even unthinkable' (*A Secular Age*, p. 556). This does not make all western people into practical atheists, but 'The immanent frame is common to all of us in the modern West.' But 'Some of us want to live it as open to something beyond; some live it as closed' (*A Secular Age*, pp. 543–4).

The immanent frame assumes a clear distinction between the 'natural' and the 'supernatural', between heaven and earth, and the existence of a separate department of life called religion, that can be taken or left as each individual prefers, a purely private matter. This amounts to a powerful and effective blindfold. It is common sense to many people who have no trouble getting by without God. But as we have already seen, Israel did not have a world view which separated the 'natural' from the 'supernatural' (or a separate department of life called 'religion'), but 'a cosmology where heaven and earth, though very different, were made for one another and were able, under certain circumstances, to come together ... normally with the Temple' (N. T. Wright, *History and Eschatology*, p. 160). So the church, as the temple of the Spirit, is called to be and offer an alternative plausibility to the immanent frame. To be a people who believe that the future of the world has already broken into it in foretaste and who demonstrate in their life and witness together the transformation which this empowers. The combination of what Jesus has done, is doing and will do means his church has a partnership in his bringing the future into the present, as his body, and the Holy Spirit's temple.

As Jesus' disciples continue on mission with him, they view the present in the light of the future he has secured. This affects how they see people and what those people can become. 'From now on, therefore, we regard no one from a human point of view; even though we once knew Christ from a human point of view, we know him no longer in that way. So if anyone is in Christ, there is a new creation: everything old has passed away; see, everything has become new!' (2 Cor. 5.16–17).

This affects discernment and the praxis of local mission, shaping how they, and we, see our contexts and community, viewed not as they are at present, but in the light of how they will be, when heaven and earth are made new. Jesus' disciples then seek to be and bring foretastes of that future into the present, by the power of the Holy Spirit. Their mission involves 'drawing down unexpected opportunities from God's future' more 'than recognizing opportunities within the constraints of the present' (Moynagh, *Church in Life*, p. 320), believing that 'the Spirit enables the potentialities of God's future to transform the actualities of the present' (p. 29). Disciples on mission with Jesus are future in advance people.

Notes

1 'The word *revolution* seems calculated to shock and makes the apolitical Christian hearer uneasy. But is that not exactly what Jesus' kingship of God language was bound to do? Kingship no less than revolution was a political term; and to establish a kingship which is not as yet effective *is* to bring about a revolution' (France, *Divine Government*, p. 22).

2 In the Old Testament the divine glory is described as filling the tabernacle and the temple, but then as filling the whole earth (Ps. 72.18–19; Isa. 6.3; Hab. 2).

7

On Mission With Jesus: Joining the Family Business

> Participation in the new creation rescues our stewardship of creation from the self-serving turn that it took at the Fall ... We can become again the faithful self-sacrificing stewards we were originally created to be. (Moo, *Creation and New Creation*, p. 254)

The family of God

The church is also the family of God. Jesus continually referred to God as Father. The kingdom he was initiating was the gift of the Father (Luke 12.32). His disciples were to pray to the Father and trust the Father for their needs (Matt. 6). His call to discipleship created a new family. His brothers, sisters and mother were 'whoever does the will of my Father in heaven' (Matt. 12.46–50). This new family could divide blood families and had priority over them (Matt. 10.34–38) although Jesus was scathing about those who made devotion to God an excuse for not caring for their families (Mark 7.9–13). In John's Gospel, following the resurrection, the disciples are called 'my brothers' for the first time (John 20.17). In Hebrews, Jesus is not ashamed to call his disciples 'his brothers and sisters' having 'become like them in every respect' for their salvation (Heb. 2.10–18). The community of disciples on mission with Jesus is a family.

Paul similarly describes the church as 'the household of God' (Eph. 2.19) and 'the family of faith' (Gal. 6.10). We who belong to Christ are 'in the bosom of God's family' (Lincoln, *Ephesians*, p. 152). In the ancient world, membership of a household provided identity, protection and belonging. It implied a home but also a history (O'Brien, *Ephesians*, p. 212). We are 'children of God' because we have been adopted into God's family and the family history becomes our history (Gal. 4.4–7; Rom. 8.14–17). As a family we are on the move with Jesus into the next phase of that story.

The evidence of our belonging to the family is that the Holy Spirit has put Jesus' personal 'Abba' word on our lips. Through him, we now share his intimate relationship with the Father. 'God was known in an intimate, familial relationship for which this term (abba) used by adults as well as children, but still tender and personal, was entirely appropriate ... It was a way above all of making Jesus' prayers one's own and hence of sharing sonship with Jesus' (N. T. Wright, *Romans*, p. 593). The Holy Spirit's presence is both the evidence of our membership of God's family, and our means of participating in it:

> But when the fullness of time had come, God sent his Son, born of a woman, born under the law, in order to redeem those who were under the law, so that we might receive adoption as children. And *because* you are children, God has sent the Spirit of his Son into our hearts, crying, 'Abba! Father!' So you are no longer a slave but a child, and if a child then also an heir, through God. (Gal. 4.4–7)

As members of the family we are to recognize our fellow believers as brothers and sisters and treat them accordingly. Paul uses the term brothers (meaning brothers and sisters) 64 times in his letters. This new relationship takes priority over all other cultural markers of status or worth. 'For in Christ Jesus you are all children of God through faith. As many of you as were baptized into Christ have clothed yourselves with Christ. There is no longer Jew or Greek, there is no longer slave or free, there is no longer male and female; for all of you are one in Christ Jesus' (Gal. 3.26–28). Of course believers normally retain their nationality and gender and often their place in society (although Paul is content for slaves to get their freedom if they can – see 1 Cor. 7.21). But these indicators of status are relativized within the church, the family of God, which is the community of the new creation. 'For whoever was called in the

Lord as a slave is a freed person belonging to the Lord, just as whoever was free when called is a slave of Christ' (1 Cor. 7.22; see Barclay, *Paul and the Gift*, chs 13 and 14). The world's valuation of a person has no place in the family of God, and we do not choose our fellow travellers. In seeking to understand this our imaginations should not be misled by our modern practice of nuclear families, limited to parents and their children. The background here is drawn from both the extensive kinship networks and obligations seen in the Old Testament, and the large households of the Roman world household, including relatives, freemen, clients and slaves. Nor should we be misled by our modern practice of adopting (primarily) young children and babies. The Romans adopted adults, often, as we shall see, with a view of the future well-being of the household and its purpose. In Roman culture an adopted son was taken out of his previous situation and placed in an entirely new relationship to his new adopting father. He started a new life as part of his new family, with all his old debts cancelled. An adopted son was considered no less important than any biologically born son in his adopting father's family. This amounted to a changed status, with his old name set aside and a new name given him by his adopting father (Longenecker, *Romans*, p. 704).

The 'Abba' Father language is not just about intimate relationship. It is that, because we share Jesus' intimate relationship with the Father. It was indeed used as a loving term by children, but in the ancient world fathers were also to be obeyed. In God's family intimacy has to be partnered by awe, and a life of obedience. The 'paterfamilias' really was in charge. And 'Abba' has a deeper resonance which connects it to suffering. The gospel writers translated Jesus' original Aramaic words into Greek, but Mark preserved the original Aramaic term *abba* in just one place – Gethsemane, where Jesus prays, 'not what I want but what you want' (Mark 14.36). The letter to the Hebrews makes a similar connection to Gethsemane. We read that, 'In the days of his flesh, Jesus offered up prayers and supplications, with loud cries and tears, to the one who was able to save him from death, and he was heard because of his reverent submission. Although he was a Son, he learned obedience through what he suffered' (5.7–8). For Christians, 'Abba' is a Gethsemane word. To be joined to Christ, Paul says, involves suffering with him (8.17).

In Romans, Paul quickly moves from our adoption into God's family to our being 'joint heirs with Christ – if, in fact, we suffer with him so that we may also be glorified with him' (Rom. 8.17). Adoption has a privilege and a cost. Membership of this family involves suffering. This is because this family has a purpose, a vocation. When you join this family, you are recruited to its cause. To join the Father's family is to join our older brother's continuing mission until it is complete. Suffering comes because our older brother's mission is contested. The kingdom he brings is both already and not yet. There has been a tendency in parts of the church to ignore the second part of our calling as God's family: to read Romans 8.14–17 (leaving out the suffering part) as our privilege, and then to jump over verses 18–27 as 'too difficult', then landing on verse 28 as assurance that all will be OK in the end. But, as we shall, see Paul's argument is that our ultimate transformation to be Christlike, 'conformed to the image of his Son, in order that he might be the firstborn within a large family' (verse 29), is inseparably linked to the healing of creation 'set free from its bondage to decay' (verse 21) because, through Christ, it will share 'the freedom of the glory of the children of God' (verse 21). This is the scale of God's salvation and the nature of our vocation in the family of God. As Paul says we are 'called according to his purpose', which gloriously includes us, but goes much further (Eph. 1.10; Col. 1.15–20; 1 Cor. 15.28).

So if we are joint heirs with Christ, what do we inherit? The answer is creation healed. The whole created order 'set free from its bondage to decay'. 'The kingdom of God is creation healed' (Küng, *On Being a Christian*, p. 231). The household business of the royal family of heaven is the healing of all creation! 'A disciple is an apprentice of the family business' (Peppiatt, *The Disciple*, p. 1). We are adopted into this family for two inseparable purposes. The first is for love of us alone. Like Paul we can say 'the Son of God loved me and gave himself for me' (Gal. 2.20). The second is that this love does more than just forgive and restore us, it turns us from part of the problem to part of the solution. You would not expect to share in the incarnate Son of God, your elder brother's, intimate relationship with the Father, without sharing in his mission from the Father to the world. It's what good families do! The Holy Spirit is given for both dimensions of the family relationship. 'The reason for human salvation is not simply to rescue us out of a messy world, but so that through our salvation the world itself might be healed' (Tom Wright, *The Crown and the Fire*, pp. 87–8).

Two words appear three times in this part of Romans (8.18–30), 'glory' and 'groaning'. As far as Paul is concerned you can't have one without the other! 'Glory' provides the boundary markers of this stage of his argument. The glory which, according to earlier chapters, fallen humans have exchanged for different forms of idolatry (Rom. 1.23), 'worshipping the creature rather than the Creator' (verse 25), rather than being the responsible tenants of God's creation, being both a full part of it but also imaging the creator in it, as Genesis 1 and 2 teach, and as a consequence, falling short of the glory of God (3.23). But through Christ, glory is restored. We have hope of sharing the glory of God (5.2). So in Romans 8 we are 'heirs of God and joint heirs with Christ – if, in fact, we suffer with him so that we may also be glorified with him'. Note that in this life suffering (groaning) and glory are inseparable. So in verse 18, 'the sufferings of this present time are not worth comparing with the glory about to be revealed to us.' In verse 30, 'And those whom he predestined he also called; and those whom he called he also justified; and those whom he justified he also glorified.' But in between (verse 21), 'the creation itself will be set free from its bondage to decay and will obtain the freedom of the glory of the children of God.' It seems that glory restored to human is inseparable from the healing of the whole creation. In fact creation waits for what the children of God have. With the waiting comes the groaning. In verse 22, 'the whole creation has been groaning in labour pains until now' but not only the creation; verse 23 says, 'but we ourselves, who have the first fruits of the Spirit, groan inwardly while we wait for adoption, the redemption of our bodies.' We who are already adopted (verse 15) are waiting for the final outcome of that adoption – transformed bodies like that of our risen Lord. Our destiny is, verse 29, 'to be conformed to the image of his son' but we are still far from that, and we know it, alongside the certainty that, because of him, it is our assured destiny. This mutual groaning, a shared sense of not yet being what we were created to be, allows Christians the most profound identification with the brokenness of the world, the human race and the wider creation. We share it, we are part of it, but with one profound difference, we are bearers of hope (verses 24–25), not wishful thinking but an assurance of the future.

Patience sustains us in the groaning. Because the promise is that the whole creation is waiting for what we, the children of God, already have or know we are promised (verse 21). This introduction of hope into a world subject to decay and death turns the groaning of the world into labour pains (verse 22), as God brings his new creation to birth through his Son and in his family (verse 29). If part of our calling is a profound identification with the pain of the world in hope, we will be driven to prayer, because we share the same brokenness and it cannot bear it in our own strength. That is where the third groaning comes in (verses 26–27): 'Likewise the Spirit helps us in our weakness; for we do not know how to pray as we ought, but that very Spirit intercedes with sighs ['groans', the same Greek word] too deep for words. And God, who searches the heart, knows what is the mind of the Spirit, because the Spirit intercedes for the saints according to the will of God.' We have already been told that the Spirit lives in us and assures us of our adoption into God's family. Now the same Spirit living in us, takes our inadequate prayers about our incompleteness and the world's pain to the heart of God, so that they come out 'according to the will of God'.

> We are inundated by the cries of an entire creation ... We are so interconnected with all of life that we cannot help being touched by the pain of all that suffers ... We human beings are far too frail and tiny to bear all this pain ... We need to experience it: it is a part of our reality. Our task in praying is

precisely that of giving speech to the Spirit's groanings within us. But we must not try to bear the sufferings of the creation ourselves ... Only the heart at the center of the universe can endure such a weight of suffering ... so the Holy Spirit helps us in our weakness. (Wink, *Engaging the Powers*, pp. 304–6)

If we delight to cry out 'Abba' we also are called to cry *for* the lost, the poor and a broken creation! Believers have no future apart from a transformed world, and the world has no future apart from the Church. Being conformed to the image of God's Son is not possible apart from the transformation of the world. It has been described as like three Russian dolls (see Tom Wright, *The Crown and the Fire*, ch. 10). First, the broken world, within which, second, the church exercises its ministry, indwelt, third, by the praying Holy Spirit. Only thus can Jesus continue his ministry of bringing foretastes of a promised and secured future into the present.

Later in Romans, Paul bears witness to 'what Christ has accomplished through me to win obedience from the Gentiles, by word and deed, by the power of signs and wonders, by the power of the Spirit of God' (15.18–19). But this breaking in of Christ's power with transforming signs which anticipate the future, has already been given is given its location in chapter 8, with the church's identification with the brokenness of the world. Just as Christ's ministry in the power of the Spirit was incarnational, so is his continuing ministry through his church. 'Prophecies, exorcisms, and miracles signify the reign of God breaking into the world. Yet these must be accompanied by a deeper sign: the witness of our lives committed to those in need' (Crosby, *Spirituality of the Beatitudes*, p. 31).

A community on mission with Jesus in a broken creation

Martin Luther is alleged to have said, 'If you preach the gospel in all aspects with the exception of the issues which deal specifically with your time, you are not preaching the gospel at all.'

As climate change is one of, if not the, great crises of our time, how could a community of disciples on mission with Jesus not engage with it?

If what it means to be the church 'is embodied in Jesus walking' (Hardy), we need to note Jesus' awareness and appreciation of the creation all around him: of the value of birds (Matt. 6.26; 10.29–31; Luke 12.6–7; 12.24) and flowers (Matt. 6.28; Luke 12.27), of sun and rain and of the seasons (Matt. 5.45), of the fruitfulness of fields and lakes, and the dependence of farmers and fishermen on the natural world; all of which he saw as his Father's gifts. He assumed the proper care of domestic animals (Matt. 12.11–12; Luke 13.15–16; 14.5), and the wild animals sustained him in the wilderness (Mark 1.13). He withdrew to the hills to pray. He taught by the lake and in the fields and used the lake as a way of creating space from the demands of the crowds. He recognized and was unfazed by the destructive capacity of fire and storms. 'Who then is this, that he commands even the winds and the water, and they obey him?' (Luke 8.25). He looked forward to 'the renewal of all things' (Matt. 19.28; for more on this, see Bauckham, *Living Among the Creatures*). Those who walk with him today need to see and value the natural world as he saw it, and still sees it.

This promised renewal of all things is picked up in St Paul's great statements about the purposes of God through his Son. The earth where Jesus walked was created through him, for him and it has its coherence only in relation to him. 'All things have been created through him and for him. He himself is before all things, and in him all things hold together' (Col. 1.16–17). In Rowan Williams' words, Jesus is 'the heart of creation, the one on whom all the patterns of finite existence converge to find their meaning' (Williams, *Christ the Heart of Creation*, p. xiii). And he came to his broken creation to restore it. 'He has made known to us the mystery of his will, according to his good pleasure that he set forth in Christ, as a plan for the fullness of time, to gather up *all things* in him, things in heaven and things on earth' (Eph. 1.9–10). 'And through him God was pleased to reconcile to himself *all things*, whether on earth or in heaven, by making peace through the blood of his cross' (Col. 1.20).

James Dunn commented:

> The vision is vast. The claim is mind blowing. It says much for the faith of these first Christians that they could see in Christ's death and resurrection quite literally the key to resolving the disharmonies of nature and the inhumanities of humankind, that the character of God's creation and God's concern for the universe in its fullest expression could be so caught and encapsulated for them in the cross of Christ. (Dunn, *Colossians*, p. 104)

If 'all things on earth' – 'the disharmonies of nature and the inhumanities of humankind' – are to be reconciled it means that the healing of a creation broken through human activity has to be on the agenda and part of the vision of any community of disciples on mission with Jesus today.

When Paul speaks of 'creation' in Romans 8 he means more than the whole human race, although we are indeed to identify with all human brokenness. He means 'the world of nature, both animate and inanimate' (Longenecker, *Romans*, p. 721, quoting Cranfield) because 'Paul could no more think of persons apart from their environment than he could of them apart from their bodies' (Longenecker, *Romans*, p. 722, quoting Talbert). When he speaks of creation being released from its 'bondage to decay' (verse 21), it is in parallel to the promised 'redemption of our bodies' (verse 23) and part of the same transformation to be brought through Christ. But creation is also damaged by human failure to care for it responsibly. In Genesis 1 humans are both fully part of the creation and simultaneously God's image bearers, called to live in it as responsible stewards and tenants. In Genesis 2 that is developed further with the call to 'till it and keep it' (verse 15). It has been described as 'dominion (Ch. 1) exercised through servanthood (Ch. 2)' (Christopher Wright, *Old Testament Ethics*, p. 126). Both creation chapters make it clear that the earth is not ours to do as we wish. 'The creation exists for God – for God's praise and glory and also for God's delight. To imagine that it all exists for us is an absurd arrogance.' 'The earth is the Lord's and all that is in it, the world, and those who live in it' (Ps. 24.1; see also Exod. 19.5 and Deut. 10.14).

Paul would have been aware of the prophets' teaching about the impact of human sin on the rest of creation. 'Covenantal Israel held the staggering notion that human conduct matters for the wellbeing of creation' (Brueggemann, *Jeremiah 1–25*, p. 56). In a most striking way, Jeremiah describes creation in reverse. At the beginning of creation, according to Genesis 'the earth was a formless void'. The Hebrew words are *tohu bohu* (1.2). But Jeremiah says:

> I looked on the earth, and lo, it was *waste and void*
>   [*tohu bohu*];
> and to the heavens, and they had no light.
> I looked on the mountains, and lo, they were quaking,
>   and all the hills moved to and fro.
> I looked, and lo, there was no one at all,
>   and all the birds of the air had fled.
> I looked, and lo, the fruitful land was a desert,
>   and all its cities were laid in ruins
>   before the LORD, before his fierce anger.
> For thus says the LORD: The whole land shall be a
>   desolation; yet I will not make a full end.
> Because of this *the earth shall mourn*, and the heavens above
>   grow black. (4.23–28)

In similar vein Hosea declared:

> Hear the word of the LORD,
>   O people of Israel;
> for the LORD has an indictment
>   against the inhabitants of the land.
> There is no faithfulness or loyalty,
>   and no knowledge of God in the land.
> Swearing, lying, and murder,
>   and stealing and adultery break out;
>   bloodshed follows bloodshed.

Therefore *the land mourns*,
   and all who live in it languish;
together with the wild animals
   and the birds of the air,
   even the fish of the sea are perishing. (4.1–3)

In the biblical context none of this is strange or arbitrary:

> In the prophetic texts ... the relationship between human and non-human is part of the fundamental order in the world. When this works well both human society and the rest of creation flourish (e.g. Isa 32:16–20, Hosea 2:20 [18]); when the order breaks down everything suffers (e.g. Isa 24:3–6, Hos 4:1–3) ... this is part of the moral order of the universe. (Marlow, *Biblical Prophets*, p. 263)

The commission for humankind to 'have dominion' as bearers of God's image in creation was fatally undermined in the Fall: expulsion from the Garden and 'cursed is the ground because of you' (3.17). In Romans, Paul revisits this narrative. Genesis 1—3 underlies much of his argument. So it is notable that in chapters 5 and 6 the language of 'dominion' returns. What Adam lost, Christ regained – those who receive God's free gift in Christ will reign in life. Sin will no longer have 'dominion' over them (6.14); rather they can be 'instruments of righteousness'. This has a vastly wider application than the care of the earth, but it does mean that in Christ humans are being restored to what they were created to be and do, which includes the care of creation. If this is the case there may be nothing as green as evangelism, restoring the stewards to their proper stewardship. 'Participation in the new creation rescues our stewardship of creation from the self-serving turn that it took at the Fall. ... We can become again the faithful self-sacrificing stewards we were originally created to be' (Moo, *Creation and New Creation*, p. 254). Slaves to sin become family members of the family of God whose feature is inseparably tied to the healing of creation. As with all dimensions of the kingdom this is already and not yet, but in our day it makes the care and healing of creation part of the vocation of communities of disciples on mission with Jesus:

> Creation is waiting for the earth creatures to be revealed, waiting for us to fulfill our calling, waiting with longing for us to claim our identity. We are the earth creatures, come to serve and observe, to tend and keep the earth and those who live in it. Creation is waiting for us to remember who we are. (Keesmaat and Walsh, *Romans Disarmed*, p. 193)

This is not the place to develop a Christian response to climate change or to propose appropriate courses of action. That can be found helpfully elsewhere.[1] But such a response will be based on hope, not fear, will be realistic about the already and not yet shape of the kingdom, and will be rooted in prayer (Rom. 8.18–27). But disciples on mission with Jesus, to be part of the Father's family, are called share his view and valuing of the creation, as an essential part of their discipleship, and, in our day, must engage with the climate crisis in his name.

Notes

1 See David Atkinson, 2008, *Renewing the face of the Earth: A Theological and Pastoral Response to Climate Change*, London: Canterbury Press; Richard Bauckham, 2010, *Bible and Ecology: Rediscovering the Community of Creation*, London: Darton, Longman & Todd; Colin Bell and Robert White (eds), 2016, *Creation Care and the Gospel*, Hendrickson/Lausanne; Dave Bookless, 2008, *Planetwise*, Leicester: IVP; Douglas Moo and Jonathan Moo, 2018, *Creation Care: A Biblical Theology of the Natural World*, Grand Rapids, MI: Zondervan; Jonathan Moo and Robin Routledge, 2014, *As Long As The Earth Endures: The Bible, Creation and the Environment*, Downers Grove, IL: Apollos; Hilary Marlow, 2020 (2009), *Biblical Prophets and Contemporary Environmental Ethics*, Oxford: Oxford University Press; Michael Northcott, 2007, *A Moral Climate: The Ethics of Global Warming*, London: Darton, Longman & Todd; Michael Northcott, 2014, *A Political Theology of Climate Change*, London: SPCK; Sandra Richter, 2020, *Stewards of Eden*, Downers Grove, IL: IVP; Ruth Valerio, 2020, *Saying Yes to Life*, London: SPCK.

8

On Mission With Jesus: A Pilgrim People

> The Church is the pilgrim people of God. It is on the move – hastening to the ends of the earth to beseech all men to be reconciled to God, and hastening to the end of time to meet its Lord who will gather all into one. Therefore the nature of the Church is never to be finally defined in static terms, but only in terms of that to which it is going. (Newbigin, *The Household of God*, p. 22)

If the church is a community of disciples on mission with Jesus, it is essentially a people on the move, a pilgrim people. This does not mean it cannot be a stable community established in a particular place, but as we have already seen, it cannot be too settled. It has a primary responsibility to be alert to the initiatives of the missionary Spirit. But it is a pilgrim people in a number of senses. To be a disciple involves having found or been found by 'the road that leads to life' in Christ (Matt. 7.14). Our Lord is 'the Way' and his followers were known as 'the Way' (Acts 24.14). The metaphor of 'walking' is a standard one for going about one's life according to God's ways. The people of Israel were to 'walk in all his ways' (Deut. 10.12), to 'walk in the law of the Lord' (Ps. 119.1). Isaiah foresaw the time when 'many peoples' would come to mount Zion 'to the house of the God of Jacob; that he may teach us his ways and that we may walk in his paths'. Those who are baptized in Christ 'walk in newness of life'. They 'walk by faith, not by sight' (2 Cor. 5.7). They are encouraged to 'walk by the Spirit' (Gal. 5.16) and be 'guided by the Spirit' (Gal. 5.25). This certainly sounds like a mobile faith.

The most significant stages in the biblical narrative begin with a call to move. Abraham's call from Ur of the Chaldees to the promised land was the precursor of God promise that through him all nations would be blessed (Gen. 12.1–3). The people of Israel's journey from slavery in Egypt to the promised land was so that they could be 'a priestly kingdom and a holy nation' (Exod. 19.5). The return from exile was with the intention that they should be 'a light to the nations' (Isa. 42.6, 49.6). The disciples by the sea of Galilee had to follow if they were to fish for people. After the resurrection they are commissioned to go and make disciples of all nations – which certainly implied travel!

According to Lesslie Newbigin, the church on earth is a pilgrim people for two reasons: 'It is on the move – hastening to the ends of the earth to beseech all men to be reconciled to God, and hastening to the end of time to meet its Lord who will gather all into one' (*Household of God*, p. 25). The first movement is the consequence of the continual mandate to reach those we are not reaching now, whether that requires crossing the street, or local cultural divides or crossing national borders. The second movement is its orientation through time, in each generation, towards the climax of history and the future which Christ has secured, and which, by the Spirit, it is called to anticipate. That future functions as a magnetic pull built into its DNA. 'Even so, come, Lord Jesus.' Thus, according to Newbigin, it is 'never to be defined in static terms'.

Both of Newbigin's orientations are missional, because as the church travels through time it quickly discovers that the culture in which it is located never stays the same for long. 'Society and culture, like language, retain their distinctiveness – their "identity" – but this distinctiveness is never "the same" for long. It lasts through change' (Bauman, *Culture as Praxis*, p. xxix). In a local church's lifetime, particularly in our day, it will find itself having to change, because its context is not likely to stay the same. The church's incarnational ministry, in rapidly changing times, has to be a dynamic one. It is necessary to change to stay the same.

The church is pilgrim because there is a profound sense in which it does not belong in the world as the world is now. There is a whole tranche of biblical language which conveys this. We are to build up 'treasures in heaven' rather than 'treasures on earth' (Matt. 6.19–21). We are to set our minds on 'things that are above, not on things that are on earth' (Col. 3.2). Christians are 'aliens and exiles' (1 Peter 2.11). 'Here we have no lasting city, but we are looking for the city that is to come' (Heb. 13.14). The church has to be distinctive if it is to be effective. It is to be 'in the world but not of the world' (John 17.14–16). Its calling is to be the salt of the earth and the light of the world. So it must stay salty and visible (Matt. 5.13–16). It must be dissatisfied with the state of the world because it has a vision of what the world will one day be. By faith we 'desire a better country' (Heb. 11.16). This sense of not belonging has often been misunderstood. It is never to be world escaping but world transforming. Disciples on mission with Jesus travel through this world as it is, out of commitment to what it will be. They are given a gift of godly dissatisfaction with the way things are because they see the way things will be. Moltmann drew an analogy for this from Saul's experience on the Damascus road:

> Faith, wherever it develops into hope, causes not rest but unrest, not patience but impatience. It does not calm the unquiet heart, but is itself this unquiet heart in man. *Those who hope in Christ can no longer put up with reality as it is*, but begin to suffer under it, to contradict it, peace with God means conflict with the world, for the goad (Acts 26:14) of the promised future stabs inexorably into the flesh of every unfulfilled present. (*Theology of Hope*, p. 21)

The 'aliens and exiles' referred to in 1 Peter are 'a chosen race, a royal priesthood, a holy nation, God's own people, in order that you may proclaim the mighty acts of him who called you out of darkness into his marvellous light' (1 Peter 2.9). Aliens were resident foreigners. The Greek word is *paroikos* from which we get 'parish'. It would be interesting to treat the parish, the place where many of us exercise long term ministry and witness, as 'the place where we resident aliens live'! In the Greek Old Testament the word is used by Abraham, who is an alien in the promised land, generations before it becomes the home of his descendants. 'I am a stranger and an alien residing among you' (Gen. 23.4). But the promise to Abraham was that through him all the nations would be blessed. Blessing for many came from God's servant obeying the call to be on the move.

Many centuries later, when God's people were sent into exile in Babylon, God told these exiles to be a blessing where they were exiled. Their gift of not belonging was to bless others, even the ones who took them captive. 'But seek the welfare of the city where I have sent you into exile, and pray to the LORD on its behalf, for in its welfare you will find your welfare' (Jer. 29.7). Drawing on this, Peter calls the churches he is addressing 'the exiles of the Dispersion' (1 Peter 1.1). A famous passage from the Epistle to Diognetus shows how this was understood in the post-apostolic years. 'They dwell in their own countries, but simply as sojourners. As citizens, they share in all things with others, and yet endure all things as if foreigners. Every foreign land is to them as their native country, and every land of their birth as a land of strangers' (*Epistle to Diognetus*, ch. 5).

This pattern of not belonging but remaining committed is seen in Paul's correspondence with the church in Corinth. I have previously summarized his counsel about their public discipleship in a pluralistic pagan city as a combination of 'involved distinctiveness' and 'subversive engagement':

> 1 Corinthians culminates in an extensive chapter on the nature and significance of the resurrection of Christ. Chapter fifteen towers over the whole letter. It provides, not merely the final issue to be addressed but the key underlying conviction which gives coherence to all the diverse teaching on discipleship throughout the letter.
>
> In chapter fifteen the resurrection provides a vision of this life in the light of the next. The future includes not only a personal resurrection, but an era in which Christ rules over the whole creation, without any enemy resisting him. It is this hope which makes the hard work of serving God worthwhile.
>
> Involved distinctiveness can be summed up as a call to be countercultural community which also seeks common ground

with its society whenever possible. This community is to be involved in, rather than withdrawn from, society.

Subversive engagement involves a proactive community, actively doing good in its society (because the good can last, in the light of the kingdom of God), while subverting many of its societies key social values (because they cannot last, in the light of the kingdom of God). (Cray, *Disciples and Citizens*, ch. 3)

Two other New Testament letters are particularly helpful, for contexts where the church's witness encounters persecution, or is seen as profoundly alien to its missionary context. They are Hebrews and 1 Peter.

Hebrews

In the letter to the Hebrews, beneath its language of Old Testament sacrifice and priesthood fulfilled by Christ, is a narrative of a stalled pilgrimage. Christian discipleship is portrayed as a journey following Christ who is both apostle and pioneer. In particular it is portrayed as a race, a marathon, to be run by faith and requiring endurance. (The race metaphor is also used by Paul in Philippians 3.12–14.) But the community of Jewish believers, whom the letter addresses, is finding the going too tough, and is in danger of dropping out, of reverting to their old faith before the coming of the Messiah. It is as they share in the worship of their great high priest that they will find the grace and strength to continue to join him in his mission. The impression is given that the costliness of discipleship has begun to wear this community down. They had received God's 'great salvation' gladly, with powerful evidences of God's presence. 'It was declared at first through the Lord, and it was attested to us by those who heard him, while God added his testimony by signs and wonders and various miracles, and by gifts of the Holy Spirit, distributed according to his will' (Heb. 2.3–4). But it had been at a cost.

> Recall those earlier days when, after you had been enlightened, you endured a hard struggle with sufferings, sometimes being publicly exposed to abuse and persecution, and sometimes being partners with those so treated. For you had compassion for those who were in prison, and you cheerfully accepted the plundering of your possessions, knowing that you yourselves possessed something better and more lasting. (Heb. 10.32–34)

Now they are in danger of abandoning that first confidence (10.25). Their commitment to meeting together as a community is flagging (10.24) and they are in danger of falling away: but have not done so yet (6.4–10). In their journey of discipleship they are in danger of being more like the children of Israel who failed to have faith in God for the journey into the promised land (3.7–18) than like Abraham in his journey of faith to the promised land (11.8–12). Their great need is of endurance (6.15; 10.36) if they are to run the race that is set before them (12.1).

The key question which their experience raises is, how do disciples on mission with Jesus keep going? What makes the long haul possible? The answer given is that Jesus has travelled the road before them, and he is both the proper object of their faith, and the source of the help that they need. Jesus is variously described as, pioneer, apostle, perfecter and high priest. These titles are paired. Jesus is 'the apostle and high priest of our confession' (3.1), sent from the Father as the leader of the mission of the church, and the means and facilitator of its worship. Hebrews teaches that it is as we engage with him in worship that we develop the endurance for missionary discipleship. But he is also 'the pioneer and perfecter of our faith' (12.2). As our forerunner (6.20), he has pioneered, blazed the trail into the Father's presence, so that we can follow. He has pioneered the life of discipleship, completing the race, despite its cost. And thus he is the perfecter, fully able to see us through to the end as we join him in his mission 'outside the camp' (13.13).

These interdependent dimensions of Christian discipleship, worship and mission, deserve further exploration. First, worship: what Jesus has done and still does for us is multifaceted. The author takes what these disciples know, the worship, temple and priesthood of the Old Covenant, and shows them that in Jesus they have something far better. That he is the fulfilment, the real thing, which the covenant given to Moses foreshadowed. Jesus is the once and for all sacrifice for sin, the source and guarantee of forgiveness, who 'has taken his seat at the right hand of the throne of God' (12.2). But he is also the High Priest, the chief and representative worshipper. Through his death, resurrection and ascension he has blazed the way into the Father's presence. 'When Christ came as a high priest of the good things that have come ... he entered once for all into the Holy Place ... with his own blood, thus obtaining eternal redemption (Heb. 9.11–12). He has pioneered the way into the very presence of God for all who believe in him (4.14; 8.11–12; 9.24). Christopher Cocksworth comments, 'A human being enters the heavenly place of God's presence and sits at his right hand. Jesus remains our brother. His humanity is no discarded' (Cocksworth, *Holy, Holy, Holy*, p. 157). The invitation of the book of Hebrews is to go where he goes (*Holy, Holy, Holy*, p. 159).

> Therefore, my friends, since we have confidence to enter the sanctuary by the blood of Jesus, by the new and living way that he opened for us through the curtain (that is, through his flesh), and since we have a great priest over the house of God, let us approach with a true heart in full assurance of faith, with our hearts sprinkled clean from an evil conscience and our bodies washed with pure water. (Heb. 10.19–21)

In that presence he leads our worship of the Father. He is described as 'a minister in the sanctuary' (8.2; The Greek word is *leitourgos*, from which we derive 'liturgist'). Words from Psalm 22 are put on his lips: 'I will proclaim your name to my brothers and sisters, in the midst of the congregation I will praise you' (Heb. 2.12; Ps. 22.25). Calvin, in his commentary, writes, 'Christ leads our songs and is the chief composer of our hymns' (Cocksworth, *Holy, Holy, Holy*, p. 159). And he intercedes for us (6.24). This is the foundation of hope in testing times. 'We have this hope, a sure and steadfast anchor of the soul, a hope that enters the inner shrine behind the curtain, where Jesus, a forerunner on our behalf, has entered, having become a high priest for ever' (6.19–20). Through and from him we have access 'in time of need' (4.14–16). Joining Jesus in worship and prayer sustains us for joining Jesus in discipleship and mission.

Then mission: at first glance there is little about mission in Hebrews. But the whole purpose of the letter is that they should maintain their public witness to Christ. Private religion does not usually attract persecution. Athletics races are not private, they are run for others to see. The challenge to these Christians is to maintain 'lips that confess his name' (13.15) and the deeds which should accompany that public confession (13.16). They are to 'hold fast' to their confession (4.14; 10.13) because God is faithful. In an extraordinary statement they are told that Jesus is to be found, not only at the Father's right hand (1.3; 8.1), but 'outside the gate' (see Costas, *Christ Outside the Gate*, pp. 188–94). 'Let us go to him outside the gate' (13.13), that is, 'the place for those who were polluted and defiled, the place for things of no further use, the place where rubbish was dumped and criminals executed' (Tetley, *A Way Into Hebrews*, p. 17). This was to step again into the place of abuse, the 'abuse he endured'. Missional discipleship is potentially costly.

So what could sustain these disciples and help them to maintain their faith and their witness? One thing was the evidence of God's faithfulness in previous generations. Hebrews implies the image of a great arena or stadium. It is packed with those who have completed the race. The runners are 'surrounded by so great a cloud of witnesses' (12.1). It is as though the stadium is rocking with cries of encouragement. Even if they won't encourage one another (3.13; 10.24–25), the saints will! The saints of Hebrews 11 are not like armchair pundits, who know better than the runners, they are witnesses to the faithfulness of God and encouragers of the current generation of athletes to get fit and continue in the race. 'Let us also lay aside every weight and the sin that clings so closely, and let us run with perseverance the race that is set before us' (12.1). Another source of strength is a vision of a future which is both promised – it is the finishing line – yet in another sense it is already theirs. Hebrews speaks of 'the coming world' (2.5). That 'here we have no lasting city, but we are looking for the city that is to come' (13.14). It recognizes that 'we do not yet see everything in subjection ... but we do see Jesus' (2.8–9). Yet through Jesus that future promise is already a spiritual reality. Just as in Jesus' teaching about the kingdom, and Paul's teaching about the Spirit, there is an already as well as a not yet. You may be looking for a city that is to come, says the writer:

> But you have come to Mount Zion and to the city of the living God, the heavenly Jerusalem, and to innumerable angels in festal gathering, and to the assembly of the firstborn who are enrolled in heaven, and to God the judge of all, and to the spirits of the righteous made perfect, and to Jesus, the mediator of a new covenant, and to the sprinkled blood that speaks a better word than the blood of Abel. (Heb. 12.22–24)

On that basis faith can be exercised because 'faith is the assurance of things hoped for, the conviction of things not seen' (11.1). On that basis, 'You may not become sluggish, but imitators of those who through faith and patience inherit the promises' (6.12). Faith and patience together produce the endurance that they need. (See Alan Kreider, *The Patient Ferment of the Early Church* for the significance of patience in the growth of the church in the first centuries.)

Above all it is the example of Jesus, who has endured all, and more than, they are going through, that is the source of strength and the foundation of hope. In him they can find help in time of need. Missionary discipleship is all about 'looking to Jesus'. Towards the end of the letter the writer reinterprets the struggle and suffering they are experiencing and gives it a purpose. Jesus 'endured the cross, disregarding its shame ... for the sake of the joy that was set before him' (12.2). And so it is with his brothers and sisters (2.11). In the same way God turns the shame and scorn with which their society treats these Christians into training, into discipline, producing the endurance they need. For which father doesn't discipline his children? It is in facing into this suffering that endurance is born. These athletes are to exercise their muscles, through obedience and faith so that they can 'lift' their 'drooping hands and strengthen' their 'weak knees, and make straight paths for [their] feet, so that what is lame may not be put out of joint, but rather be healed' (12.12–13). The community of disciples on mission with Jesus will sometimes face suffering, as its Lord did, but grace is available in its time of need.

1 Peter

Nowhere is the apparent ambiguity of the vocation of the church – as a community of disciples on mission with Jesus for its context – set out more clearly than in Peter's first letter. Peter describes the churches in a group of provinces in Roman Asia Minor as 'the Dispersion': the term used of Jews living away from their ancestral homeland (John 7.35). Its origins lay in the exile of God's people to Babylon (a term used to describe Rome, from which the letter was written, in 5.13), and it carried a sense of longing for home. Hence these communities of disciples are 'exiles'. But these exiles are not Jews longing to relocate to Israel. Most of them at least are not ethnically from there. They are exiles because they have experienced a change of spiritual status. Irrespective of their ethnic origins, which in these Roman provinces may well have been diverse, when it came to relationship with God, they had been 'not a people', but now they are 'God's people' (2.10, referencing Hosea 1 and 2).

Remarkably, they are exiles *because* they have been set free. Redeemed slaves were free to go to wherever they wished, but these redeemed people remain as exiles. They are to 'live in reverent fear during the time of your exile. You know that you were ransomed from the futile ways inherited from your ancestors, not with perishable things like silver or gold, but with the precious blood of Christ' (1.17–19). Through Christ's death they have been set free from the dominance of the patterns of life in which they were raised. Through his resurrection they have a future kept safe for them:

> Blessed be the God and Father of our Lord Jesus Christ! By his great mercy he has given us a new birth into a living hope through the resurrection of Jesus Christ from the dead, and into an inheritance that is imperishable, undefiled, and unfading, kept in heaven for you, who are being protected by the power of God through faith for a salvation ready to be revealed in the last time. In this you rejoice. (1 Peter 1.3–6a)

As a consequence, they have become resident 'aliens' (2.11) in the communities where many of them were raised. 'Christians are the *insiders* who have diverted from their culture by being born again' (Volf, 'Soft Difference', p. 18).

But their new status as God's people gives them a vocation to those same communities. Their new identity is as 'a spiritual house, to be a holy priesthood, to offer spiritual sacrifices acceptable to God through Jesus Christ (2.5) and 'a chosen race, a royal priesthood, a holy nation, God's own people' and the vocation of God's own people is to 'proclaim the mighty acts of him who called you out of darkness into his marvellous light' (2.9). This is the fulfilment in Christ of the vocation and identity of God's people in the Old Covenant. 'The whole earth is mine, but you shall be for me a priestly kingdom and a holy nation' (Exod. 3.5–6). They are the local spiritual house, the true ('holy') temple where sacrifices are offered to the true God – in the midst of the range of local temples (an image also used by St Paul). They are priests of the true God revealed in Christ. This is not a reference to 'the priesthood of all believers'. It is about the corporate identity and vocation of the whole church. Just as Aaron and his descendants represented the people to God and God to the people, so the whole people of Israel had this role for the rest of the world. In Christ, the whole community of disciples functions as 'a royal priesthood' for the community in which it lives. 'The priestly church ... represents the people to God and God to the people' (Paas, *Pilgrims and Priests*, p. 303). Although Peter refers to the priesthood of the whole nation, not that of the priests and Levites, I could not help but note that the tribe of Levi received no land of its own when the promised land was settled (Deut. 18.1). They lived among the tribes they served.

This priestly ministry has two interdependent dimensions – worship and witness. They 'offer spiritual sacrifices acceptable to God through Jesus Christ' (2.5) and they 'proclaim the mighty acts of him who called you out of darkness into his marvellous light' (2.9). Jews of the Diaspora, distant from the Temple in Jerusalem, used 'spiritual sacrifices' to describe many acts of spiritual discipline and devotion. Here, in the light of Christ's sacrifice, it means that 'the whole of life is offered up in sacrifice' (McKelvey in Jobes, *1 Peter*, p. 151). Equally, their witness can only have integrity if there is evidence in their lives of the consequences of their discipleship. Being a 'holy priesthood' (2.5) demands holy lives. 'As he who called you is holy, be holy yourselves in all your conduct; for it is written, "You shall be holy, for I am holy"' (1.15–16). They are not conformed to the desires that they formerly had in ignorance (1.14). Rather they are to live for the rest of their earthly life 'no longer by human desires but by the will of God'. They had already 'spent enough time in doing what the Gentiles like to do, living in licentiousness, passions, drunkenness, revels, carousing, and lawless idolatry' (4.2–3). This change of behaviour can result in misunderstanding. 'They are surprised that you no longer join them in the same excesses of dissipation' (4.4). But the purpose of the change of behaviour is positive behaviour, 'good conduct in Christ' (3.16). When their way of life is being challenged or questioned, they are to be alert for opportunities to witness. 'Always be ready to make your defence to anyone who demands from you an account of the hope that is in you; yet do it with gentleness and reverence' (3.15–16). Above all their purpose is to bless. 'Do not repay evil for evil or abuse for abuse; but, on the contrary, repay with a blessing. It is for this that you were called' (3.9). They are to 'seek peace (well-being) and pursue it' (3.11) and to be 'eager to do what is good' (3.13).

It is clear that as spiritual 'sojourners' and 'alien residents' they must withdraw from the self-indulgent lifestyle of their contemporaries (2:11) and seek the welfare of the society in which they live. They were instructed to spend their days in this earthly city seeking the blessing of its inhabitants (2:11ff.). (Winter, *Seek the Welfare of the City*, p. 17)

The word variously translated as 'conduct' (2.12, 15; 3.1, 16), 'ways' (2.18) or 'lives' (3.2) or even 'during the time' (1.17; all NRSV) has a root meaning of 'walk'. '"Walk" is the way the *Christian community* lives in the world' (Volf, 'Soft Difference', p. 20). As this pilgrim church 'walks' through its context and community according to the way of Christ, it gets a range of responses:

> We encounter evil people who persecute Christians and who will continue to do the same, blaspheming what is most holy to Christians (4:4,12). We come across ignorant and foolish people who will be silenced by Christian good behaviour (2:15). We meet people who know what is wrong and what is right and are ready to relate to Christians accordingly (2:14). Finally, we encounter people who see, appreciate, and are finally won over to the Christian faith (2:12) (Volf, 'Soft Difference', p. 26)

Clearly these communities of disciples were not to see their culture, context and surrounding communities as essentially hostile. They were not to be surprised by the 'fiery ordeal' of persecution (4.12), but it was not the only response they received. Stephan Paas, who has written insightfully about the relevance of 1 Peter for highly secular contexts, says:

> I want to stress that this pilgrimhood of the Church does not necessarily imply a 'counterculture'. In that case the metaphor of alienhood would mean that Christians are constantly in an antagonistic relation with their context. In spite of the tense relation with wider society that Peter assumes, the letter never suggests that his readers should simply oppose the world. (Paas, *Pilgrims and Priests*, p. 245)

Rather they are to bless it, according to the way of Christ. 'Priests are a minority community by definition, who find their calling in seeking the peace of the city' (Paas, *Pilgrims and Priests*, p. 297).

John

The vocation to be different, for the sake of being a blessing, is informed by Israel's exile and dispersion, but for Christians its primary source is the incarnation of the Son of God:

> The root of Christian self-understanding as aliens and sojourners lies not so much in the story of Abraham and Sarah and the nation of Israel as it does in the destiny of Jesus Christ, his mission and his rejection which ultimately brought him to the cross. 'He came to what was his own, and his own people did not accept him' (John 1:11). (Volf, 'Soft Difference', p. 17)

As Jesus walked the through Galilee or Jerusalem with his disciples, he received the same range of responses as is found in 1 Peter. We are repeatedly told that there were divisions among the responses to him (for example, 7.40–44; 10.19–21; 11.45–46). Then he clearly warns his disciples that they can expect similar treatment (see 15.18–20). This is made clear in his high priestly prayer (17.11–18). The disciples do not belong to the world, because Jesus' kingdom does not have its origin in this fallen world (Later he says to Pilate, 'My kingdom is not from this world. If my kingdom were from this world, my followers would be fighting to keep me from being handed over to the Jews. But as it is, my kingdom is not from here' (John 8.36).) They do not belong because, in this sense, Jesus does not belong. 'They do not belong to the world, just as I do not belong to the world.' But they are in the world, not as an unfortunate occurrence of fate, but as a vocation. They have been sent there. So Jesus prays for their unity and their protection, not from the world, even though he says it hates them, but from the evil one. Again this parallels 1 Peter, where, 'Like a roaring lion your adversary the devil prowls around, looking for someone to devour' (5.8). The evil one is real, but in Christian mission, people, even persecutors, are not the enemy. They are people for whom Christ died, and for whose sake the church is sent into the world. The disciples' mission will not be fruitless. As there were different responses to Jesus' message, so there would be to that of his followers, some embracing the faith. 'If you forgive the sins of any, they are forgiven them' (20.23). This gospel record is written, 'that you may come to believe that Jesus is the Messiah, the Son of God, and that through believing you may have life in his name' (20.31).

Conclusion

The church is a community which cannot settle and fit in, because if it does it has nothing distinctive to offer the world. It has been sent into the world by Jesus, as he was sent into the world. To fulfil its ministry it is called into a liminal place. 'Liminality ... applies to that situation where people find themselves in an in-between, marginal state in relation to the surrounding society' (Hirsch, *The Forgotten Ways*, p. 220). This is the norm for the church and it is made possible by a deep-rooted relationship to Christ and a quality of community of disciples on the move, sharing his mission together (*Epistle to Diognetus*). Johnny Baker has described 'pioneer ministry' as 'the gift of not fitting in' (Baker, *Pioneer Gift*, p. 9). Pioneers are a vital part of God's equipping the church for mission, but not everyone is a pioneer – it is a distinctive gift. But the whole church has been given an uncomfortable vocation, to share Christ's vocation of not fitting in – of Godly distinctiveness for the sake of the salvation of the world. 'This distance is a presupposition of mission ... To make a difference, one must be different' (Volf, 'Soft Difference', p. 24).

9

On Mission With Jesus: Identifying Jesus in the Church

[T]he Church is a kind of historical image of the figure of Jesus. (Radner, *Church*, p. 10)

If 'church' is what happens when people encounter the Risen Jesus and commit themselves to sustaining and deepening that encounter in their encounter with each other, there is plenty of theological room for diversity of rhythm and style, *so long as we have ways of identifying the same living Christ* at the heart of every expression of Christian life in common.' (Williams, Foreword, *Mission-Shaped Church*, p. v)

One reason to review the appropriateness of our default settings concerning the church is that our familiarity with the church can obscure Jesus, more than reveal him. In Terry Pratchett's Discworld novels there are many gods, and their power or lack of it depends on the scale of faith, of belief, that people have in them. In *Small Gods* there is a vast institution around 'The Great God Om', but there is only one novice left who actually believes in him, rather than his institution. The practices and practicalities of the church do not exist for their own sake. They exist to reveal Jesus, but they can sometimes obscure him, if their purpose is not properly understood.

One of the great strengths of Archbishop Rowan Williams' teaching about the church, which will inform much of this chapter, is his focus on the centrality of Jesus. He sees through the church to Jesus and looks to see Jesus in the church:

'Because ecclesia in the Greek is a word that simply means a calling together. What calls? Who calls? Jesus. When he calls, this is what happens and if we have to stick a label on it, we call it Church. Church is what emerges under the pressure of Jesus' presence.'

'That's the Church. It is what happens when the call of Jesus is definitively heard.' 'The church begins where Jesus is with others.' (Fresh Expressions Conference, May 2011)

'Church' is what happens when people encounter the Risen Jesus and commit themselves to sustaining and deepening that encounter in their encounter with each other. (Foreword, *Mission-Shaped Church*, p. v)

In baptism and Holy Communion, the nature of the Church is laid bare for us. What is the Church? It is simply those who have been immersed in, soaked in the life of Jesus, and who have been invited to eat with him, and pray to the Father with him. (*Tokens of Trust*, p. 113)

The Church ... is meant to be the place where Jesus is visibly active in the world. ... Where Jesus is visibly active something very like the church must be going on. (*Tokens of Trust*, p. 128)

If the church is a community of disciples on mission with Jesus, the place where he is 'visibly active in the world', how do we ensure that we do not obscure him or misrepresent him? How can we ensure that we are bearing witness to Jesus as he is, not a Jesus to suit our own convenience? How can Jesus be visible in the church? The Anglican Communion has recently given priority to intentional discipleship,[1] with a clear emphasis on mission, under the title of 'Living and Sharing Jesus-Shaped Life'.[2] The Church of England has a national vision and strategy to be 'Jesus Christ Centred and Shaped by the 5 Marks of Mission', which have been reframed as discipleship practices, namely, 'Tell, Teach, Tend, Transform and Treasure'. It is obvious that what is required therefore is Christlikeness: in the church as a whole, in each local church and in each believer. Dr John Stott's final public sermon affirmed that, 'God wants

His people to become like Christ. Christlikeness is the will of God for the people of God' (Stott, 'John Stott's final sermon'). But this raises a problem, for to become like Christ is a journey, not a tick-box characteristic. It will only be complete when we see him face to face (1 John 3.2). Those who we regard as most like Christ are usually the ones most aware of how little they resemble their Lord. Furthermore it is a corporate quality, not just a personal one (Eph. 4.13). Christlikeness is a vision we live towards. It is displayed as much in the direction of travel as in any current attainment. But that does not excuse us from making progress on the journey. 'It is enough for the disciple to be like the teacher' (Matt. 10.25).

Just as the kingdom of God, and the kingdom ministry of the Holy Spirit are both present realities in foretaste, and assured promises for the future – both already and not yet – so it is with our conformity to Christ. This means that to truly reveal Jesus, the church, which in many ways is evidently not yet like him, must also be and be seen as a community of grace. It is because of our unChristlikeness that we need Christ. Grace both receives us now, as we are, and assures us and ensures that on the final day we will be like our master. 'Through whom we have obtained access to this grace in which we stand; and we boast in our hope of sharing the glory of God' (Rom. 5.2). One danger is that becoming more like Christ is viewed as a matter of purely personal, often private, piety, isolated from the overall purpose of the church. But our becoming Christ-like is central to God's purposes for the church. Humans were created in the image of God, living masterpieces reflecting the character, the image, of our creator, in all our relationships with the rest of creation and with one another. But through our sin the image is defaced and the relationships broken. We are profoundly damaged masterpieces in need of costly restoration. That restoration is brought about through Jesus, who is 'the image of the invisible God' (Col. 1.15). Christlikeness is central. Because in Jesus we see the image of God. We see what God is truly like. 'God is Christlike, and in him is no un-Christlikeness at all' (Ramsey, *God, Christ and the World*, p. 98). And we see what we are to be like: the image restored in a human life. His achievement, through his life, death and resurrection (Col. 1.19–20), creates our destiny. He is our example. God's purpose is that we are 'to be conformed to the image of his Son, in order that he might be the firstborn within a large family' (Rom. 8.29). We saw in an earlier chapter that God's family business is the healing of the whole creation, heaven and earth made new. The vocation of the church is to be image bearers of Christ, a community like Jesus.

If the church is 'a community of disciples on mission with Jesus', then each part of this definition contributes to the Church's vocation for Christlikeness. Each of these have been addressed as this book has progressed, but it is time to bring them together, but in a different order.

Disciples

It should be obvious, but there is no Christlikeness without discipleship. The gift of forgiveness should never be separated from the call to follow. The old life is left behind as the new is embraced. Jesus is both Saviour and Lord. The words I speak to each candidate when, as a bishop, I confirm them, bring both comfort and challenge. 'God has called you by name, and he has made you his own.' The call to follow is profoundly personal. 'God has no grandchildren.' The love and grace of Jesus Christ is for each one, and God knows and calls each by name. Each is called personally, just as and just who they are. But each one stops being their own! 'You are not your own. For you were bought with a price' (1 Cor. 6.19–20). It is fundamental to Christian faith that we belong to Jesus. 'Christ Jesus has made me his own' (Phil. 3.12).

Community

According to David Bosch, 'The disciple follows the Master but he/she never follows him alone.' And 'disciples belong together in an indestructible fellowship' (Bosch, *The Scope of*

Mission, p. 5). Christian discipleship is always personal, but it is essentially corporate. The church is the body of Christ, and 'the measure of the full stature of Christ' can only be achieved 'as each part is working properly' (Eph. 4.12–16). 'The slogan of the Church's life is "not without the other", no I without you, no I without a we' (Williams, *Tokens of Trust*, p. 106). Growth into Christlikeness is never a solo flight, however much it also needs some disciplined solitary time (Matt. 6.6). Fellow disciples are God's gifts for our growth in Christlikeness. 'So believing in the Church is really believing in the unique gift of the other that God has given you to live with' (Williams, *Tokens of Trust*, p. 106). My fellow disciples are essential for my growth in Christlikeness. Perhaps the greatest challenge to discipleship in the Western world is to escape the corrosive power of individualism, and flourish in the gift of community with and in Christ. The placing of discipleship before community is deliberate. The community is a community of disciples. Its purpose is defined by its founder and master. It is his body in each place where he has summoned it in to being. In each place where he has sent it to do his will. It is not community for the sake of community. It is not a religious club, nor simply a meeting of those with a common belief. It must be open and accessible, but at its heart is a profound commitment to follow wherever Jesus calls.

'With Jesus'

'Jesus' needs no further explanation at this point, but it's the 'with' that matters. According to Paul, 'your life is hidden *with* Christ in God' (Col. 3.3), or more frequently, disciples are 'in Christ' (Rom. 6.11, 23; 8.1). Christ is our environment. Our present and our future are entirely bound up with him. The key to discipleship is found in his words 'abide in me as I abide in you. Just as the branch cannot bear fruit by itself unless it abides in the vine, neither can you unless you abide in me' (John 15.4). The invitation is to go beyond merely believing that out eternal security is in Jesus, to depending on him moment by moment. Leaning into him. Making him our daily environment. But a question remains: 'If we are in and with Jesus, where is Jesus?' Since his ascension there have been two, equally correct answers to that question. He is at the right hand of the Father, interceding for us, and in him we have access to the Father. But by the Spirit he is also continuing his mission from the Father to the world. So where is Jesus?

He is 'on mission' – to abide in Christ and to bear fruit from him is not just about personal piety. It involves sharing in his mission. Being with him wherever his mission takes us. Seeking the company that he seeks and those with whom he identifies (Luke 4.17–21; 19.10; Matt. 9.12; 25.31–46). Disciplined and prayerful study of the Gospels will show the sort of people whose company Jesus seeks. The church is a missional community, because while it is on the earth it is on mission with Jesus. It can only sustain that mission by drawing its strength from him, in the presence of the Father. 'We are to be where he is not only in terms of mission and outreach and service in the world, in serving and accompanying the outcast; we are also to be where he is, "close to the Father's heart"' (Williams, *Being Disciples*, p. 13). It is not just that disciples accompany their Lord in his mission, but that discipleship deepens, and flourishes best, in the context of mission. To be truly a community of disciples involves being on mission with Jesus. But that carries a particular challenge. In the Gospels responses to Jesus are mixed. In introducing the kingdom of God – the new age – he was a threat to those who benefitted from the old or existing age. Britons, perhaps particularly the English, tend to regard religion as a private matter, and want to be liked. The health warning is that the public following of Jesus can get you loved or loathed, as our loyalty is to him and his kingdom.

If the church is on mission it will not stay the same – it will change as it follows its Lord through time, unexpected events and cultural transitions. As the *Fresh Expressions in the Mission of the Church* report states, 'From a fresh expressions perspective, all forms of the Church are provisional, and will continue to adapt in response to their changing context as new Christians enter the Church' (p. 153).

Worship 'on the way'

The major emphasis of this book has been on the missionary nature of the church and of its being a movement of missionary disciples. But where does that leave worship? We saw in Chapter 2 that worship and mission are inseparable aspects of our participation in Christ, that 'Worship is joining with Jesus as he praises his Father.' And mission is 'joining with Jesus in his mission from the Father to the world'. In Chapter 3, from Matthew 28 we saw that the commission to make disciples is given in the context of worship:

> Worship and mission are inseparable, they are parallel responses to Jesus, they form the rhythm of church life, the ecology of the life of the church. They are not two gifts but one gift, Christ by the Spirit in two dimensions. Neither part can be addressed apart from its relation to the other. Each is shaped in relation to the other. Each provides evidence of the authenticity of the other. Authentic worship leads to mission. Authentic mission wins worshippers.[3]

Authentic worship leads to mission. Worship could rightly be called the sixth mark of mission, as we 'proclaim the Lord's death until he comes' (1 Cor. 11.26). My colleague in York, David Watson, often said, 'A praising community preaches to answer the questions raised by its praise' (Watson, *I Believe in Evangelism*, p. 166). To David Ford and Daniel Hardy, 'Evangelism as the horizontal dimension of praise – the content of praise repeated and explained to others so that they can join the community of praise' (Ford and Hardy, *Knowing and Praising God*, p. 19). My former colleague in Kent, Robin Gill, states that, 'Worship makes strong demands upon us. It requires no less than we should go out into the world to love, serve and care' (Gill, *Moral Communities*, p. 23). To Archbishop William Temple, 'The proper relation in thought between prayer and conduct is not that conduct is supremely important and prayer may help it, but that prayer is supremely important and conduct tests it' (*Christus Veritas*, p. 45). Conduct in mission and other forms of discipleship 'tests' prayer and worship, and the reverse applies. Authentic mission wins worshippers. It involves initiation into the worshipping community, into the body of Christ.

If we return to the Gospels, the most explicit worship of Jesus comes after his resurrection (Matt. 28.17; John 20.28; Luke 24.52). This is understandable, as only at that point do the disciples have a grasp of Jesus' full identity. But Matthew's Gospel in particular (see also John 9.38) recounts how, during his ministry, various people pay homage to him or kneel before him: a leper seeking cleansing (8.1–2), a synagogue leader whose daughter had just died (9.18), the disciples, following the stilling of the storm (14.33), the Canaanite woman whose daughter is tormented (15.25), James and John's mother, with inappropriate aspirations for her sons (20.20). There is also the slave who begs the king for patience in Jesus' parable (18.26). In each case Matthew uses the same word (*prosekunei*) as when the disciples worship the risen Lord (28.17).[4] Matthew's Gospel begins with the birth of Emmanuel, God 'with us'. The child is worshipped (*prosekunei*) by the Magi (2.11), who are representative Gentiles. Matthew's Gospel concludes as Jesus is worshipped and sends his disciples to the Gentiles, saying I am 'with you' always.

A community on mission with Jesus will always be a worshipping community. Wherever Jesus is recognized, there will be worship. Mission and worship are an integrated response to the Holy Spirit's revelation of Jesus Christ. My purpose is not to demean worship compared to mission, but to relocate our primary instincts about the church from meetings (for whatever purpose) to a movement in mission. The children of Israel worshipped as a travelling people with a travelling tabernacle. Before them, the patriarchs built altars at key places of encounter with God as they travelled through a land which they did not yet possess. Missional worship is worship 'on the way' by the people of the Way, as the church responds to the leading of the missional Spirit. The pilgrim people of God is both a gathered and a scattered people. Disciples on mission with Jesus re-gather together regularly to offer praise and adoration, to intercede together, to refocus their calling and their devotion to their Lord, to welcome new disciples, to attend to the guidance of the Holy Spirit together, to be refreshed by the Lord's teaching and to be sent out again.

In these re-gatherings, the Eucharist, the holy communion, has a central and pivotal place. In it we are drawn back into the story of God in Christ as the story where we find our meaning. We are refocused not only on the historical fact of the death and resurrection of Christ for us, but on our dependence on him and what he has done, receiving again the invitation to feed on him, both personally and together. 'We may identify the eucharist as the dominically appointed context both for the renewal of our identification with Christ's death and for the intensification of our participation in his life' (Cocksworth, *Evangelical Eucharistic Thought*, p. 221). Many Western people, particularly in urban contexts, have largely lost their sense of being rooted in the past. Any sense of history is provided by a tourist or heritage industry. All well and good while there was confidence in continual progress, but we now live in an age deeply uncertain about the future, and highly aware of the double-edged nature of science and technology. This questioning about the future has led to an overemphasis on the present. We live for now because now is all we can be sure of. But in each Eucharist (each giving of thanks for what God had done in Christ) the Church proclaims an alternative perspective, a three-dimensional gospel for a one-dimensional society. Christian worship, and especially the Eucharist, links past, present and future. 'It is the appointed place at which the past, present and future of God's dealings with man in Christ come to clear, concrete and climatic expression' (Cocksworth, *Evangelical Eucharistic Thought*, p. 190). In the Eucharist we are celebrating the Lord's death in the past, but we do so in his risen presence and in anticipation of his return. Christians' claim that what God has done in Christ restores both a rootedness in the past and a hope for the future. Both are necessary for any sense of meaning in life beyond the here and now. 'In order to have a sense of who we are, we have to have a notion of how we have become, and of where we are going' (Taylor, *Sources of the Self*, p. 47). As people with no history with the church are drawn into its life and story they will often need 'waymarkers, public opportunities to take to take a step nearer to Christian commitment ... as and when each is ready' (Cray, 'Doors to the Sacred', p. 10) as a journey into full sacramental participation. Tradition is not a term taken seriously by those raised to seek continually after the latest fashionable experience, but 'to live in tradition is about living an authentic life in which our present is given coherence from our past and hope from our future' (Stevenson, *Handing On*, p. 128). Such a tradition is renewed each time we share Holy Communion.

Worship is to, for and about God as revealed in Jesus Christ. Worship only 'works' when it is authentically offered to God. It has significant benefits but all are lost when we worship for what *we* can get out of it. 'The principal object of liturgy is to worship God. Values that are generated in the process are a consequence of worship and not its object' (Gill, *Moral Communities*, p. 67). But authentic worship does generate values. Alan Kreider has pointed out that people did not become Christians in the early church because of the attractiveness of the worship, they were not allowed to attend it. But he says:

> And yet I think there was a connection. I believe that worship, to which pagans were denied admission, was all-important in the spread of the church. It was important not because it was attractive, but because its rites and practices ... made a difference in the lives and communities of the worshippers. It performed the function of re-forming those pagans who joined the church into Christians, into distinctive people who lived in a way that was recognizably in the tradition of Jesus Christ. (Kreider, *Worship and Evangelism in Pre-Christendom*, p. 10)

According to Robin Gill, 'Within worship moral values take on a more demanding and insistent shape, than they do outside worship: they change the very way we see the world' (Gill, *Moral Communities*, p. 81). So the overflow of worship is Christian character, is discipleship, is Christlikeness. Making it a fundamental aspect of being a community of disciples on mission with Jesus.

Identifying Jesus

In *Mission-Shaped Church*, Archbishop Rowan spoke of 'ways of identifying the same living Christ at the heart of every expression of Christian life in common'. Primary among these are word and sacrament. The scriptures and the dominical sacraments are mandated by Jesus. They are his gifts to the church. So is the Jesus we claim to worship recognizably the Jesus of the Gospels? Does the public and personal reading of Scripture, and the related teaching, given and received, consistently inform and revise our understanding of him and the life of our churches? For years Archbishop Stuart Blanche had a discipline of daily study in the Greek text of St Mark's Gospel. Memorably he told our congregation, 'Every time I think I have grasped him, I find something else that astounds me.' Are we still surprised by Jesus, as the scriptures reveal him? Does God's word through scripture renew our understanding of him? Or does our default setting for the church restrict our vision? The dominical sacraments are the means by which we are initially joined to Jesus, and to one another, through baptism, and then regularly renew and refocus our belonging through Holy Communion. Both are inseparably linked to Jesus' death and resurrection. Dominical sacraments 'covenanted'. When entered upon with faith they minister Jesus, irrespective of the appropriateness of the form of church, or spiritual health of the person administering them.

Marks of the church

The marks of the church from the Nicene creed 'one holy catholic and apostolic' are 'about Jesus Christ. The church is one in Jesus and holy in Jesus; the church is catholic in Jesus and it is sent in mission in Jesus' (Rowan Williams, 'Archbishop's Address to the 3rd Global South to South Encounter – Ain al

Sukhna, Egypt – 28th October 2005'). These are authentic marks of the church, recognized and valued down the centuries. They are aspects of Christlikeness, but as with the church's Christlikeness as a whole they are as much indicators of the church's failings as of its character. Despite the great gains in ecumenical relationships in recent decades the church is clearly not one. Disputes between different traditions within denominations provide further evidence. Some very public failings, in particular in the area of safeguarding, show that it is not consistently holy. Too often 'catholic' is used to name one tradition in contrast to others, rather than 'the universal scope of the church as a society instituted by God in which all sorts and conditions of humanity, all races, nations and cultures, can find a welcome and a home' (Avis, *The Anglican Understanding of the Church*, p. 65). Apostolicity can be reduced to the validation of forms of ministry, or checks on doctrinal orthodoxy, rather than the dynamic of a church sent into the world.

Nevertheless, with their origin in Jesus, these marks also represent essential characteristics of the church and are evidenced in its life, however imperfectly. Stephen Pickard helpfully 'signals a move from marks as fixed points of measure to marks as dynamic qualities encoded into the very DNA of the ecclesia of God ... In this sense, the marks identify a journey to be travelled, rather than a place of rest' (Pickard, *Seeking the Church*, p. 129). But where Jesus is honoured as Lord, people gather around him who would not otherwise identify with one another. When Jesus is honoured as Lord, lives are transformed. When Jesus is honoured as Lord, the cultural hospitality of the church expands. When Jesus is honoured as Lord, his disciples cross boundaries to reach those who would otherwise be beyond the reach of the church as it is. Apostolicity has at its heart a community of disciples on mission with Jesus, going wherever Jesus leads them. If the marks are an invitation to a journey with Jesus, then the journey is worth the effort.

One small application uses them to test dimensions of maturity in a local church: its depth of fellowship (In), worship and discipleship (Up), connection to the rest of the church (Of) and its mission (Out) (*Mission-Shaped Church*, pp. 98–9).

One of Canon George Lings' many contributions to the *Mission-Shaped Church* report (of which he wrote the first draft) was his insight that, 'God's church should and can reproduce' (Lings, *Reproducing Church*, p. 11). The underlying assumption is that the Church is God's community with a divine mandate to reproduce. It is intended by God to multiply, by the Spirit, and to fill all creation. This is an essential dimension of any missionary ecclesiology. Churches are created by God to grow:

> We do not argue that it is the natural condition for every local church to be growing. But we do argue that it is the normative condition for the national church in normal times if it keeps the faith and keeps up with the culture. (*Mission-Shaped Church*, p. 93)

Every church was planted. They did not appear by spontaneous combustion. It's just that some have been in existence for so long they have forgotten how they began (or that they began!). To give birth to the next generation is normal. Few parents have identical twins. My two daughters are and look very different, but they are sisters and fiercely loyal to one another. Church planting is non-identical reproduction. Churches should not expect the churches they plant to be carbon copies, either of themselves or all the same, but to have their own character and identity, hopefully appropriate to their context. (For a detailed exploration of this theme, see Lings, *Reproducing Churches*.)

Models of the church

If there is 'plenty of room for diversity of rhythm and style' to embody and manifest the risen Christ, then a whole range of models of the church, in the fresh expressions sense[5] or as described by Avery Dulles,[6] can be established, as appropriate to context. A mixed ecology of models of church is at the heart of the Church of England's vision for its current and future mission:

IDENTIFYING JESUS IN THE CHURCH

In the Church of England today, bishops undertake to pursue and support the full range of contributions to mission and church growth ... creating and normalizing a pattern of diversity, of parish and other traditional forms alongside newer forms. This pattern of diversity is *the 'new normal'*.[7]

Historically this level of diversity is not new:

Go back 600 years. You'd have monasteries of different kinds You'd have the enclosed orders. You'd have the friars, the preaching orders. You'd have local guild churches, and parish churches and chantry chapels, and cathedrals and minsters, not just the parish church. And we've airbrushed that variety out of the picture. (Rowan Williams, quoted in Taylor, *First Expressions*, p. 121)

As Archbishop Stephen Cottrell has said: 'The Church of England has too many churches, and I think the answer is we need more, but of a different kind.'[8]

But no model in itself, be that an inherited or a more recently pioneered approach, carries an automatic guarantee that people will encounter Jesus through it. There must be some underlying qualities which allow for this spaciousness and contextual diversity of forms of church. For *Mission-Shaped Church*, I drafted five values of a missionary church, with a nod towards the five marks of mission (*Mission-Shaped Church*, pp. 81–2). The purpose was to identify common missional factors which might underlie the wide range of models of fresh expression which we had discovered in our research. They were drafted to be equally applicable to traditional or inherited forms of church as well. Twenty years on, reflecting on considerable experience of fresh expressions, I would draft them a little differently, but the main points would remain. For this book they revisit various themes addressed in earlier chapters, but still repay careful attention.

A missionary church is focused on God the Trinity:
Worship lies at the heart of a missionary church, and to love

and know God as Father, Son and Spirit is its chief inspiration and primary purpose. It worships and serves a missionary God, and understands itself to share in the divine mission. All of its life and activity is undergirded by prayer.

I was never entirely comfortable with the word 'focus', but could not improve on it at the time. Worship and mission are more than focused on God the Holy Trinity, they are a participation in the divine life, and need to be understood in this way, not simply as duties or tasks to be performed by the church. By grace, and through the Spirit, they are a share in the Son's communion with and mission from the Father. This is not simply a piece of theological theory, it is the spirituality which sustains the church day by day. As we saw in Chapter 2, we join Jesus as he worships the Father, and in his continuing mission from the Father to the world.

A missionary church is incarnational:
A missionary church seeks to shape itself in relation to the culture in which it is located or to which it is called. Whenever it is called to be cross-cultural then its long-term members or initial team lay aside their cultural preferences about church to allow the emergence of a form or style of church to be shaped by those they are seeking to reach. If a church is long established, then it evaluates itself in relation to the culture of the community it serves, and strips away whatever is not required by the gospel. An incarnational church seeks to be responsive to the activity of the Spirit in its community.

The incarnational character of carrying out 'Christ's mission in Christ's way' was addressed in Chapter 5 and the need to respond to the leading of the Spirit in each context in Chapter 4. The praxis described will be elaborated in the next chapter. But the fundamental truth is that the church is not tied to a single cultural form, however much it has been loved by previous or current generations of Christians.

IDENTIFYING JESUS IN THE CHURCH

The Church does not really have a single culture. On the other hand, it has a single transformative energy, the Spirit of Christ figured in the Scriptures, which, in the process of time, is constantly assimilating, perhaps strengthening, perhaps re-ordering the multiple cultures of Adam's children. (Radner, *Church*, ch. 7)

It has received a commission to take a Jesus-shape in each time and space. 'Jesus Christ is the same yesterday and today and for ever' (Heb. 13.8), but to embody him, to be the body of Christ in each place, requires engagement with that place: 'the Church is a kind of historical image of the figure of Jesus' (Radner, *Church*, p. 10).

The Jesus who is ever the same looks different in different time, cultures and places for him to be trusted and followed in each place. One of the most significant lessons from the practice of planting fresh expressions of church is the significance of context. To repeat a quote from Andrew Walls, 'Christian faith is embodied faith; Christ takes flesh among those who respond to him in faith. But there is no generalized humanity; incarnation has always to be culture specific' (Walls, *The Missionary Movement in Christian History*, p. 47). Being 'on mission with Jesus' is never generic. It is always contextual.

A missionary church is transformational:
A missionary church exists for the transformation of the community that it serves, through the power of the gospel and the Holy Spirit. It is not self-serving, self-seeking or self-focused. The kingdom of God is its goal, and church is understood as a servant and sign of God's kingdom in its community, whether neighbourhood or network.

This was addressed in Chapter 3. The church does not exist for itself. 'The church gets in trouble when it thinks it is in the church business rather than the Kingdom business' (Snyder, *Liberating the Church*, p. 11). It is to be world transforming, not world withdrawing. But a Church of England report warned that, 'There are parts of the Church which primarily serve as a club for their existing members without any obvious commitment to mission.'⁹ During times of numerical decline this can be an understandable, if mistaken, response. More of a reflex than a thought-out decision. The wagons are circled and the purpose of the church becomes the survival of the church. Thriving churches can also demand so much of their congregation that all their time and energy is sucked into maintaining church life, much of which has little connection to mission. The church's purpose is not to be a whirlpool, drawing people into another world, but a launch pad, equipping each member for whole life discipleship. Church gathered is for the sake of church scattered. If redrafting this value today I would add that the church's ministry is ultimately for the glory of God, not just the well-being of a local community. It is not the kingdom of God if God is not acknowledged and worshipped as king. Disciples on mission with Jesus are told that, 'My Father is glorified by this, that you bear much fruit and become my disciples' (John 15.8).

A missionary church makes disciples:
A missionary church is active in calling people to faith in Jesus Christ, and it is equally committed to the development of a consistent Christian lifestyle appropriate to, but not withdrawn from, the culture or cultures in which it operates. It engages with culture, but also presents a counter-cultural challenge by its corporate life based on the world view and values of the gospel. It encourages the gifting and vocation of all the people of God, and invests in the development of leaders. It is concerned for the transformation of individuals, as well as the transformation of communities.

The theme of discipleship was addressed extensively in Chapter 3 and in various other parts of this book. The essence of the church is to be a community of disciples. When it fails to make disciples and to grow disciples into maturity, it fails to be true to itself. Evangelism is a subset of the larger process of disciple making. This value connects directly to the previous one. Individuals can flourish in Christ because of, not in spite of, the fact that the church is not to be self-serving. Just as Jesus made dis-

IDENTIFYING JESUS IN THE CHURCH

ciples during the day to day activity of his mission, so disciples grow best when they are 'on mission with Jesus'.

A missionary church is relational.
In a missionary church, a community of faith is being formed. It is characterized by welcome and hospitality. Its ethos and style are open to change when new members join. Believers are encouraged to establish interdependent relationships with fellow Christians as they grow into Christ. As a community it is aware that it is incomplete without interdependent relationships with other Christian churches and communities. It does not seek to stand alone.

The church is a *community* of disciples on mission with Jesus. It is 'a people sent to the Peoples, a nation for the Nations' (Radner, *Church*, p. 156). According to Rowan Williams' definition, those who have encountered the risen Christ 'commit themselves to sustaining and deepening that encounter in their encounter with each other'. As such each local church needs a genuine corporate life. It is a community not just a regular meeting. Nor can it stand alone with no relationship with other churches. The mixed economy, or mixed ecology concept assumes this.

Much more could be said about a missionary church. These five principles provide a broad standard to help discernment at a time when the shape of the church in the UK is increasingly varied and in flux. None of these qualities is automatically guaranteed by particular structures of mission or strategies for church or church planting. Neither do any of these qualities automatically flow from a particular church tradition or 'type'. These five marks are not 'pass' or 'fail' criteria, but may be a helpful way of highlighting or identifying a church's missionary purpose and qualities. Eddie Gibbs has proposed two additional values: 'A missionary church is reproducible' and 'a missionary church combines local engagement with global concerns and commitment' (*Churchmorph*, p. 66).

Resilience and flexibility

During the substantial times of change we have been and will continue to be living through, churches on mission with Jesus will need to demonstrate both resilience and flexibility.

Resilience (deep roots in Christ) and *flexibility* (the capacity to respond quickly and appropriately to changes in a context or new opportunities created by the Holy Spirit).

As those born of the Spirit, we are to be responsive to 'The wind [that] blows where it chooses, and you hear the sound of it, but you do not know where it comes from or where it goes' (John 3), but as those growing to maturity within the body of Christ we are not to be 'tossed to and fro, and blown about by every wind of doctrine' (Eph. 4). The two are inseparably linked. If flexibility, openness to change, and the ability to respond to the unexpected are genuine responses to the missionary Spirit, they can provide the context for deepening discipleship. To quote Bishop Stephen Pickard, 'The more deeply the people of the Church enter into the slipstream of the Spirit's work the more profound the emergence of holy life becomes' (*Seeking the Church*, p. 138). Equally it is deep roots in Christ which create the capacity for responsive change.

Flexibility

Cultures are never stable, they are in a constant process of change. But our current global context is one of accelerating and discontinuous change. The accelerated speed of change, the complexity of a joined-up multicultural world and the fluidity of the resulting local and national cultures make our times profoundly unpredictable. Consequently we live at a time when previous experience, and previous models, are very fallible guides to the future or to reaching a changing culture (see Tod Bolsinger, *Canoeing the Mountains*). We have also seen that the Holy Spirit often leads the church's mission in unexpected or unpredictable ways. The church needs to develop practices of discernment, but also an agility in response to the

Spirit's initiatives. This is very different from strategic planning. More often than not, the Spirit reveals the next step, not the final destination. Over-fixed ideas about the 'proper' shape of the church for a context are of little help. Existing models of church are a resource to draw on, not blueprints to start from. With change as the new status quo the church frequently finds itself in a liminal state. But such liminal periods can prove to be the occasions when we are prepared for guidance we would otherwise find hard to hear or receive (as in Acts 16.6–10 when a period of frustration leads to an unexpected call to Macedonia). This requires the church to develop a flexibility which has not been characteristic of the Church of England in previous eras. The House of Bishops' statement on church planting warns that, 'Church planting will continue to change and evolve in the coming years, in ways that have yet to be imagined, as the Church responds to the movement of the Spirit in mission.'

Which brings us to resilience.

Resilience

Such times of instability require an investment in the local church's resilience, ensuring that it is deeply rooted in Christian practice. Robin Greenwood has called this a move 'from strategies to virtues: choosing and living practices to build the Church's character and purpose' (Greenwood, *Being Church*, p. 68). What the local church looks like can and should be flexible to change and context. But it is the depth of each expression of church's habits of discipleship which are crucial in a seductive consumer society, irrespective of the model of church. When my colleague Andrew Roberts moved on from his role as Director of Training for Fresh Expressions, he wrote his book *Holy Habits*, which I commend warmly. The effectiveness of a local church is deeply related to its capacity to discern the actions of the missionary Spirit, but that discernment depends on its habits of discipleship and disciple making. What personal and, above all, shared practices of devotion and discipleship are in place, to form a contextual community of disciples, that can recognize the call of Jesus by the Holy Spirit?

When Jesus was on mission with his disciples he led them day by day wherever he wished. But as he took them to sometimes unexpected places – through Samaria, across the lake to Gadara, and so on – their relationship with him grew deeper. Flexibility – 'Where on earth will he take us today?' – was the context for deepening resilience. The same is required of today's communities of disciples.

But it is easy for any church to lose its original missional edge and kingdom focus. Daniel Hardy proposed four dimensions which provide an appropriate health check for any congregation, whether fresh expression or in an inherited mode (Hardy, *Finding the Church*, pp. 147–8).

The first he called 'intensification'. To what extent is this community still being formed by the gospel? Is there a deepening and maturing in the faith? Accompanying this deepening, and as evidence of it, is 'range'. Is there an effective and appropriate contribution to the global issues now confronting the world? The assumption here is that powerful global issues always have local force. Professor Eddie Gibbs has suggested that the marks of any missional church today should include local, commitment to global issues (*Churchmorph*, p. 66). Mission and ministry are 'glocal'. The integrity of this global concern is demonstrated by 'affinity' (effectively a synonym for incarnational). Is the ministry of this church 'close enough to the hearts and minds of those to whom they speak'? The final dimension is 'mediation', which draws all the dimensions together. It involves, 'placing the intensity of the gospel in the closest affinity to those lives and societies to which it is addressed'.

This vision should be the aspiration of any church that wishes to be a community of disciples on mission with Jesus. It also provokes a longing for the Spirit. To Daniel Hardy again, the church is called 'to participate more fully in the energy of the Spirit of Christ by which God, through his church, is drawing all human society to its fulfilment in the kingdom of God' (Hardy, *Finding the Church*, p. 4, quoted in *Mission-Shaped Church*, p. 86).

IDENTIFYING JESUS IN THE CHURCH

Duerksen and Dyrness (*Seeking Church*, pp. 151–73) identify five 'ecclesial markers' that signal the transformative presence of the church – normative markers of the church, common across time and location:

- Wherever the story of Christ is heard and obeyed.
- Wherever a community forms around the story.
- Wherever this community responds to this story in prayer and praise.
- Wherever this community seeks to live in peace with each other and their wider community.
- Whenever an impulse drives this community to witness to Christ and the transformation the Spirit has brought about.

There we can say the emergent dynamic of the church is present.

These are excellent as markers of individual churches or congregations, but they fail to address issues of accountability, historic tradition, or mutual recognition and the need to receive from other churches. The Anglican Communion addresses these through the Lambeth Quadrilateral, which upholds the Holy Scriptures as containing all things necessary for salvation; the Creeds (and in particular the Apostles' and Nicene) as a sufficient statement of faith; the dominical sacraments of Baptism and Holy Communion; and the historic episcopate, locally adapted.

So when the priest who planted Harvest New Anglican Church's cell church on the Island of Thanet was asked in what way his church was Anglican, his reply was, 'We teach the scriptures, believe the creeds, celebrate baptism and holy communion using the (simplified) rites of our denomination and are accountable to and licenced by our bishop.' The plant was also a deanery-approved initiative. The Quadrilateral, of course, includes word and sacrament. Not as tick-box markers of an authentic church, but as the primary means of grace. (For a contemporary exposition of word and sacrament, see Pickard, *Seeking the Church*, pp. 190–208.) The Quadrilateral should not be seen as substitute for the characteristics identified by Duerksen and Dyrness, rather it provides the denominational tradition and structure within which they can flourish.

Bishop Pickard writes of 'the unfinished, future oriented, joyful freedom into which the church is called as it follows the ways of God in the world' (*Seeking the Church*, p. 210). It is this deeply rooted joyful freedom in Christ in which we are invited to participate as a community of disciples on mission with Jesus.

Notes

1 Anglican Communion, 'Season of Intentional Discipleship and Disciple-Making', *Anglican Communion*, https://www.anglicancommunion.org/mission/intentional-discipleship/discipleship-path/discipleship.aspx, accessed 30.08.2023.

2 Anglican Communion, 2019, 'Living and Sharing Jesus-Shaped Life', London: Anglican Consultative Council, available from https://www.anglicancommunion.org/media/424526/jsl-booklet-2019_en.pdf, accessed 20.08.2023.

3 See Ruth A. Meyers, 2014, *Missional Worship, Worshipful Mission*, Grand Rapids, MI: Eerdmans; Alan Kreider and Eleanor Kreider, 2009, *Worship and Mission after Christendom*, Milton Keynes: Paternoster Press.

4 For this paragraph on worship in Matthew, I acknowledge the insights of Marcus Green in his excellent 2004 book on worship, *Salvation's Song*, Eastbourne: Survivor.

5 Church Army research unit report 'The Day of Small Things' recognized 20 models of fresh expression of church (using models in a different sense) and focused on the most frequent 14.

6 Avery Dulles, 1986, *Models of the Church*, 2nd edn, Dublin: Gill & Macmillan; 5 out of his 6 had arisen since the middle of the twentieth century.

7 House of Bishops 'Church Planting and the Mission of the Church', formerly available at https://www.churchofengland.org/sites/default/files/2018-06/CHURCH%20PLANTING%20AND%20THE%20MISSION%20OF%20THE%20CHURCH%20-%20June%202018_0.pdf.

8 Talk given at the national Multiply Conference, 25 June 2020.

9 Resourcing Mission Group Interim Report 2005, available at https://www.churchofengland.org/sites/default/files/2018-10/gs1580a-with-annexes-accountability-and-transparency-within-the-church-of-england-report-of-the-group-established-by-the-archbishops.pdf, accessed 01.11.2023.

10

Becoming a 'Jesus on Mission'-Shaped Church

> The church is apostolic in its being and in its doing when it embodies Jesus' mission and patterns its actions after his. (Guder, *Missional Church*, p. 133)

'Together as the Church we are the Body of Christ, a community of missionary disciples. This missionary discipleship is the foundation of every Christian's vocation to work and service' (General Synod, 'Developing Discipleship', quoting Pope Francis, *Evangelii Gaudium*). If we are committed to the church being 'a community of disciples on mission with Jesus', how could that become a reality? How do we become a 'Jesus on mission'-shaped church? What is needed? Eventually there will likely be some re-organization, but changing structures changes very little, unless it comes as a result of a new vision of the church. What is needed first is a deep engagement with the Scriptures – the Gospels in particular, and the most careful attention to the local missionary leadership of the Holy Spirit. My hope is that this process will lead to a congregational pattern or rhythm of life and witness, made up of 'Jesus on mission'-shaped habits. Ultimately it is new habits which change the default setting as they establish the new normal.

Scripture

The Bible is a missional book. Christopher Wright begins his exposition of 'the Bible's Grand Narrative' by stating 'Mission is what the Bible is all about; we could as meaningfully talk of the missional basis of the Bible as of the biblical basis of mission' (*Mission of God*, p. 29). The Bible sets out the grand narrative of the mission of God and of our reception of it and participation in it. But the Bible is not merely a source of revelation, let alone of theological propositions. It is also a text through which God acts. The Old Testament prophets frequently recall that 'the word of God came to me.' In the same tradition the letter to the Hebrews recognizes 'the word of God' as 'living and active, sharper than any two-edged sword ... able to judge the thoughts and intentions of the heart' (Heb. 4.12). It is well put by Clark Pinnock:

> Scripture is a means of grace by which God's Word continues to come to us. It is not so much a static collection of timeless oracles as it is the place to stand when one wants to be in God's presence and learn of him. Through the Bible we can orient ourselves to the objective revelation that has been given and through the Spirit enter into it personally and dynamically. (Pinnock, *Flame of Love*, p. 164)

As Pinnock says, it is through the work of the Spirit that the text of Scripture becomes reality in life and mission. The Spirit is both the inspirer of scripture (2 Peter 1.21) and its illuminator in each context:

> A consequence of ... the Spirit's necessary role in biblical construction and interpretation is illumination: the need to pray that God reveal anew through his written Word. Human understanding of God's written revelation is 'not a secure possession, or a merit, but a gift from the divine mercy, continually to be received as such, and only as such.' Nor is this merely a once-for-all gift. It is always on loan, radically contingent on the Son's and Spirit's action. (Work, *Living and Active*, p. 272, quoting Barth, *Church Dogmatics*, 1.2.697)

Any church which wishes to be a 'Jesus on mission'-shaped church needs to give regular disciplined attention to Scripture, particularly the Gospels, as 'the place to stand'. This place to stand is the only place to start. The Holy Spirit is not only the

BECOMING A 'JESUS ON MISSION'-SHAPED CHURCH

illuminator, but also the missionary leader. We have already seen, in a previous chapter, that the inspired interpretation of Scripture is a primary feature of the church's mission in Acts. So if the missionary Spirit is both the illuminator of Scripture and the leader of local mission, then the attentive reading of Scripture, as a corporate discipline, is vital for the local church's faithful participation in that mission. Scripture reveals the Holy Spirit to be both profoundly trustworthy, a stable, reliable, Christlike presence; and yet, in the mission of the church, an unpredictable actor who continually takes the church by surprise. The Spirit is the 'Boundary-Breaker', the 'Plan-Disruptor' and the 'Surprise-Bringer' but also the 'Communicative Spirit' (Guthrie, *Creator Spirit*, pp. 9–12). The Spirit speaks. Jesus promised, 'He will take what is mine and declare it to you' (John 16.14). The Spirit speaks through scripture, and scripture is the ultimate test of any claim to the Spirit's speech.

The purpose of such attentive corporate reading is not merely pragmatic – the need for immediate discernment. It is transformative; to shape us into those who are able to discern:

> The Spirit who inspired and preserved the scriptures illuminates, teaches, guides convicts and transforms through that Word today. The Word is alive quick and powerful because of the Holy Spirit's ministry. The relation of the Spirit to Scripture is based on that of the Spirit to Christ. Even as the Spirit formed Christ in Mary, so the Spirit uses Scripture to form Christ in believers. (Land, *Pentecostal Spirituality*, p. 100)

Scripture after all is the 'word about the Word'. The 'one thing' for which Jesus commended Mary of Bethany was attentiveness to his teaching (Luke 10.38–42). As the New Testament church grew, its leaders were soon aware of the danger of being diverted from that primary task. 'It is not right that we should neglect the word of God order to wait on tables ... we, for our part, will devote ourselves to prayer and to serving the word' (Acts 6.2–4).

The disciplined reading of scripture has played a central role at various times of transition in the church's mission to the world. It lies at the heart of monastic life, and has done so from its beginning. 'Whatever you do, do it according to the testimony of the holy Scriptures', said Abba Antony (Harmless, *Desert Christians*, p. 168). Monastic missional movements from Columba to Boniface were sustained by this and other disciplines. The monastic practice of *Lectio Divina* was developed by Benedict in the sixth century, from earlier traditions, although it did not take its full current form until the twelfth century. The monastic life which renewed church and society, and was critical for mission, was soaked in scripture through disciplined reflective reading. Thanks to the development of printing, and the first legal translation of the Bible into English, the Reformation emphasis on *sola scriptura* took cultural shape in England, with Archbishop Thomas Cranmer's daily offices. Cranmer took the monastic disciplined reading of scripture into the pattern of worship of the parish churches – a missional gift which we need to reappropriate for the mission of the church today. A century before the birth of the Protestant missionary movement, it was Ignatius of Loyola's Jesuits who initiated a programme on international cross-cultural mission. In this they were resourced by their founder's spiritual exercises, particularly his emphasis on the imaginative reading of scripture.

Every major cultural shift has required a reappropriation of scripture in response to new situations and the new questions they raise. So today, if Jesus is still on mission with his disciples, then the four Gospels (supplemented by Luke's second volume, Acts) become our primary sources. For those Christian traditions who use the Revised Common Lectionary, it is a gift, as we read from the Gospels at each communion service and focus on one each liturgical year.[1] The Church of Scotland's 'A Church Without Walls' report proposed that:

> The shape of the church in each village, town and city of Scotland will emerge as we take time to 'follow Jesus' through a saturation in the Gospel stories. We recommend that each congregation choose one of the Gospel writers as their pastor for the coming year and let them teach us about following Jesus. (pp. 17–18)

BECOMING A 'JESUS ON MISSION'-SHAPED CHURCH

Sermons from the Gospels will help. Consistent teaching based on sound scholarship is essential, but is not sufficient on its own. Discernment is a communal exercise. It has to be supplemented by gatherings for meditation and sharing. There are number of practices which can facilitate this – *Lectio Divina*, Ignatian imaginative reading, various forms of scripture meditation, and most recently 'Dwelling in the Word' (developed in the USA by Church Innovations, but championed in the UK by the Church Mission Society).[2] If the gift of missional illumination through the Scripture is 'always on loan' it requires a permanent practice of attentive reading, not just at the beginning of a new initiative, but throughout a church's life.

Whichever practice is chosen, the purpose has to be an 'inside-out' one: how to learn from scripture to join in with what Jesus is doing by the Spirit in the community or communities where we are located or to which we are sent. This will involve bringing questions to the text which arise from living out the faith in these communities. To repeat a quotation from Chapter 3, 'Discipleship emerges out of prayer, study, dialogue, and worship by a community learning to ask the questions of obedience, as they are engaged directly in mission' (Roxburgh, *The Missionary Congregation*, p. 66). This places reflection on scripture at the very heart of discipline and discernment.

Discernment

'The church is called and sent to participate in God's mission in the world. The responsibility of the church is to discern where and how this mission is unfolding' (Van Gelder, *The Ministry of the Missional Church*, p. 59). If God the Holy Trinity is active in mission in the world, and the church is both the fruit of God's mission, and finds its identity through participating in it, then discernment is the primary capacity required to join in with that mission in each context. (For more on discernment and leadership see Cray, *Discerning Leadership*.)

The church itself must continually undergo the process of discerning the spirits and of distinguishing what is essential and what is peripheral to Christian belief and practice, as the early church did. They must continually discern how the universal promise in Jesus might best be enacted in each particular context. (Lois Malcolm in Dehmlow-Dreier, *Created and Led by the Spirit*, p. 65)

This process of discernment will normally be corporate. Ownership normally comes through participation. There are no short cuts in the discernment process. There is a danger of cloning previous experience rather that doing the patient work of listening to the Holy Spirit in the context. Cloning happens when church leaders try to reproduce something which has proved effective in one context, without paying proper attention to the new context and the activity of the Holy Spirit in it. Or it happens when an old, well-established practice which is no longer fruitful is continued or revived without any attempt at prior discernment. All neighbourhoods and networks change over time, and inattention to such changes can easily result in a loss of touch. Discernment involves a faithful stewardship of the gospel we have received, combined with attentiveness to its engagement with its current context. This may result in discoveries of facets of our great tradition that had not previously been grasped or understood as we see it engage and transform in settings with which we were not previously familiar: a phenomenon which has occurred many times before in the history of Christian mission.

We western people love predictability. It is part of our scientific methodology and one of the ways we seek to control our environment and circumstances. But we should not be surprised at the unpredictability of the Holy Spirit's actions. The Holy Spirit is wiser than us, and we are not the ones in control. The Spirit is the active local leader of the church's mission! Unpredictability is not the same as unreliability. 'The Holy Spirit is not tame – and therefore he is not completely predictable. However, the Holy Spirit is the Spirit of Jesus Christ, and

BECOMING A 'JESUS ON MISSION'-SHAPED CHURCH

therefore he does bring wisdom, truth and power' (Sunquist, *Understanding Christian Mission*, p. 234).

If God is living and active, then ... church planting (or revitalizing) should attend to discerning God's initiatives in their lives and contexts ... It requires that we engage the living Trinity now, on the ground, in the mission that is around us and ahead of us. (Branson in Branson and Warnes, *Starting Missional Churches*, p. 37)

the energy intensive task of building new households of faith is initiated and undergirded by the primary agency of the Spirit. (Dehmlow-Dreier, 'Planting Missional Congregations', p. 4)

The church needs navigators, tuned to the voice of God, not map-readers. (Gibbs, *Leadership Next*, p. 58)

Lessons from fresh expressions

After several years of observing the birthing of fresh expressions of church in the UK, the ecumenical Fresh Expressions Team developed a recommended 'journey', a process for planting, which it depicted diagrammatically (for more detail, see www.freshexpressions.org.uk; Cray, 'Communities of the Kingdom', pp. 19–26; Moynagh, *Church for Every Context*, pp. 208–20):

The listening process is not just a starting point, but the ongoing foundation for all that develops. Discernment is the key capacity from start to new start. Serving – being good news before sharing good news – provides the points of contact and establishes the new congregation as one seeing the kingdom for and in its community. The essence of the church itself is community. Building community and mutual relationships, rather than just ministering to unconnected individuals, is vital if the fresh expression is to be a real community rather than a weekly event. From the beginning, the call is to long-term discipleship within a community of disciples. A public gathering for worship can then be shaped which takes proper note both of the gospel and its traditions *and* of the specific people and context for whom it is intended. (A frequent mistake is to start with an act of worship before relationships have been formed that would guide the design of that act of worship.) This is an incarnational approach, not an attractional one.

The intention is not to impose a strict linear approach – which would be counter-intuitive to the emphasis on discernment – but rather to demonstrate from experience of the Spirit's leading why 'normally' certain things are best done before others. Once these underlying values become instinctive a more flexible journey becomes possible. The suggested sequence is like the scales which musicians have to master before they can improvise. Discernment is necessary at every stage and every transition in this model. It underpins the whole.

'The shape of empowered mission is not arrived at ideologically, or even pragmatically. In mission we ask not just "Is this action good and necessary?" We also ask, "Where is God leading? Is this God's undertaking?" ... Spirit leadership is central' (Pinnock, *Flame of Love*, p. 145). Local contextual discernment has a number of different dimensions. (For more detail, see Cray, *Discerning Leadership* and 'Discernment as the Key to Planting Missional Churches'.) All are for the purpose of listening to God; but some are direct, through prayer, scripture, prayer walking and so forth, and some are indirect: listening to him through our fellow church members, and above all through the local community. 'Knitworking' (Brown in Branson and Warnes, *Starting Missional Churches*, p. 68) is networking with people and their local connections, forming community as you network – gathering local history and published census information, listening to the memories of local history keepers and the stories of the people we meet. All these provide the raw material for discernment, which involves analysis as well as prayer and spiritual intuition. 'We began with meeting people and learning to listen to their stories' (MacMillan in Branson and Warnes, *Starting Missional Churches*, p. 112). The aim is to identify needs that can be met, appropriate opportunities to exercise the gifts the team bring, and to identify doorkeepers to the community or network, sometimes known as 'people of peace'. If this is to be achieved successfully, 'Church planters need to engage the practices that tune our lives to God' (Branson in Branson and Warnes, *Starting Missional Churches*, p. 38). This approach, equally applicable to the renewal of contextual mission, requires a congregation to develop some spiritual skills and qualities to enhance their capacity for discernment. John V. Taylor wrote that, 'The main concerns of any missionary training ... should be to help people to become more receptive to the revelation of God. We have greatly extended out power to transmit, to communicate ... but not our power to receive' (Taylor, *The Go-Between God*, pp. 65 and 70). These principles are equally applicable to any church trying to reconnect to the mission of God in its context.

In response to Pentecost, and in preparation for following the missionary Spirit, the early church 'devoted themselves to the apostles' teaching and fellowship, to the breaking of bread and the prayers' (Acts 2.42). They paid disciplined attention to the means of grace in order to cultivate their rootedness in Christ – their spiritual immune system – and so increased their flexibility, their capacity to identify the Spirit's leading. Openness to the new leading of the Spirit requires deep roots in the ways of the Spirit in the Church. Appropriate spiritual disciplines help develop 'the personal and corporate characteristics needed for a ... group to be vulnerable to God, sensitive to the Spirit's initiatives, constantly reflecting and learning, and ready to be engaged in God's initiatives' (Warnes in Branson and Warnes, *Starting Missional Churches*, p. 139). As discernment proceeds, often one step at a time, the further requirement is faith, the willingness to follow courageously into where that Spirit is leading.

Learning missional habits from Jesus

> We cannot mimic Jesus' earthly mission in a one-to-one fashion. Nor can we afford to confuse our mission with his singular role in God's saving purpose. Nevertheless, if we truly believe that Jesus' mission is the concrete and climactic expression of the mission of God in history, then how can we *not* let it profoundly shape us? (Flemming, *Recovering the Full Mission of God*, p. 82)

How do churches located in, and called to, a specific place continue to learn from the itinerant ministries of Jesus and the apostles? In Chapter 4 we learned that the successor to physical itinerancy is attentiveness to the leadership and initiatives of the Holy Spirit (Johnson, *Prophetic Jesus*, p. 127). The contrast between residential and itinerant ministries is not as substantial as it may seem. Jesus had a home base in Capernaum for part of his Galilean ministry (Ghering, *House Church and Mission*, pp. 31ff.) and probably another in Bethany for his visits to Jerusalem (pp. 43–4). Paul spent 18 months in Corinth (Acts 18.11). Church gatherings, I have suggested, are to be seen as fuel stops along the way and part of the rhythm of being on mission with Jesus.

It is Spirit-empowered habit that will establish a new default setting. The consequence of the outpouring of the Spirit at Pentecost was a set of habits that were consistent with the teaching of Jesus (Acts 2.42). But Acts is the second volume of two, and it needs to be read in the light of the first, Luke's Gospel. For many of that initial group, empowered by the Spirit that day,

BECOMING A 'JESUS ON MISSION'-SHAPED CHURCH

these were the second set of habits that had been formed in them by Jesus. Some of them had experienced three years of discipleship in mission in his company: a three-year training in missional practice with Jesus.

From the Gospels we learn some core practices that are characteristic of a community of disciples on mission with Jesus. It is through practices like these that a church can act its way into a new way of seeing and being the church.

'Good news bearers'

It is easy to forget that 'gospel' means 'good news'. Disciples on mission with Jesus are good news bearers. Jesus, and John the Baptist before him (Matt. 3.2), defined that good news as 'the kingdom of God has come near' (Mark 1.14–15). When the disciples were sent out, the message was the same (Luke 9.2; 10.9). The forgiveness of sins is, of course, good news, but the kingdom is more than that. God has intervened in Christ to restore his rule and put his world right, and part of it is a reality now. Communities of disciples are 'for' their communities, they want God's best for their communities in the light of the kingdom. By the presence and power of the Holy Spirit, the kingdom of God is 'now' as well as 'not yet' and these disciples have a glimpse of what the kingdom can mean in their contexts and, by the Spirit, seek to bring it to bear in their contexts. Jesus called them the salt of the earth – referring to their influence scattered through society, and the light of the world – referring to their impact as a community. Yes, it requires repentance, as well as faith, to enter the kingdom. But repentance is turning to something better, as in the parables of the treasure in field and the pearl of great price. Disciples on mission with Jesus seek to bring foretastes of that better way into the present, and provide opportunities to turn to it. They are good news bearers in word and deed.

'Boundary breakers'

Jesus' ministry was characterized by his commitment to those who were weaker, considered of less worth, alien or in some way 'other':

> This approach is what Jesus modelled to us in his incarnation. Jesus poured himself out for the sake of the world. Jesus befriended disreputable people and refused to condemn the unrighteous. Jesus loved women and children and the poor – the hidden ones, the little ones, the marginalized, the outsiders. (Ross, 'Pioneering Missiologies', p. 31)

His disciples accompanied him and were on a learning curve in all these incidents. To be disciples on mission with him today requires the same. No one is excluded from the offer of good news, but carrying the good news to the excluded in any place requires the crossing of whatever social, cultural or religious boundaries are in place at the time. The gut instinct and motivation for this is compassion, as it was for Jesus (Mark 6.34; Matt. 9.33–38), who, out of compassion, still sends labourers into his harvest field. The Holy Spirit is given to disciples for this very purpose (Acts 1.8). Disciples on mission with Jesus are boundary breakers.

'Slow walkers'

On a pilgrimage to the Holy Land, Daniel Hardy remarked on the significance of Jesus walking. 'He was walking, step by step through the land, and after every set of steps he met someone, stood by someone, one to one' (Hardy, *Wording a Radiance*, pp. 79–83). It was on my own pilgrimage that I realized how much and how far Jesus walked. Mission with Jesus is at walking pace. I was introduced to the practice of slow walking when we protested about proposed fracking outside our village in North Yorkshire. Walking as a group, as slow as we possibly could, in front of the lorries bringing in the equipment to drill and frack for shale gas. Slowing the progress of something we considered a threat to our community and our climate. Disciples on mission with Jesus go slowly, not just to challenge evil, but because like him they wish to attend fully to the people they meet along the way. Jesus' ministry is person-centred and interruptible (Mark 5.21–43; see Barrett and Harley, *Being Interrupted*). Hardy observed, 'The Church's walking is not haphazard: it is *careful walking*, for it is walking by the Spirit, displaying Jesus' care to whoever follows' (*Wording a Radiance*, p. 85). This challenges the rush, pressure and stress of much of modern life. As a balance, Jesus' frequent crossing of the lake also created space away from the continual demands of the crowds, showing how he dealt with the constant expectation and pressure put upon him. Disciples on mission with Jesus are slow walkers.

'Grateful guests, generous hosts'

In how many homes were the disciples given hospitality, simply because they were with Jesus? He received hospitality from friends (Mary, Martha and Lazarus), new followers (Zacchaeus) and sometimes from critics (Simon the Pharisee). Many of his conversations were over meals, rarely in his own space. When the disciples were sent out by Jesus, they were to accept the hospitality of whatever home was opened to them. Disciples on mission engage with people in the spaces where those people are comfortable and are the hosts.

But at the same time, 'Jesus is portrayed as a gracious host, welcoming children, tax-collectors, prostitutes and sinners into his presence and therefore offending those who would prefer such guests not to be at his gatherings' (Ross, 'Pioneering Missiologies', p. 34). Similarly, his disciples are to offer hospitality to 'the poor, the crippled, the lame, and the blind … because they cannot repay you' (Luke 14.12–14). Hospitality is a core practice in mission and it is an exchange, not a one-way process. 'This intermingling of guest and host roles in the person of Jesus is part of what makes the story of hospitality so compelling for Christians. Jesus welcomes and needs welcome. Jesus requires that followers depend on and provide hospitality' (Pohl, *Making Room*, p. 17). Sometimes, those who receive Jesus or his disciples as their guest discover him as their host, as with the disciples on the road to Emmaus. 'Think of Jesus on the Emmaus road as travelling pilgrim and stranger, recognized as host and who he was in the breaking of bread during a meal involving an act of hospitality' (Ross, 'Pioneering Missiologies', p. 34).

David Fitch proposes that Christians are to be a 'faithful presence' in three different locations. We gather around the table where Jesus is the host ('The Lord is here, his Spirit is with us') to break bread and share wine in remembrance of him, as he commanded. Here we are refocused and re-envisioned, as were the two disciples in their home at Emmaus where Jesus took the role of the host. The second space is where we Christians are the hosts, the faithful presence, and open our homes to friends, neighbours and strangers. The third space is when we come as guests dependent on our hosts hospitality, being the faithful presence of Christ there (Fitch, *Faithful Presence*). Disciples on mission with Jesus are to be generous hosts and grateful guests.

'Cross bearers'

There is no escaping the fact that discipleship is cross-shaped and costly. 'Then he said to them all, "If any want to become my followers, let them deny themselves and take up their cross daily and follow me"' (Luke 9.23). St Paul wrote, 'And he died for all, so that those who live might live no longer for themselves, but for him who died and was raised for them' (2 Cor. 5.15). There is a public costliness involved in living for him. Although the kingdom of God offers the world something far better than anything else it prizes, it also involves a surrender to the king. 'Christianity is a way of seeing the world which may go against the grain. This is what Jesus offers us – an upside-down kingdom, an alternative reality, a remedial perspective' (Ross, 'Pioneering Missiologies', p. 30). The good news of a better way was and is bad news to those who were invested in the way things were. The call to discipleship can create misunderstanding and cause division. Jesus warned that it could divide families. Disciples are vulnerable, 'Sheep among wolves'. In many parts of the world, public Christian faith results in persecution. Those whom Jesus calls must count the cost. The daily denying of self, for the love of Christ and the love of others is a hallmark of the Christian life. Disciples on mission with Jesus are cross bearers.

'Disciple makers'

Disciples on mission with Jesus make disciples. They are 'fishers of people'. They help others to respond to Jesus' invitation to follow, just as they had responded themselves. This should be seen as a natural consequence of the habits already outlined. When disciples bear good news, go out of their way to engage with the marginalized, attend patiently to people and give and receive hospitality generously, while publicly owning their faith even when that is costly, they establish a setting for faith sharing that has integrity and has demonstrated the fruit of lives committed to Jesus. Disciple making involves sharing ourselves as much as our beliefs (1 Thess. 2.8). Nor is it a matter of standard phrases. Jesus' public teaching had variety. It used questions and parables, engaging the imagination of his listeners, making his hearers question the way they saw the world and opening their eyes to the kingdom of God.

Disciple makers are always concerned that their conversation partners become Jesus' disciples, and not their own disciples. Becoming a disciple always involves an encounter with the cross. But the gracious offer of forgiveness should never be separated from the call to follow, but not to follow alone. This call is into a community of followers. Discipleship is always personal, but essentially corporate. Disciples on mission with Jesus are disciple makers.

'Jesus dwellers'

Most important of all, disciples on mission with Jesus stay close to Jesus. He called the twelve to 'be with him'. Much of the time they were with him on mission, sometimes he called them apart for focused time with him (not always successfully!). They see Jesus at prayer and ask him to teach them. On the night before he was betrayed, he told them to abide in him, to make him their environment, and that apart from him they could do nothing (John 15). When he commissioned them, he promised he would always be with them. Proximity, intimacy with Jesus is the key to discipleship. This intimacy is sustained by the traditional means of grace and by the habits taught in the Sermon on the Mount (Matt. 6) and those established by the Spirit on the day of Pentecost (Acts 2.42). Disciples on mission with Jesus stay close. They are 'Jesus dwellers'.

Rhythm of life

Some churches are developing a rhythm of life, a shared pattern of missional practices to sustain that church's shared life and mission.

> This is not intended as a list of rules as much as a healthy and holistic framework for living. A rule captures and articulates the core values and vocation of a community. It is stable but not static ... to equip those who live by it to serve the kingdom of God, and engage with mission and discipleship wherever Christ sends them. (Cray, Mobsby, Kennedy, *New Monasticism*, pp. 152–3)

One example from Australia is called BELLS:

> *Bless* I will bless three people this week, at least one of whom is not a member of our church.
> *Eat* I will eat with three people this week, at least one of whom is not a member of our church.

BECOMING A 'JESUS ON MISSION'-SHAPED CHURCH

Listen I will spend at least one period of the week listening for the Spirit's voice.
Learn I will spend at least one period of the week learning Christ.
Sent I will journal throughout the week about all the ways I alerted others to the universal reign of God through Christ.
(Frost, *Surprise the World*, pp. 21ff.)

The author, Michael Frost, points out 'that each habit is designed to release a certain value in the life of the person who practices them' (p. 23). Generosity, hospitality, being Spirit-led, and so on, grow through habit.

The Moot community in the city of London has a rhythm of life encapsulated in six words: presence, acceptance, creativity, hospitality, accountability and balance. They say:

A Rhythm of Life is not a full symphony with every instrument written up, but rather the background beat that keeps everything else in order, calling us back on track, reminding us of the type of music we want to play, and the way we want to live, creatively exploring our spirituality and the Divine. ('Rhythm', *Moot St Mary Aldermary*, https://www.mootcommunity.org)

Many of the features of mission with Jesus are practices that can become positive habits or be part of such a rhythm of life:

Good news bearers – seek to bring some aspect of Jesus kingdom to bear on your context each week.
Boundary breakers – reach to someone beyond your regular circle this week.
Slow walkers – give thoughtful attention to someone, from outside the church, this week.
Generous guests – be open to receive hospitality or welcome from somewhere where you are not in control this week.
Cross bearers – be obedient to Jesus this week, irrespective of the cost.
Disciple makers – pray for unforced opportunities to share what it means for you follow Jesus this week.

Jesus dwellers – create time and space to be alone with Jesus this week.

Church inside out

This process will require some change; some turning of the church from an inward focus to an outward one. Hopefully engagement with the Gospels will raise questions and provide the motivation for changes of emphasis and consequently of structures and patterns of church life. In *Mission-Shaped Church* we wrote, 'The change is to an outward focus: from a "come to us approach" to a "we will go to you" attitude, embodying the gospel where people are, rather than embodying it where we are, and in ways we prefer' (*Mission-Shaped Church*, p. 41). Thus opening up the congregation to a mixed economy/ecology approach. The aim is to turn a church inside out. As Archbishop Stephen Cottrell put it, making it less an 'eat in' community and more a 'take away' one. Professor Eddie Gibbs proposed a 'Focus on ministry *by* the church in the world, rather than ministry *in* the church that is largely confined to the existing members' (Gibbs, *Leadership Next*, p. 26). For example, were I to lead a local congregation again, every small group or mid-week gathering we had would have a specific missional purpose, irrespective of their other reason for gathering.

Centre and edge

Almost by definition, a community of disciples on mission with Jesus will sometimes find itself being led where it has not been before, beyond the edges of its familiar life and ministry. At a Fresh Expressions conference in Germany, Bishop Steven Croft said, 'We have learned to connect the centre to the edge', meaning that those in authority at the 'centre' were both listening to the voices from the pioneering edge of the church's mission, and were giving them greater recognition. The centre and edge language is problematic if is merely about power. But if the edge

BECOMING A 'JESUS ON MISSION'-SHAPED CHURCH

is recognized as the place where the church engages with people and contexts it would not otherwise reach, or with emerging cultural trends which may well become main stream, then the relationship between the two becomes mutual as mission at the edge informs the centre, and the centre supports and empowers mission on the edge. The dynamic becomes one of empowerment rather than control.

For Clare Watkins, the church is to be 'ek-centric': 'an "ek-centricity" in which church is both centred and called out from itself' (*Disclosing Church*, p. 121). 'The centre holds fast, whilst at the same time ecclesial dynamics work centrifugally, compelling energies out from the centre itself' (p. 128). For Watkins, this overcomes the artificial tension between mission and maintenance:

> What becomes clear is that ways of real living are needed which do not offer 'maintenance' or 'mission' as alternatives or differentiated tasks; but rather, our understanding of church needs to be construed in terms which newly identify what is to be 'maintained' and how, in order that 'mission' can be served out from the centre toward the world. (Watkins, *Disclosing Church*, p. 122)

She concludes, 'Learning this lesson "on the edges" is what can enable us to review our institutional centres as places of service to that work of the Spirit, rather than as some static tabernacle of "the true Church"' (p. 156). Bishop Croft's original statement was referring to denominational and diocesan centres, but the same principles apply to the local church.

Watkins sees mission at the edge as opening up new centres of mission which are themselves centred sets – and so on. 'It is as if we were seeing, at the places on the edge, new kinds of centres for church break open; and when they broke open, it was expressions of church without hard edges that were expressed' (p. 155). This breaking open of new kinds of centres for church is critical in the UK, where fewer than half of people in Britain said they are Christian in the latest census (Office for National Statistics, 'Religion, England and Wales', Census

2021). The majority of the majority who do not go to church show little indication that they would do so if we made it more inviting, despite our best efforts. But the research shows that the majority are not atheists and many are 'maybes, doubters and don't knows' (Linda Woodhead, 'The Rise of "No Religion" in Britain'). These, in particular, are ones to whom communities of disciples on mission with Jesus are called today.

What does this look like?

The church is essentially itinerant because it is apostolic, a sent community. The church is 'a community of disciples on mission with Jesus'. Both words, discipleship and mission, are essential, and they are inseparable. The presence of Jesus is the key to being a disciple, and Jesus is on mission.

This requires it to be a community continually open to the initiatives of the missionary Spirit. To fulfil this calling, practitioners will need to immerse themselves both in their context, and in the Gospels, to learn how Jesus engaged with Israel in his day. Because 'What Jesus was to Israel, the Church must now be for the world' (N. T. Wright, *The Challenge of Jesus*, p. 34) locally, not just in principle.

This company on mission mixes with all sorts of marginal and excluded people. Jesus continually breaks with social norms. He touches lepers. He and his disciples share meals with people well outside the socially accepted boundaries of the people of God of his day. Both within their own number, and engaging with those outside, the disciples learn, to quote Rowan Williams again:

> Being where Jesus is means finding yourself in the company of the people whose company Jesus seeks and keeps. So, when Jesus goes to be in the company of the excluded, the wretched, the self-hating, the poor, the diseased, that's where you're going to find yourself. If you are going to be where Jesus is, if your discipleship is not intermittent but a way of being, that's where you are going to find yourself, in the same sort of

BECOMING A 'JESUS ON MISSION'-SHAPED CHURCH

human company that he is in. This is once again an important reminder that our discipleship is not about choosing our company beyond choosing the company of Jesus. (Williams, *Being Disciples*, Kindle edn p. 10)

Clearly there is a distinction between the disciples being on mission with Jesus when he was physically present and with his post-resurrection unseen presence through the Holy Spirit. He prepares them for this change by sending out first twelve, then seventy. When the seventy return, he tells them he saw the consequences of their ministry as it took place (Luke 10.18). When he commissions them finally, he promises to be with them. Luke says that his first volume was about 'what Jesus began to do and teach'. His second volume is about Jesus' continuing ministry. Qualitatively there is no difference.

What does such a church 'on the move' look like? It cannot be a bounded set, made up exclusively of the totally committed.

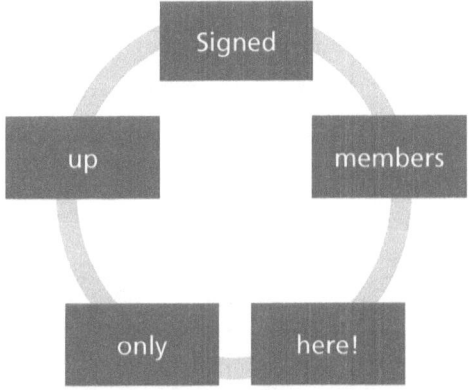

That is not what I mean by disciples on mission with Jesus. The New Testament disciples' frequent squabbles and misunderstandings would not make that a very encouraging picture.

The Gospels often chide the church for trying to act as a kind of Border Agency Police for heaven; or Christians offering their well-meaning services to Jesus as Immigration Control Officers for paradise. But Jesus isn't interested in our proposals to police the boundaries of his kingdom, thank you. (Percy, *The Humble Church*, p. 152)

There has to be a generous hospitality. There has to be the warm invitation to belong, while exploring believing. A church on the move has to be a centred set, welcoming all who are open to journey with Jesus, but with a deep underlying call to wholehearted discipleship.

Clare Watkins writes of 'an account of church which is not so much bounded as centred and edgeless' (*Disclosing Church*, p. 235). Nigel Rooms and Elli Wort's research on churches in the north of England concluded that 'churches need fuzzy boundaries. Not hard boundaries to the outside, not no boundary at all, but fuzzy ones where one can't quite tell who is "in" and who is "out"' (*Fuzzy Church*, p. xi).

In a centred set those at the heart are deeply committed to Jesus, but their community is welcoming and inviting to every sort of enquirer. 'The discipleship for which Jesus called was both open and committed', says James Dunn, adding, 'For many people today, Christians included, these two are a contradiction in terms' (Dunn, *Jesus' Call to Discipleship*, p. 126). Ultimately what will matter is not how near or far people are to Jesus, but in which direction they are travelling.

BECOMING A 'JESUS ON MISSION'-SHAPED CHURCH

This missional mobility is not at the cost of pastoral care. The church on the move cares for those in need. It is what James McClendon calls 'an open circle of care' (*Ethics*, p. 53). As Daniel Hardy observed:

> This wandering Jesus shows us what it means to care for the Church and what it means for the Church to care for its members. We learn from Jesus that deep care is right here, where he walks, and that deep care engages deeply with what we are and where we are. This shows us the way forward: not to over-analyse what the Church should do, but to learn what next to do through direct engagement with him who meets us where we are. This takes patience and waiting. (*Wording a Radiance*, p. 84)

So as Jesus goes on mission, he has the twelve with him, and a larger group of disciples, men and women, there are crowds gathering for a time, and so on. There are various levels of commitment and enquiry in this travelling company, all centred on the person of Jesus, all exposed to his mission to the villages of Galilee. They see the kingdom in action as they learn about its way of life and the person who is at its centre and consider his call to discipleship. This is a vision for church as a community of missional disciples, inviting others into their pilgrimage, and, as much as possible into their mission: serving their community alongside Christ's apprentices, to learn that service and self-sacrifice lies at the heart of that apprenticeship, and is its ethical core. To quote T. W. Manson, a scholar from a previous generation, 'In the Kingdom of God service is not a stepping stone to nobility, it is nobility, the only kind of nobility that is recognized' (Manson, *The Church's Ministry*, p. 27). Such a church proclaims Jesus and his kingdom, sets out to bless, and continually invites others to journey with them, and to explore a relationship him as they continue to journey with him in mission. But the gospel narratives move inevitably towards the cross. So missional disciples, who serve the risen Lord, will point all who would follow him to that same cross, and to baptism as the means of permanent identification with him in his death and resurrection, and as the cost of discipleship.

Postscript

What is needed, I propose, is a renewed imagination, a change of default setting about the shape of the church, in the light of its missionary nature and its current cultural context in the West. An image of the church, rooted deep into our imaginations, that is more of a movement than a meeting, more about joining Jesus in the community, than Jesus joining us in a building. We need something that is more about our following Jesus in our communities than our getting blessed in church. Something that is more about our being given to the Holy Spirit than the Holy Spirit being given to us. What is needed is to recover Christ's original call to be a community of disciples on mission with him.

This is both an ecclesiology for our current western context, and also a move to a more dynamic understanding of ecclesiology, where the key metaphors engage with one another like the colours in a kaleidoscope: always present but varying in scale and pattern depending on cultural context, though always uniting in a pattern for that time. The Spirit is the agent of transformation, but the inspiration is always to portray Christ. 'The Church is therefore a living organism, always changing, moving and growing' (Ward, *Liquid Ecclesiology*, p. 45).

In *Mission-Shaped Church* we wrote:

> The Church takes its missionary form through receiving the gifts of the past and the future. At a time of substantial change, the Church of England needs to learn from the Spirit to be more an anticipation of God's future than a society for the preservation of the past. Perhaps our greatest need is of a baptism of imagination about the forms of the Church. (p. 90)

The greatest gift from the past is this original and founding call of Jesus to follow him and join in his mission. It is the work of the missionary Spirit to bring that vocation to life in our day, not just as a contemporary reality but, as it was with Jesus, an anticipation of the future.

BECOMING A 'JESUS ON MISSION'-SHAPED CHURCH

The Spirit enables fidelity to and continuity with apostolic faith but constantly actualizes and particularizes this tradition afresh in the present, so that the truth of Christ is brought alive for ever in new situations with which the church engages in its missionary calling. This is integral to the Spirit's eschatological ministry – to carry the church forward in mission, anticipating here and now in ever-fresh ways the Father's final eschatological desire. ('Eucharistic Presidency' 2:28 quoted in *Mission-Shaped Church*, p. 90)

Incarnational mission, discerning and following the missionary Spirit, the planting of new communities of disciples by contextual mission: these are simply how we are to be the Church in western society for the conceivable future. They are to be the mainstream. We can work towards the point where the default setting for 'church' instinctively includes these values and practices. We look for the time when parish, circuit, deanery and presbytery self-evidently mean being a community of disciples on mission with Jesus.

The church thus lies ahead of us as vocation, every bit as much as it is present to us as identity, community, structure and ritual. (Watkins, *Disclosing Church*, p. 156)

Notes

1 The Revised Common Lectionary runs in three-year cycles; the Gospel readings in the first year (Year A) are taken from the Gospel of Matthew, those in the second year (or Year B) from the Gospel of Mark, and in the third year (or Year C) come from the Gospel of Luke. Portions of the Gospel of John are read throughout Eastertide, and are also used for other liturgical seasons including Advent, Christmastide and Lent where appropriate.

2 'Dwelling in the Word', *Church Mission Society*, https://churchmissionsociety.org/blog/dwelling-in-the-word/, accessed 30.08.2023.

Bibliography

Alexander, Loveday, 2005, *Acts in its Ancient Literary Context*, London: T&T Clark.

——, 2012, 'The Church in the Acts of the Apostles' in *Fresh Expressions in the Mission of the Church*, London: Church House Publishing.

Atkinson, David, 2008, *Renewing the Face of the Earth: A Theological and Pastoral Response to Climate Change*, London: Canterbury Press.

Avis, Paul, 2000, *The Anglican Understanding of the Church*, London: SPCK.

Badcock, Gary, 2009, *The House Where God Lives*, Grand Rapids, MI: Eerdmans.

Baker, Johnny, and Cathy Ross, 2020, *Imagining Mission with John V. Taylor*, London: SCM Press.

Barclay, John M. G., 2015, *Paul and the Gift*, Grand Rapids, MI: Eerdmans.

——, 2020, *Paul and the Power of Grace*, Grand Rapids, MI: Eerdmans.

Barrett, Al, and Ruth Harley, 2020, *Being Interrupted: Reimagining the Church's Mission From the Outside*, London: SCM Press.

Barth, Marcus, 1974, *Ephesians 1–3*, Anchor Bible 34, New York: Doubleday.

Bauckham, Richard, 1996, 'James and the Gentiles' in Ben Witherington (ed.), *History, Literature and Society in the Book of Acts*, Cambridge: Cambridge University Press.

——, 2010, *Bible and Ecology: Rediscovering the Community of Creation*, London: Darton, Longman & Todd.

——, 2011, *Jesus: A Very Short Introduction*, Oxford: Oxford University Press.

——, 2012, *Living Among the Creatures*, Carlisle: Paternoster.

——, and Trevor Hart, 1999, *Hope Against Hope*, London: Darton, Longman & Todd.

Bauman, Zygmunt, 1999, *Culture as Praxis*, London: Sage.

——, 2000, *Liquid Modernity*, Cambridge: Polity.

——, 2010, *44 Letters from the Liquid Modern World*, Cambridge: Polity.

BIBLIOGRAPHY

———, and Keith Tester, 2001, *Conversations with Zygmunt Bauman*, Cambridge: Polity.
Beasley-Murray, George, 1986, *Jesus and the Kingdom of God*, Exeter: Paternoster Press.
———, 1991, *John*, Dallas, TX: Word Biblical Commentary.
Beck, Ulrich, and Elisabeth Beck-Gernsheim, 2002, *Individualization*, London: Sage.
Bell, Colin, and Robert White (eds), 2016, *Creation Care and the Gospel*, Peabody, MA: Hendrickson Publishers.
Bevans, Stephen, and Roger Schroeder, 2004, *Constants in Context*, New York: Orbis Books.
Board of Mission, 2004, *Mission-Shaped Church*, London: Church House Publishing.
Bolsinger, Tod, 2018, *Canoeing the Mountains*, Expanded Edition, Downers Grove, IL: IVP.
Bookless, Dave, 2008, *Planetwise*, Leicester: IVP.
Bosch, David, 1980, *Witness to the World*, London: Marshall Morgan & Scott.
———, 1982, *The Scope of Mission*, CMS Annual Sermon.
———, 1983, 'Evangelism and Social Transformation' in Vinay Kumar Samuel and Chris Sugden (eds), *The Church in Response to Human Need*, Grand Rapids, MI: Eerdmans.
———, 1991, *Transforming Mission*, New York: Orbis Books.
———, 1995, *Believing in the Future*, Leominster: Gracewing.
Branson, Mark Lau, 'Perspectives from the Missional Conversation' in Mark Lau Branson and Nicholas Warnes, 2014 (eds), *Starting Missional Churches*, Downers Grove, IL: IVP, pp. 28–47.
Branson, Mark Lau, and Nicholas Warnes, 2014 (eds), *Starting Missional Churches*, Downers Grove, IL: IVP.
Brown, Craig, 'Gathering Neighbors' in Mark Lau Branson and Nicholas Warnes, 2014 (eds), *Starting Missional Churches*, Downers Grove, IL: IVP, pp. 66–87.
Bruce, F. F., 1959, *The Book of Acts*, Grand Rapids, MI: Eerdmans.
———, 1995, *Epistles to Colossians, Philemon, Ephesians*, NICNT, Grand Rapids, MI: Eerdmans.
Brueggemann, Walter, 1988, *To Pluck Up, to Tear Down: A Commentary on the Book of Jeremiah 1–25*, Grand Rapids, MI: Eerdmans.
Burridge, Richard, 2007, *Imitating Jesus*, Grand Rapids, MI: Eerdmans.
Campbell, Douglas, 2020, *Pauline Dynamics*, Grand Rapids, MI: Eerdmans.
Carson, Don, 'Pauline Inconsistency', *Churchman* 100:1 (1986).
Castells, Manuel, 2009, *The Rise of the Network Society*, 2nd edn, Oxford: Wiley-Blackwell.
Chilton, Bruce, and J. I. H. McDonald, 1987, *Jesus and the Ethics of the Kingdom*, London: SPCK.

Church of Scotland, 2001, 'A Church Without Walls', Edinburgh: St Andrew Press.
Cocksworth, C., 1993, *Evangelical Eucharistic Thought in the Church of England*, Cambridge: Cambridge University Press.
——, 1997, *Holy, Holy, Holy: Worshipping the Trinitarian God*, London: Darton, Longman & Todd.
Cohick, Lynn H., 2020, *The Letter to the Ephesians*, NICNT, Grand Rapids, MI: Eerdmans.
Costas, Orlando, 1982, *Christ Outside the Gate*, New York: Orbis Books.
Couldry, Nick, 2000, *Inside Culture*, London: Sage.
Couldry, Nick, and Andreas Hepp, 2017, *The Mediated Construction of Reality*, Cambridge: Polity.
Cray, Graham A., 2007, *Disciples and Citizens*, Leicester: IVP.
——, 2010, *Discerning Leadership: Co-operating with the Go-Between God*, Cambridge: Grove Leadership.
——, 2010, 'Why is New Monasticism Important to Fresh Expressions' in Graham Cray, Ian Mobsby and Aaron Kennedy (eds), *New Monasticism and Fresh Expressions of Church*, London: Canterbury Press.
——, 2012, 'Communities of the Kingdom' in Graham Cray, Aaron Kennedy and Ian Mobsby (eds), *Fresh Expressions of Church and the Kingdom of God*, London, Canterbury Press.
——, 2017, 'Doors to the Sacred through Fresh Expressions of Church' in Graham Cray, Aaron Kennedy and Ian Mobsby (eds), *Doorways to the Sacred*, London: Canterbury Press.
——, 2017, 'Discernment as the Key to Planting Missional Churches' in Coenie Burger, Frederick Marais and Danie Mouton (eds), *Cultivating Missional Change*, Wellington, South Africa: Biblecor.
Crosby, Michael, 1989, *Spirituality of the Beatitudes*, New York: Orbis Books.
Dehmlow-Dreier, Mary Sue, 2013 (ed.), *Created and Led by the Spirit*, Grand Rapids, MI: Eerdmans.
Dehmlow-Dreier, Mary Sue, 'Planting Missional Congregations: Imagining Together' in Mary Sue Dehmlow-Dreier, 2013 (ed.), *Created and Led by the Spirit*, Grand Rapids, MI: Eerdmans, pp. 3–26.
Doctrine Commission, 1991, *We Believe in the Holy Spirit*, London: Church House Publishing.
Donovan, Vincent, 2002 edition, *Christianity Rediscovered*, London: SCM Press.
Duerksen, Darren T., and William A. Dyrness, 2019, *Seeking Church*, Downers Grove, IL: IVP.
Dulles, Avery, 1986, *Models of the Church*, 2nd edn, Dublin: Gill & Macmillan.

BIBLIOGRAPHY

Dunn, James D. G., 1970, 'Spirit and Kingdom', *Expository Times* 82:2, pp. 36–40.
——, 1975, *Jesus and the Spirit*, London: SCM Press.
——, 1992, *Jesus' Call to Discipleship*, Cambridge: Cambridge University Press.
——, 1996a, *The Acts of the Apostles*, Peterborough: Epworth.
——, 1996b, *Colossians and Philemon*, NIGTC, Grand Rapids, MI: Eerdmans.
——, 1998, *The Theology of Paul the Apostle*, Edinburgh: T&T Clark.
Epistle to Diognetus, 'The Epistle to Diognetus – chapters 5–7', *Early Church Texts*, https://earlychurchtexts.com/public/epistle_to_diognetus.htm (accessed 29.08.2023).
Esler, Philip F., 1989, *Community and Gospel in Luke–Acts*, Cambridge: Cambridge University Press.
Farrow, Douglas, 2004, *Ascension and Ecclesia*, London: Bloomsbury.
Fee, Gordon, 1994, *God's Empowering Presence*, Peabody, MA: Hendrickson Publishing.
Fitch, David, 2016, *Faithful Presence: Seven Disciplines that Shape the Church for Mission*, Downers Grove, IL: IVP.
——, 2018, *Seven Practices for the Church on Mission*, Downers Grove, IL: IVP.
Flemming, Dean, 2013, *Recovering the Full Mission of God*, Downers Grove, IL: IVP Academic.
Flett, John, 2010, *The Witness of God*, Grand Rapids, MI: Eerdmans.
Ford, David, and Daniel Hardy, 1985, *Knowing and Praising God*, Philadelphia, PA: Westminster John Knox Press.
France, R. T., 1985, *Matthew*, Tyndale New Testament Commentaries, Leicester: IVP.
——, 1990, *Divine Government: God's Kingship in the Gospel of Mark*, London: SPCK.
Francis, *Evangelii Gaudium*, Vatican City: Libreria Editrice Vaticana, https://www.vatican.va/content/francesco/en/apost_exhortations/documents/papa-francesco_esortazione-ap_20131124_evangelii-gaudium.html, accessed 1.09.2023.
Frost, Michael, 2016, *Surprise the World*, Carol Stream, IL: NavPress.
Gaventa, Beverly R., 1986, *From Darkness to Light: Aspects of Conversion in the New Testament*, Minneapolis, MN: Fortress Press.
Gay, Doug, 2011, *Remixing the Church*, London: SCM Press.
General Synod, 1994, *Breaking New Ground*, London: Church House Publishing.
——, 1997, *Eucharistic Presidency*, London: Church House Publishing.
——, 2012, *Fresh Expressions in the Mission of the Church*, London: Church House Publishing.

———, 2018, *Church Planting and the Mission of the Church* and *The Mission and Ministry of the Whole Church*, London: Church House Publishing.
Ghering, Roger W., 2004, *House Church and Mission*, Grand Rapids, MI: Baker Academic.
Gibbs, Eddie, 2001, *Church Next*, Leicester: IVP.
———, 2005, *Leadership Next*, Leicester: IVP.
———, 2009, *Churchmorph*, Grand Rapids, MI: Baker.
Giddens, Anthony, 1990, *The Consequences of Modernity*, Cambridge: Polity.
———, 1991, *Modernity and Self-Identity*, Cambridge: Polity.
Gill, Robin, 1992, *Moral Communities*, Exeter: University of Exeter Press.
González, Justo L., 2001, *Acts: The Gospel of the Spirit*, New York: Orbis Books.
Gorman, Michael, 2018, *Abide and Go: Missional Theosis in the Gospel of John*, Eugene, OR: Wipf & Stock.
Green, Marcus, 2004, *Salvation's Song*, Eastbourne: Survivor.
Greenwood, Robin, 1994, *Transforming Priesthood*, London: SPCK.
———, 2013, *Being Church*, London: SPCK.
Grenz, Stanley, 1994, *Theology for the People of God*, Carlisle: Paternoster Press.
Guder, Darrell L., 1998 (ed.), *Missional Church: A Vision for the Sending of the Church in North America*, Grand Rapids, MI: Eerdmans.
———, 2004, *The Incarnation and the Church's Witness*, Eugene, OR: Wipf & Stock.
Gunton, Colin, 1991, *The Promise of Trinitarian Theology*, Edinburgh: T&T Clark.
Guthrie, Steven R., 2011, *Creator Spirit*, Grand Rapids, MI: Baker Academic.
Hardy, Daniel W., 1996, *God's Ways with the World: Thinking and Practising the Christian Faith*, Edinburgh: T&T Clark.
———, 2001, *Finding the Church*, London: SCM Press.
———, 2010, *Wording a Radiance*, London: SCM Press.
Harmless, William, 2004, *Desert Christians: An Introduction to the Literature of Early Monasticism*, Oxford: Oxford University Press.
Hauerwas, Stanley, 2006, *Matthew*, Grand Rapids, MI: Brazos Press.
Hauerwas, Stanley, and William H. Willimon, 1989, *Resident Aliens: Life in the Christian Colony*, Oxford: Abingdon Press.
Hays, Richard, 1997, *The Moral Vision of the New Testament*, Edinburgh: T&T Clark.
Healey, Nicholas, 2012, 'Ecclesiology, Ethnography and God: An Interplay of Reality Descriptions' in Pete Ward (ed.), *Perspectives on Ecclesiography and Ethnography*, Grand Rapids, MI: Eerdmans.

BIBLIOGRAPHY

Heath, Elaine, 2008, *The Mystic Way of Evangelism*, Grand Rapids, MI: Baker Academic.

Hibbert, Evelyn and Richard, 2018, *Walking Together on the Jesus Road: Intercultural Discipling*, Pasadena, CA: William Carey Library.

Hiebert, Paul, 2008, *Transforming Worldviews*, Grand Rapids, MI: Baker Academic.

Hill, Graham, 2017, *Salt, Light and a City: Introducing Missional Ecclesiology*, 2nd edn, Eugene, OR: Wipf & Stock.

Hirsch, Alan, 2006, *The Forgotten Ways*, Grand Rapids, MI: Brazos.

Hocken, Peter, 'The Holy Spirit and the Coming Kingdom', Skepsis (Anglican Renewal Ministries magazine)

Hooker, Morna, 1996, 'A Partner in the Gospel: Paul's Understanding of his Ministry' in Eugene H. Lovering and Jerry L. Sumney (eds), *Theology and Ethics in Paul and his Interpreters: Essays in Honor of Victor Paul Furnish*, Oxford: Abingdon Press.

——, and Frances Young, 2010, *Be Holy As I Am Holy*, London: SCM Press.

Horrell, David G., 2005, *Solidarity and Difference*, Edinburgh: T&T Clark.

Hurtado, Larry, 2017, *Destroyer of the Gods: Early Christian Distinctiveness in the Roman World*, Waco, TX: Baylor University Press.

Irenaeus, 'Irenaeus of Lyons. Against Heresies', *Early Christian Writings*, http://www.earlychristianwritings.com/text/irenaeus-book1.html, accessed 30.08.2023.

Irving, Alexander J. D., 2020, *God, Freedom, and the Body of Christ: Toward a Theology of the Church*, Eugene, OR: Cascade Books.

Jackson, Bob, 2002, *Hope for the Church*, London: Church House Publishing.

Jennings, Willie, 2017, *Acts*, Belief Theological Commentary, Louisville, KY: Westminster John Knox Press.

Jobes, Karen H., 2005, *1 Peter*, Grand Rapids, MI: Baker.

John Paul II, *Redemptorist Missio*, http://www.vatican.va/content/john-paul-ii/en/encyclicals/documents/hf_jp-ii_enc_07121990_redemptoris-missio.html, accessed 1.09.2023.

Johnson, Luke Timothy, 1992, *The Acts of the Apostles*, Sacred Pagina, Collegeville, MN: Liturgical Press.

——, 2011, *Prophetic Jesus, Prophetic Church*, Grand Rapids, MI: Eerdmans.

Keener, Craig, 2021, *1 Peter*, Grand Rapids, MI: Baker Academic.

Keesmaat, Sylvia C., and Brian J. Walsh, 2019, *Romans Disarmed: Resisting Empire, Demanding Justice*, Grand Rapids, MI: Brazos.

Kim, Kirsteen, 2009, *Joining in with the Spirit*, London: Epworth.

Kirk, J. Andrew, 1999, *What is Mission?*, London: Darton, Longman & Todd.

Kraft, Charles, 1979, *Christianity in Culture*, New York: Orbis Books.
Kreider, Alan, 1995, *Worship and Evangelism in Pre-Christendom*, Joint Liturgical Studies 32, Cambridge: Grove.
——, 2016, *The Patient Ferment of the Early Church*, Grand Rapids, MI: Baker Academic.
Kuhn, Thomas, 1970, *The Structure of Scientific Revolutions*, 2nd edn, Chicago, IL: University of Chicago Press.
Küng, Hans, 1968, *The Church*, London: Search Press.
——, 1977, *On Being a Christian*, Glasgow: Fount.
——, 1988, *Theology for the Third Millenium*, London: Harper Collins.
——, 1995, *Christianity*, London: SCM Press.
Ladd, George Eldon, 1974, *The Presence of the Future*, London: SPCK.
Langmead, Ross, 2004, *The Word Made Flesh: Towards an Incarnational Missiology*, Lanham, MD: University Press of America.
Land, Steven J., 1993, *Pentecostal Spirituality: A Passion for the Kingdom*, Sheffield: Sheffield Academic Press.
Levison, Jack, 2013, *Inspired: The Holy Spirit and the Mind of Faith*, Grand Rapids, MI: Eerdmans.
Lincoln, Andrew T., 1990, *Ephesians*, Waco, TX: Word Biblical Commentaries.
—— (with A. J. M. Wedderburn), 2008, *Theology of the Later Pauline Letters*, Cambridge: Cambridge University Press.
Lings, George, 2017, *Reproducing Church*, Abingdon: Bible Reading Fellowship and Church Army.
Longenecker, Richard R., 2016, *Romans*, NIGTC, Grand Rapids, MI: Eerdmans.
Lyon, David, 2000, *Jesus in Disneyland*, Cambridge: Polity.
MacDougall, Scott, 2015, *More Than Communion*, London: T&T Clark.
MacMillan, Nicki Collins, 'Creating Third Spaces' in Mark Lau Branson and Nicholas Warnes, 2014 (eds), *Starting Missional Churches*, Downers Grove, IL: IVP, pp. 106–19.
McClendon, James, 2002, *Ethics*, rev. edn, Oxford: Abingdon Press.
McFadyen, Alistair, 1990, *The Call to Personhood*, Cambridge: Cambridge University Press.
Malcolm, Lois, 'Raised for our Justification: Christ's Spirit for Us and for All' in Mary Sue Dehmlow-Dreier, 2013 (ed.), *Created and Led by the Spirit*, Grand Rapids, MI: Eerdmans, pp. 45–67.
Manson, T. W., 1948, *The Church's Ministry*, London: Hodder & Stoughton.
Marlow, Hilary, 2009, *Biblical Prophets and Contemporary Environmental Ethics*, Oxford: Oxford University Press.
Marshall, Peter, 1987, *Enmity in Corinth*, Tübingen: J. C. B. Mohr.
Meyer, Keith, 2010, *Whole Life Transformation*, Downers Grove, IL: IVP.

BIBLIOGRAPHY

Meyers, Ruth A., 2014, *Missional Worship, Worshipful Mission*, Grand Rapids, MI: Eerdmans.
Moltmann, Jürgen, 1967, *Theology of Hope*, London: SCM Press.
——, 1977, *The Church in the Power of the Spirit*, London: SCM Press.
Moo, Douglas, 2009, 'Creation and New Creation: Transforming Christian Perspectives' in Robert White (ed.), *Creation in Crisis: Christian Perspectives on Sustainability*, London: SPCK.
——, and Moo, Jonathan, 2018, *Creation Care: A Biblical Theology of the Natural World*, Grand Rapids, MI: Zondervan.
——, and Robin Routledge, 2014, *As Long As The Earth Endures: The Bible, Creation and the Environment*, Downers Grove, IL: Apollos.
Morgan, Alison, 2015, *Following Jesus*, Wells: ReSource.
Morris, Helen D., 2019, *Flexible Church: Being the Church in the Contemporary World*, London: SCM Press.
Morris, Leon, 1992, *The Gospel According to Matthew*, Leicester: IVP.
Moynagh, Michael, 2011, *Church for Every Context*, London: SCM Press.
——, 2017, *Church in Life*, London: SCM Press.
Navarro, Kevin J., 2023, *Trinitarian Doxology: T.F. and J.B. Torrance's Theology of Worship*, Eugene, OR: Pickwick Publications.
Nazir-Ali, Michael, 2001, *Future Shapes of the Church*, House of Bishops paper.
Newbigin, Lesslie, 1953, *The Household of God*, London: SCM Press.
——, 1976, *A Local Church Truly United*, Geneva: WCC.
——, 1978, *The Open Secret*, London: SPCK.
——, 1982, *The Light Has Come: An Exposition of The Fourth Gospel*, Grand Rapids, MI: Eerdmans.
——, 1982, *The Other Side of '84*, London: British Council of Churches.
——, 1987, *Mission in Christ's Way*, Geneva: WCC.
——, 1989, *The Gospel in a Pluralist Society*, London: SPCK.
Nietzsche, Friedrich, 2002, *On Truth and Lies in a Nonmoral Sense*, Delhi: Grapevine.
Northcott, Michael, 2007, *A Moral Climate: The Ethics of Global Warming*, London: Darton, Longman & Todd.
——, 2014, *A Political Theology of Climate Change*, London: SPCK.
O'Brian, Peter T., 1999, *Ephesians*, Pillar New Testament Commentaries, Leicester: Apollos.
Orr, Peter, 2019, *Exalted Above the Heavens: The Risen and Ascended Christ*, Leicester: IVP.
Paas, Stephan, 2019, *Pilgrims and Priests: Christian Mission in a Post-Christian Society*, London: SCM Press.
Peppiatt, Lucy, 2012, *The Disciple*, Eugene, OR: Cascade Books.
Percy, Martyn, 2021, *The Humble Church: Becoming the Body of Christ*, London: Canterbury Press.

Peterson, David, 2009, *The Acts of the Apostles*, Cambridge, Apollos.
Pickard, Stephen, 2012, *Seeking the Church*, London: SCM Press.
Pinnock, Clark, 1966, *Flame of Love*, Downers Grove, IL: IVP.
——, 1985, *The Scripture Principle*, London: Hodder & Stoughton.
Pohl, Christine, 1999, *Making Room*, Grand Rapids, MI: Eerdmans.
Polhill, John B., 1992, *Acts*, New American Commentary 26, Toronto: Holman Reference.
Pratchett, Terry, 1992, *Small Gods*, London: Victor Gollancz.
Radner, Ephraim, 2017, *Church*, Cascade Companions, Eugene, OR: Wipf & Stock.
Rahner, Karl, 1970, *The Trinity*, London: Burns & Oates.
Ramsey, Michael, 1969, *God, Christ and the World*, London: SCM Press.
Richter, Sandra, 2020, *Stewards of Eden*, Downers Grove, IL: IVP.
Roberts, Andrew, 2016, *Holy Habits*, Walton-on-the-Hill: Malcolm Down Publishing.
Rookmaaker, H. R., 1970, *Modern Art and the Death of a Culture*, Leicester: IVP.
Rooms, Nigel, and Wort, Elli, 2021, *Fuzzy Church: Gospel and Culture in the North of England*, Durham: Sacristy Press.
Ross, Cathy, 'Pioneering Missiologies: Seeing Afresh' in Cathy Ross and Johnny Baker (eds), *The Pioneer Gift: Explorations in Mission*, London: Canterbury Press.
Roudometof, Victor, 2016, *Glocalisation: A Critical Introduction*, Abingdon: Routledge.
Rowe, Kavin, 2010, *World Turned Upside Down: Reading Acts in the Graeco-Roman Age*, New York: Oxford University Press.
Roxburgh, Alan, 1997, *The Missionary Congregation: Leadership and Liminality*, Harrisburg, PA: Trinity Press.
Sample, Tex, 1998, *The Spectacle of Worship in a Wired World*, Oxford: Abingdon Press.
Sanneh, Lamin, 1989, *Translating the Message*, New York: Orbis Books.
Schaeffer, Francis, 1968, *The God Who Is There*, Downers Grove, IL: IVP.
——, 2014, *Escape From Reason*, Leicester: IVP.
Sennett, Richard, 1998, *The Corrosion of Character*, New York: Norton.
Shorter, Aylward, 1994, *Evangelization and Culture*, London: Geoffrey Chapman.
——, 1999, *Towards a Theology of Inculturation*, New York: Orbis Books.
Smail, Thomas, 1988, *The Giving Gift*, London: Hodder & Stoughton.
Smith, James K. A., 2014, *How (Not) to Be Secular: Reading Charles Taylor*, Grand Rapids, MI: Eerdmans.
Snyder, Howard, 1973, *The Community of the King*, Madison, WA: IVP.

―――, 1983, *Liberating the Church*, Basingstoke: Marshall, Morgan & Scott.
Stevenson, Kenneth, 1996, *Handing On*, London: Darton, Longman & Todd.
Stott, John, 2007, 'John Stott's Final Sermon: The Model – Becoming More Like Christ', 17 August, *Christian Today*, https://www.christiantoday.com/article/john.stott.final.sermon.the.model.becoming.more.like.christ/12442.htm, accessed 6.09.2023.
Sunquist, Scott W., 2013, *Understanding Christian Mission*, Grand Rapids, MI: Baker.
Tannehill, Robert C., 1994, *The Narrative Unity of Luke–Acts: A Literary Interpretation. Volume two: The Acts of the Apostles*, Minneapolis, MN: Fortress Press.
Taylor, Charles, 1989, *Sources of the Self*, Cambridge: Cambridge University Press.
Taylor, Charles, 2004, *Modern Social Imaginaries*, London: Duke University Press.
―――, 2007, *A Secular Age*, London: Harvard University Press.
Taylor, Steve, 2019, *First Expressions: Innovation and the Mission of God*, London: SCM Press.
Taylor, John, 1998, *The Uncancelled Mandate*, London: Church House Publishing.
―――, 1972, *The Go-Between God*, London: SCM Press.
Temple, Willliam, *Christus Veritas*, London: Macmillan, 1939.
Tetley, Joy, 1988, *A Way Into Hebrews*, Grove Biblical Series 8, Cambridge: Grove.
Thiselton, Anthony C., 2000, *The First Epistle to the Corinthians*, Grand Rapids, MI: Eerdmans.
―――, 2015, *Systematic Theology*, London: SPCK.
Thompson, John, 1994, *Modern Trinitarian Perspectives*, Oxford: Oxford University Press.
Tomlin, Graham, 2006, *Spiritual Fitness*, London: Continuum.
Torrance, Alan J., 1996, *Persons in Communion*, Edinburgh: T&T Clark.
Torrance, James B., 1981, 'The Vicarious Humanity of Christ' in T. F. Torrance (ed.), *The Incarnation: Ecumenical Studies in the Nicene-Constantinopolitan Creed AD 381*, Edinburgh: Handsel.
―――, 1991, 'The Doctrine of the Trinity in our Contemporary Situation' in *The Forgotten Trinity* (Selection of Papers), London: British Council of Churches/Council of Churches in Britain and Ireland.
―――, 1996, *Worship, Community and the Triune God of Grace*, Carlisle: Paternoster Press.
―――, 2014, *Participatio* supplement to Volume 3.
Torrance, Thomas F. 1975, *Theology in Reconciliation* (reprint 1996), Eugene, OR: Wipf & Stock.

———, 1993, *Royal Priesthood: A Theology of Ordained Ministry*, Edinburgh: T&T Clark.
Valerio, Ruth, 2020, *Saying Yes to Life*, London: SPCK.
Van Gelder, Craig, 2000, *The Essence of the Church*, Grand Rapids, MI: Baker Academic.
———, 2007, *The Ministry of the Missional Church*, Grand Rapids, MI: Baker.
Vanhoozer, Kevin, 2007, 'One Rule to Rule Them All' in Craig Ott and Harold Netland (eds), *Globalizing Theology: Belief and Practice in an Era of World Christianity*, Nottingham: IVP.
Van Unnik, Willem C., 1973, in *Sparsa collecta, Part 1. Evangelia, Paulina, Acta* in *Novum Testamentum Supplements* vol. 29.
Vatican Council, 1965, '*Ad Gentes*: On the Mission Activity of the Church', http://www.vatican.va/archive/hist_councils/ii_vatican_council/documents/vat-ii_decree_19651207_ad-gentes_en.html, accessed 30.08.2023.
Volf, Miroslav, 1996, *Exclusion and Embrace*, Nashville, TN: Abingdon Press.
———, 1998, *After Our Likeness: The Church as the Image of the Trinity*, Grand Rapids, MI: Eerdmans.
———, 'Soft Difference: Theological Reflections on the Relation Between Church and Culture in 1 Peter', https://www.pas.rochester.edu/~tim/study/Miroslav%20Volf%201%20Peter.pdf, accessed 1.09.2023.
Wallis, Jim, 1976, *Agenda For Biblical People*, New York: Harper & Row.
———, 1981, *The Call to Conversion*, New York: Harper & Row.
Walls, Andrew, 1996, *The Missionary Movement in Christian History*, Edinburgh: T&T Clark.
———, 2002, *The Cross-Cultural Process Christian History*, Edinburgh: T&T Clark.
———, 2002, 'Christian Scholarship and the Demographic Transformation of the Church' in Rodney L. Peterson and Nancy M. Rourke (eds), *Theological Literacy for the 21st Century*, Grand Rapids, MI: Eerdmans.
Ward, Pete, 2017, *Liquid Ecclesiology*, Boston, MA: Brill.
Warnes, Nick, 'Growing Roots in a Secularized Context' in Mark Lau Branson and Nicholas Warnes, 2014 (eds), *Starting Missional Churches*, Downers Grove, IL: IVP, pp. 120–39.
Warren, Max, 1978, 'The Fusion of I.M.C. and W.C.C. at New Delhi: Retrospective Thoughts After a Decade and a Half' in *Zending op weg Naar de Toekomst*, Kampen, Netherlands: J. H. Kok.
Watkins, Clare, 2020, *Disclosing Church: An Ecclesiology Learned from Conversations in Practice*, Abingdon: Routledge.

BIBLIOGRAPHY

Watson, David, 1976, *I Believe in Evangelism*, London: Hodder & Stoughton.
Webster, John, 2005, 'The Visible Attests the Invisible' in Mark Husbands and Daniel J. Treier (eds), *The Community of the Word: Toward an Evangelical Ecclesiology*, Downers Grove, IL: IVP.
Wells, Samuel, 2017, *Incarnational Ministry*, London: Canterbury Press.
———, 2018, *Incarnational Mission*, London: Canterbury Press.
White, James R., 1998, *The Forgotten Trinity*, Minneapolis, MN: Bethany House.
Willard, Dallas, 1998, *The Divine Conspiracy*, London: Fount.
———, 2009, *The Great Omission*, San Francisco, CA: HarperOne.
Williams, Rowan, 2002, *On Christian Theology*, Oxford: Blackwell.
———, 2007, *Tokens of Trust*, London: Canterbury Press.
———, 2016, *Being Disciples: Essentials of the Christian Life*, London: SPCK.
———, 2018, *Christ the Heart of Creation*, Bloomsbury: Continuum.
Wink, Walter, 1992, *Engaging the Powers*, Minneapolis, MN: Fortress Press.
Winter, Bruce, 1994, *Seek the Welfare of the City*, Carlisle: Paternoster Press.
Witherington III, Ben, 2001, *The Acts of the Apostles*, Carlisle: Paternoster Press.
Wittgenstein, Ludwig, 2009 edition, *Philosophical Investigations*, Oxford: Wiley-Blackwell.
Work, Telford, 2002, *Living and Active: Scripture in the Economy of Salvation*, Grand Rapids, MI: Eerdmans.
Wright, Christopher, 2004, *Old Testament Ethics for the People of God*, Leicester: IVP.
———, 2008, *The Mission of God*, Leicester: IVP.
Wright, N. T., 1992, *The New Testament and the People of God*, London: SPCK.
———, 1996, *Jesus and the Victory of God*, London: SPCK.
———, 2002, *Romans*, New Interpreter's Bible Vol. X, Nashville, TN: Abingdon Press.
———, 2013, *Paul and the Faithfulness of God*, London: SPCK.
———, 2015, *The Challenge of Jesus*, 2nd edn, London: SPCK.
———, 2019, *History and Eschatology*, London: SPCK.
Wright, Tom, 1995, *The Crown and the Fire*, London: SPCK.
———, 1997, *What St Paul Really Said*, Oxford: Lion.
———, 2002, *Matthew for Everyone Pt. 2*, London: SPCK.
———, 2012, *How God Became King*, London: SPCK.
Yates, Tim, 1988, 'Anglicans and Mission' in Stephen Sykes and John Booty (eds), *The Study of Anglicanism*, London: SPCK.
Zizioulas, John, 1993, *Being as Communion*, New York: SVS Press.

Index of Names and Subjects

Ad Gentes 91–2
Alexander, Loveday 82, 86
Avis, Paul 177

Badcock, Gary 134
Baker, Johnny 165
baptism 48, 59–60, 111–12, 151, 167, 176
Barclay, John 107, 141
Barth, Karl 23
Barth, Marcus 109
Bauckham, Richard 44–6, 49, 60, 146
Bauckham, Richard and Hart, Trevor 122, 131
Bauman, Zygmunt 5–6, 152
Beasley-Murray, George 49, 69, 123
Beck, Ulrich 3
Bevans, Stephen and Roger Schroeder 12, 23, 24, 36, 90
Body of Christ 8, 11–12, 37, 72, 87–9, 108–13, 115, 117, 133, 170, 173, 181, 184, 189
Bosch, David 2, 12, 13, 14, 22, 23, 24, 26, 28, 43, 53, 87, 90, 123, 169

Branson, Mark Lau and Warnes, Nicholas 197
Bruce, F. F. 76, 108
Burridge, Richard 40, 43–4, 48, 49

Campbell, Douglas 102, 104–5
Carson, Don 104–5
Castells, Manuel 3
Chilton, Bruce and McDonald, J. I. H. 123
Christology 87, 89, 92, 95, 108, 111
'Church Without Walls' report 45, 47, 56
Cocksworth, Christopher 31, 33, 37, 174
Cohick, Lynn 109
community 4, 7, 9, 12, 13, 15, 20–1, 25, 29, 31, 35, 38, 43–6, 55, 57, 59, 60, 65, 66, 70, 81, 83, 84, 87, 89, 91, 97, 108, 110–11, 112, 114–16, 118, 120, 122, 127, 129–30, 135, 138, 140, 145–6, 147, 151, 154–5, 156, 160–1, 163, 164–5, 167–70, 172–3,

176–8, 180–3, 186, 187, 194, 196–7, 203, 204, 206, 208, 210, 211–13
consumerism 3, 4, 6, 13, 93, 185
context 1, 3, 7–9, 10–13, 15–17, 36, 47, 59, 60, 77, 83, 87, 88–9, 90, 93, 96, 97, 98, 99, 106, 110, 113–16, 120, 126, 128, 131, 135, 138, 152, 160, 163, 178, 180–1, 184–6, 190, 193–7, 199, 205, 207–8, 212
Cottrell, Stephen 179
Couldry, Nick 4
Couldry, Nick and Hepp, Andreas 115
Cray, Graham 7, 26, 93, 112
Crosby, Michael 145

default setting 1, 10, 13–16, 20, 22, 31, 35, 36, 38, 57–8, 62, 66, 68, 166, 176, 189, 198, 212–13
Dehmlow-Dreier, Mary Sue 83, 194, 195
discernment 7–8, 12, 18, 78–9, 89, 114, 138, 183–4, 191, 193–5
discipleship 16, 21, 38–63, 65–7, 84, 98, 104, 105, 120, 139, 150, 154–5, 160–2, 167, 169–70, 175–7, 179, 182, 184–5, 188, 191, 195–6, 199, 202–4, 208–11
Doctrine Commission 132

Donovan, Vincent 91
Duerksen, Darren and Dyrness, William A. 8, 9, 10
Dulles, Avery 21, 178
Dunn, James 74–5, 112, 123, 127, 130, 147, 219
dying to live 96

Ecclesiology 6, 10, 11, 16, 17, 18, 24, 28–9, 37, 47, 64, 90–1, 93, 99, 108, 178, 212
Esler, Philip 76
Eucharist (Holy Communion) 112, 167, 174–5, 176
Eucharistic Presidency 38, 58, 129, 213

family of God 139–45
Farrow, Douglas 110
Fee, Gordon 69, 127, 130, 135
Fitch, David 202
Flemming, Dean 38, 39, 40, 44, 46–7, 49, 198
Flett, John 26
Ford, David 79, 172
France, R. T. 62
Fresh Expressions, fresh expressions 1, 7, 9, 10, 11, 15, 19, 20, 119
Fresh Expressions in the Mission of the Church 18, 171
Frost, Michael 204–5

Gaventa, Beverley 77

INDEX OF NAMES AND SUBJECTS

Gay, Douglas 7
Ghering, Roger 198
Gibbs, Eddie 12, 55, 57–8, 60
Giddens, Anthony 3–7
Gill, Robin 172, 175
González, Justo 82
Grenz, Stanley 132
Guder, Darrell 94, 97, 98, 114
Gunton, Colin 128

Hardy, Daniel 22, 30, 39, 41, 47, 79, 200–1, 211
Hauerwas, Stanley 47, 51
Hauerwas, Stanley and Willimon, William 111
Hays, Richard 106
Healey, Nicholas 8
Heath, Elaine 14, 28
Hibbert, Evelyn and Hibbert, Richard 55, 58, 60
Hiebert, Paul 15
Hill, Graham 64, 99
Hirsch, Alan 55, 165
Hocken, Peter 130, 131
Holy Spirit 10, 11, 20, 24, 26, 27, 30, 33–4, 49–50, 52, 55, 59, 60, 64–86, 88, 111, 116, 120, 122–38, 140, 143, 145, 155, 168, 173–4, 181, 184–5, 186, 189, 190–1, 194, 198, 199, 200, 209, 212
Hooker, Morna 90, 100–4
Horrell, David 112
House of Bishops 7
Hurtado, Larry 85

imagination 15–16, 20, 36, 212
immanent frame 5, 137
Incarnation(al) 8, 58, 66, 89–107, 102, 105, 114
Irving, Alexander 35

Jackson, Bob 116
Jennings, Willie 65, 70
Jesus still on mission 21, 34, 37, 38, 49–52, 66, 110, 142, 158–60, 170–1, 172
Johnson, Luke Timothy 52, 66, 73, 78, 198

Keesmaat, Sylvia and Walsh, Brian 150
Kim, Kirsteen 64
Kingdom of God 39–41, 46, 48, 68, 69, 89, 94, 118, 122–31, 133, 136, 142, 155, 164, 168, 171, 181, 182, 186, 199, 202, 203, 204, 211
Kirk, Andrew 23
Kraft, Charles 8
Kreider, Alan 159, 175
Kuhn, Thomas 12
Küng, Hans 2, 12, 64, 142

Ladd, George Eldon 123
Langmead, Ross 91
Levison, Jack 79–80
Lincoln, Andrew 108, 109, 111, 139
Lings, George 178
Longenecker, Richard 141, 147

Lyon, David 3

MacDougall, Scott 15, 29
Manson, T. W. 211
marks of the church 11, 176–8
Marlow, Hilary 149
Marshall, Peter 196
McClendon, James 211
McFadyen, Alistair 30
missional practices 16, 185, 198–206
mission of God 22–8, 35, 37, 38
'Mission-Shaped Church' report 6–7, 17, 20, 58, 63, 93, 96, 97, 116, 119, 166, 176, 177, 178, 179–83, 206, 212, 213
Moltmann, Jurgen 29, 35–6, 65, 122, 128, 130, 153
Moo, Douglas 139, 149
Morgan, Alison 47
Morris, Helen 11, 113
Morris, Leon 40
Moynagh, Michael 26, 114, 138

Nazir-Ali, Michael 114
Newbigin, Lesslie 2, 28, 64, 89, 90, 94, 114–16, 117–18, 123, 132, 151–2
Nietzsche, Friedrich 11

O'Brien, Peter 139
Orr, Peter 50

Paas, Stephan 161, 163–4

Pannenberg, Wolfhart 87
participation in Christ 31–5
people of God 11–12, 153
Peppiatt, Lucy 4, 142
Percy, Martin 210
Peterson, David 70, 82
Pickard, Stephen 177
pilgrim people 151–65
place 4, 8, 13, 46, 52, 59, 89, 95–6, 109, 110, 113–16, 120, 129, 133–4, 135, 151, 153, 165, 167, 170, 181, 186, 198, 200, 207
Polhill, John 77
Pope Francis 48, 60
Pratchett, Terry 166

Radner, Ephraim 20, 66, 88, 90, 91, 120, 166, 181
Rahner, Karl 26
Ramsey, Michael 168
Redemptoris Missio (Pope John Paul II) 91
Rookmaaker, Hans 2
Rooms, Nigel and Wort, Ellie 210
Ross, Cathy 37, 98, 200, 201–2
Roudemetof, Victor 4, 115
Rowe, Kavin 67, 83, 84–5, 98
Roxburgh, Alan 59

Sample, Tex 58
Schaeffer, Francis 2
Scripture 7, 8, 10, 26, 66, 68, 75, 78–9, 80, 88, 120, 131–3, 176, 181, 187, 189–93, 196

INDEX OF NAMES AND SUBJECTS

Shorter, Aylward 90, 95–6
Smail, Thomas 88
Smith, James K. A. 5
Snyder, Howard 111, 181
social imaginary 15
Stevenson, Kenneth 175
Stott, John 168
Sunquist, Scott 36, 83, 92

Tannehill, Robert 81
Taylor, Charles 5, 15, 137, 174
Taylor, John V. 25, 31, 66, 83, 89, 130, 197
Taylor, Steve 11
Temple, William 172
temple of the Spirit 11–12, 133–8
Thiselton, Anthony 13, 105, 112
Tomlin, Graham 54
Torrance, Alan 32, 36
Torrance, James 23, 31–4
Torrance, Thomas 31–4
tradition 7, 8, 9, 10, 13, 17, 19–20, 45, 58, 64, 75–6, 79, 91, 93, 116, 175, 177, 179, 183, 187, 194, 204, 213
Trinity, trinitarian 23–4, 26, 28–32, 33, 132, 179–80, 193, 195

van Gelder, Craig 36
Van Unnik, Wilhelm 74
Vanhoozer, Kevin 4, 115
Volf, Miroslav 29, 49, 90, 98, 161, 163, 164, 165

Wallis, Jim 53, 56
Walls, Andrew 88, 90, 97–8, 117, 118, 181
Ward, Pete 1, 6, 13, 212
Warren, Max 86
Watkins, Clare 207–8, 210, 213
Watson, David 57, 172
Webster, John 65
Welby, Justin 20
Wells, Samuel 93
Willard, Dallas 42, 46, 53
Williams, Rowan 11, 39, 42, 63, 90, 146, 166–7, 169, 171, 176, 179, 208
Wink, Walter 145
Winter, Bruce 163
Wittgenstein, Ludwig 14–15
Woodhead, Linda 208
world view 14
worship 11, 13, 16, 29, 32–3, 35, 37, 56–7, 59, 68, 134, 155, 156–8, 172–6, 179–80, 182, 193, 196
Wright, Christopher 54–8, 147
Wright, Tom (N. T.) 14, 39, 44, 46, 62, 72, 83, 101, 112–13, 122, 127, 132, 133, 136, 137, 140, 143, 146, 208

Yates, Timothy 18

Zizioulas, John 64, 87, 128

www.ingramcontent.com/pod-product-compliance
Lightning Source LLC
Chambersburg PA
CBHW031105080526
44587CB00011B/827